T0383125

Business School Research

This second book in the EFMD Management Education series explores business schools' increasing focus on, and search for, meaningful societal and economic research impact. This involves, in particular, co-operation and collaboration in both knowledge creation and implementation of the findings of academic research in practice.

Business schools have a critical role to play in 'rewiring' our missions for research relevance, impact and reach, and in recognising needs and addressing real issues of society and economy. With cases from a range of international business schools, the book doesn't simply highlight the need for the dominant research model in business schools to evolve, but illustrates how this can happen in practice. In so doing, it opens the discussion on how the business school can contribute in very real ways to solving global and complex challenges such as climate change, rising inequalities, international isolationism, eroding democratic systems, and the spread of fake news.

These are goals that the EFMD has championed since its inception, and this book will be of value and interest to policy makers and business leaders seeking insight into how management education will be shaped to support business and wider society, as well as those working in business schools and higher education leaders.

Eric Cornuel has been President of EFMD Global since 2000. He is an acknowledged leader, expert and authority on management education and a recipient of the Légion d'honneur & Magnolia Award from the city of Shanghai for services to education. He is a Professor at the University of Louvain, Belgium and holds an Honorary Doctorate from Kozminski University, Poland.

Howard Thomas is a 'serial dean' having held deanships in Asia, Europe and North America. He is a well-regarded and highly cited scholar in the fields of strategic management and management education. He is an Emeritus Professor and former Dean at LKCSB, Singapore Management University, and currently a Special Advisor at EFMD Global.

Matthew Wood is Director, Operations and *Global Focus* Magazine Editor at EFMD Global.

Business School Research

Excellence, Academic Quality and Positive Impact

Edited by
Eric Cornuel, Howard Thomas and
Matthew Wood

LONDON AND NEW YORK

Cover design: © Jebens Design

First published 2024
by Routledge
4 Park Square, Milton Park, Abingdon, Oxon OX14 4RN

and by Routledge
605 Third Avenue, New York, NY 10158

Routledge is an imprint of the Taylor & Francis Group, an informa business

© 2024 selection and editorial matter, Eric Cornuel, Howard Thomas and Matthew Wood; individual chapters, the contributors

The right of Eric Cornuel, Howard Thomas and Matthew Wood to be identified as the authors of the editorial material, and of the authors for their individual chapters, has been asserted in accordance with sections 77 and 78 of the Copyright, Designs and Patents Act 1988.

Funded by EFMD Global.

Trademark notice: Product or corporate names may be trademarks or registered trademarks, and are used only for identification and explanation without intent to infringe.

British Library Cataloguing-in-Publication Data
A catalogue record for this book is available from the British Library

ISBN: 978-1-032-73456-9 (hbk)
ISBN: 978-1-003-46741-0 (ebk)

DOI: 10.4324/9781003467410

Designed and typeset in Roboto
by Jebens Design

Contents

Global Focus:
Annual Research Volume 2 2023

Business School Research: Excellence,
Academic Quality and Positive Impact

*Eric Cornuel, Howard Thomas and
Matthew Wood - Editors*

Editors
Eric Cornuel
Howard Thomas
Matthew Wood

Design & Art Direction
Jebens Design / www.jebensdesign.co.uk

Photographs & Illustrations
©Jebens Design Ltd / EFMD unless otherwise stated

www.globalfocusmagazine.com
www.efmd.org

©EFMD
Rue Gachard 88 – Box 3,
1050 Brussels, Belgium

More ways to read *Global Focus* publications

Go to
globalfocusmagazine.com
to access the online library
of *Global Focus* publications

Your say

We are always pleased to hear your
thoughts on our publications.

Please address comments and
ideas to Matthew Wood at EFMD:
matthew.wood@efmdglobal.org

EFMD
GLOBAL

Introducing Business School Research and Positive Impact

HOWARD THOMAS

Introduction

The first, inaugural EFMD annual research volume, 'Perspectives on the impact, mission and purpose of the business school', was launched as a special issue of Global Focus magazine in November 2022 and was subsequently published in book form in 2023 by Routledge (Cornuel et al., 2023). It examined how impact has become an increasingly important theme in addressing the purpose and value of the modern business/management school. Typically debates about impact have involved such issues as the 'rigour/relevance debate' (Irwin, 2023) and the co-production of research knowledge through business school collaboration with agencies of business, government and civil society. Partly because of the influence of media rankings and a discernible 'market managerialism' orientation in business schools' leadership (Locke and Spender, 2011), business school impact performance has been measured primarily in terms of 'league table' outputs (e.g. citation counts and media rankings) rather than through assessment of meaningful outcomes relative to societal and economic impact (which cannot be measured quite as succinctly and neatly as performance metrics and media rankings). Indeed, Eric Cornuel (2023) in his role as EFMD President, re-emphasised the adoption of the principle of 'stakeholder' rather than shareholder value maximisation in order to advance research ideas that benefit society as well as fulfilling the clear scientific mission of academia. He reinforced responsible impact goals by stressing the importance of business and management schools producing positive impacts through clear academic research findings which can then be interpreted, understood and implemented by applied practitioners.

Therefore, in rereading the perspectives in the EFMD Research Volume 1 (Cornuel et al., 2023), you will notice comments amongst its authors about the need to address more closely issues of the societal and economic impact of business school research. Suggestions for topics included corporate social responsibility, sustainability, the ESG (economic, social and governance) agenda and collaboration both between business schools as well as with business and governments. External environments in a precarious world were seen as equally challenging with political issues of concern such as inequality, populism, decoupling and de-globalisation becoming more critical. Further, building entrepreneurship programmes and developing ecosystems between schools and their stakeholders has become a strategic imperative. There was also a sense that future research should be even more interdisciplinary and integrative.

Hence, the broad theme of this second stand-alone annual EFMD 'research' volume will be to debate business schools' increasing focus on, and search for, meaningful societal and economic research impact involving, in particular, co-operation and collaboration in both knowledge creation and implementation of the findings of academic research in practice. Examples of this societally-oriented applied research can already be found in publications of EFMD, which have reported the results of their annual 'Excellence in Practice' (EiP) prize-winning awards in Global Focus special issues over the last decade, (also see the Ginneberge paper on the evolution of EiP in this volume) as well as more recently GBSN (the Global Business School Network) with its 'Going Beyond' awards. Further, the RRBM (Responsible Research in Business and Management) community examined, in the paper 'Which business topics should we research?' (Tsui et al., 2023), award-winning RRBM articles and books and outlined their impacts. The Financial Times in its recent sustainability series provided summaries of impactful research in the field. AACSB International have also produced a recent white paper on business schools and societal impact.

DOI: 10.4324/9781003467410-1

Consequently, there has been much more interest in the broad spectrum of academic research activities and the issue of assessing research outputs using more qualitative performance assessment(s). In particular, the trade-offs between the *value* and the costs of teaching/learning efforts and academic research are being scrutinised carefully and cost/benefit analysis of the impact of research and its influence on societal and economic performance is now more closely evaluated. During this evaluation, interested parties have been asking a fundamental question, namely, how can we measure the outputs, and hence impact, of academic research in business and management schools more meaningfully? And how can schools build up research capabilities both in academia and, particularly, in collaborating more effectively with the tri-sectors of business, government and civil society? This, in turn suggests at least two key questions about appropriate research performance metrics, namely, first, "what are other ways of measuring meaningful and rigorous research besides high impact publications and citation scores?" Second, "how can measures of success and collaborative impact between business schools and the 'tri-sectors' of business, government and industry be devised?" Hence, it is now essential for business school leaders to examine how business schools should shift from simply counting research citations to assessing impacts in a more comprehensive fashion. How can business schools communicate their impact clearly to all their stakeholders and demonstrate their ability to catalyse strategic development and social change?

MEASURING BUSINESS SCHOOL IMPACT

Typically, there are three main priorities, and dimensions, which interact with each other as business schools frame their visions and missions of enhancing management knowledge and producing distinctive management theories and insights (Thomas *et al.*, 2023). First, the processes of knowledge generation and development to produce high quality, often multi-disciplinary research outputs involving academic faculty, doctoral students and 'tri-sector' participants. Second, knowledge dissemination in teaching and learning activities enabling the growth of quality education at undergraduate and postgraduate levels and thus contributing to student intellectual growth and societal socio-economic development and advancement. Third, knowledge transfer through 'tri-sector' collaboration, engagement and practice enhancements, i.e. translating academic knowledge into meaningful impacts for potential implementation by key stakeholders. The key strategic question is how does a business school know it has achieved its vision and mission goals in terms of the three

main targets and objectives of academic excellence, student learning success and meaningful, positive socio-economic impact? We examine each element in turn.

MEASURING ACADEMIC EXCELLENCE

Internationally the standard quantitative output measure for research merit and excellence is the number, and citations, of so-called high impact publications in leading A-star journals (often measured by Google Scholar, Scopus, ResearchGate and other bibliometrics). These measures are widely critiqued by many academics, who are against the use of journal impact factors as a measure of research quality (arguing that such A-star papers are not read much by other academics and even less by practicing managers). A specific academic criticism is that a citation is a measure of impactful publication at a single point in time (usually at the end of a project) but often fails to capture the scholarly academic impact that becomes evident over time. For that reason, as a scholar's work evolves, and becomes increasingly recognised as influential and significant, it is argued that measurement of impact should at least focus on the creation of field, or discipline, weighted citation measures which capture both longer-term intellectual influence and impact rather than immediate publication or citation impact (other bibliometric agencies e.g. Altmetrics, also offer a more long-term view of citation metrics). Further, from a policy perspective, measurement of scholarly impact should also track a scholar's impact in terms of such important factors as the number, and scale, of research grants received and outstanding Ph.D. students mentored and produced, as well as the receipt by such first-rate scholars of lifetime achievement or leadership awards from the leading professional or learned societies in their fields.

MEASURING TEACHING AND LEARNING SUCCESS

Excellent faculty who teach very well and typically produce more applied forms of research involving practicing managers and organisations, are rarely as highly valued as distinguished academic scholars. They are variously described as adjunct, clinical, or practice faculty yet they are extremely important in developing new pedagogical approaches, in writing insightful case studies and in encouraging linkages between students and companies, entrepreneurial start-ups and public sector organisations. They tutor and lead students in action and experiential learning projects and provide expertise as they train them to organise and manage applied projects in teams. They also prepare students for oral presentations in external case study competitions as well as mentoring them while undertaking internships with companies and learning from innovative entrepreneurs. In essence, they provide a bridge between the classroom and practice and generate a range of important insights and experiences for both students and more research-oriented faculty. It is clear that their contributions should be measured more broadly via teaching awards (investigating why and how they inspire students) and their development, and creation of award-winning case studies and simulation models which illustrate the implementation of management tools, theories and planning approaches. Many of these faculty also produce excellent text books which prepare the students to be highly effective in their careers. Student feedback about courses is often sought retrospectively from alumni who frequently mention particular courses and teachers who strongly influenced the development of their own careers. Such feedback is a strong reminder for schools to measure the value and performance of excellent teachers and mentors, judging how they improve the educational quality of curricula and inspire students to build lifelong skills and capabilities (in fairness, it should also be pointed out that some outstanding scholars are also great teachers – a 'win-win' outcome - but it is often the value of the 'rump' of excellent applied faculty that must also be measured and assessed even more carefully).

MEASURING SOCIAL AND ECONOMIC IMPACT: KNOWLEDGE TRANSFER AND ENGAGEMENT

While acknowledging the need to measure the scholarly and pedagogical value and performance of academic faculty, governments across the world have become increasingly interested in the cost-benefit trade-offs between the value and costs of investments in academic research and teaching, and the extent and importance of academic influence on society and economic growth pathways. Indeed, there have been an increasing number of studies focusing on the value of academic research relative to socio-economic impact (e.g. governments in France, Ireland, the Netherlands, Norway, Sweden, Australia, the US and the UK). These studies have adopted similar frameworks for evaluating research impact. The main aim is to complement a continued strong focus on rigorous, relevant high-quality research with more detailed assessment of its meaningful socio-economic impact to all stakeholders in society.

Hence, all countries tend to favour a more balanced assessment of outputs, often with bibliometric measures, in order to judge research quality in terms of rigour, originality, significance, and reach. Some, such as the USA, continue to rely, and focus, mainly on citations and publication metrics and advocate the construction of, for example, 4-year H-index measures to address longer-term value. Further, they stress that publications for assessment should normally be located in the top academic field journals which offer relatively few qualitative statements about the potential

value of such research to societal objectives. Other countries notably Australia and the UK, have constructed more comprehensive research evaluation frameworks which also include similar quantitative output measures to those used in the USA but add much stronger qualitative assessment dimension methods which involve expert assessment of the reach and significance, of research studies, and which seek to explain the impacts, societal and economic, of these research studies and institutes over a longer time horizon. These expert assessors also evaluate the research institutes in relation to such important factors as their innovativeness, vitality and sustainability. Typically, in such cases as Australia and the UK, around 30% of the overall research assessment framework evaluation analyses the socio-economic impact, research environment and culture of the research institution.

More generally, these frameworks have provided important information and insights about how researchers have attempted to stimulate and grow the spectrum of research activity from their research units and universities. They point out how efforts to improve quality, to develop emerging areas of research, to promote integration between disciplines (e.g. healthcare and digitisation methodologies) and to incentivise interdisciplinary research have been nurtured. In addition, it is clear that governments have encouraged the development of ecosystems for collaborative research whether cross-disciplinary within a given institution or across different educational institutions and research institutes as well as collaborations with industry and government in order to improve co-production of knowledge and opportunities for applied research. In turn, such collaborative research often leads to effective strategic implementation of new ideas and innovations in communities, business and governmental contexts.

(Note: for those interested in examining the conduct and findings of recent research excellence frameworks (REF) in the UK, see Pidd and Broadbent (2015), Hughes, Webber and O'Regan (2019) for REF 2014 and for REF 2021 see REF impact case study database, UKRI, 2022: (https://results2021.ref.ac.uk/impact) as well as a recent article by Blackburn et al. (2023).

OTHER PERSPECTIVES ON SOCIETAL IMPACT

Many recent papers have attempted to define and identify approaches for measuring the societal impact of research (e.g. Haley and Jack (2023); Kalika (2023)). Kalika's (2022) book is also particularly useful as it catalogues a decade of impact resulting from the evolution of BSIS (the Business School Impact System) (a partnership between EFMD and FNEGE (the French Foundation for Management Education)). BSIS was the first framework to propose a global view of positive business school impact based upon seven school impact influence dimensions, namely, financial, educational, business development, intellectual, ecosystem, societal and image impact. BSIS has been used by over 60 schools globally to understand, and communicate their real impact to their stakeholders. Some of the challenges of measuring societal impact (based upon Kalika (2022) and suggestions in an AOM survey by Haley and Jack (2023, pp.20-23)) are indicated below:

Challenges

- "Most of the scholars stated that the present system for faculty evaluation led to over reliance on more traditional techniques and methodologies and what journal editors find acceptable"
- Further "most faculty in business schools tend to conduct rigorous research that speaks to just a few people as such research advances their careers"
- Will universities and professional organisations such as EFMD and AACSB measure scholarly impact more closely aligned with their own academic visions/ missions? For example, will universities adjust their academic evaluation and promotion criteria to incorporate all their strategic priorities – research, teaching and learning, and stakeholder engagement?
- Will journal editors demand impact statements as an integral part of articles about specific research studies?
- Will the spread of US standards (e.g. citation metrics, H-indices, etc.) globally amount to imperialism with disregard of context, culture and country characteristics?

Despite the challenges most current business school academics would, however, agree with researchers such as Renate E Meyer (from WU, Vienna), (Haley and Jack, 2023, p.5) who stresses that "scientifically rigorous research is and has to remain academia's core currency". She adds that "societal impact refers to the lasting efforts that our research has on the attainment of societal goals such as equality, sustainability, or less poverty … impact is not equal to sitting on advisory boards, counselling politicians, or being present in the media."

Meyer also points out a real concern, that societal impact, especially in the social sciences, is hard to pin down. "It unfolds in a non-linear way and causality can hardly ever be attributed to a specific publication … to summarise, when assessing societal impact, we are faced with a non-linearity, a temporality, and a visibility (or better: vanity) challenge."

Nevertheless, despite the elusiveness of the concept of

societal impact Haley and Jack (2023, p.22) advocate modifications of short-term metrics in order to acquire more complete data and measure a wider range of scholarly impact. Their suggestions include some of the following:

- Standardised, broadly adopted, open-access classification systems for journal articles and books/ reports
- Refinements of citations data (e.g. self-citations; positive/negative citations; H-indices; field-weighted indices)
- Greater emphasis on contributions to some of the more significant applied journals, (e.g. HBR (Harvard Business Review), SMR (Sloan Management Review), CMR (California Management Review) and LRP (Long-Range Planning))
- Co-production of knowledge/research with practitioners to ensure practical relevance and reach of the findings
- Recognition of the value of inter-disciplinary research within and across institutions

We may not agree with any or all of these metrics but interdisciplinary research may yet prove to be more impactful than research which draws on just one discipline.

Indeed, to quote Arnoud de Meyer (2011), former president of Singapore Management University (SMU) "the business world exists as an ecosystem of business, government, NGOs and non-profits, each interlocking with the other. This is also why research has to be interdisciplinary, to consider the impact across different stakeholders."

Interdisciplinarity as a concept should, or could, also be nurtured by transnational alliances of 'like-minded' universities, which have a strong orientation in the social and management sciences (as an example perhaps schools like Copenhagen Business School, LSE, Paris Dauphine and WU Vienna). Such alliances might involve open collaboration across a range of activities, leading to enhanced networks and a research ecosystem which could collectively achieve greater impact, recognition and influence. And other researchers such as Tima Bansal and her colleagues at the interdisciplinary 'Innovation North lab' at Ivey Business School in Canada are working together to provide frameworks to address so-called 'wicked problems' or societal grand challenges. Bansal says her lab "does not seek to solve specific wicked problems, but to develop the tools and protocols, so that innovators can tackle the wicked problems they choose."

PERSPECTIVES ON MEANINGFUL, POSITIVE RESEARCH IMPACT FROM PAPERS AND AUTHORS IN THIS VOLUME

Authors in this volume have been carefully selected from a range of distinctive global business schools and research institutes to present their perspectives on meaningful research impact. Writers such as Haley and Jack (2023), Kalika (2022) and Tsui (2023) have pointed out how business school research has changed, and expanded, over the last decade. There has clearly been an increasing commitment to responsible management research and an emphasis on identifying meaningful research impacts for all stakeholders particularly in relation to achieving socio-economic impact goals. While the pursuit of high-quality, rigorous research impact is still a dominant core academic value, efforts to attack more complex issues such as so-called grand challenges (e.g. climate change, sustainability, etc.) have required cross-disciplinary and cross-institutional collaboration between business schools and their core stakeholders in business, government and civil society. Such efforts have generated greater understanding of how research insights, ideas and approaches can be translated effectively to solve practical management problems in business, government and society.

After the introduction to this volume, important papers on EFMD and Societal Impact (by Eric Cornuel and Howard Thomas, and Jan Ginneberge) succinctly review EFMD's perspectives on practice and societal impact.

Indeed, Cornuel and Thomas point out that "EFMD has constantly focused on linking European educational experience and innovative ideas with meaningful impact on management practice and learning." They argue that "European management education has thus developed a clear identity and a balanced relationship with government and society" which leads to a strong "belief in socially responsible management education that is endemic" and is "deeply embedded in its EQUIS accreditation peer review standards for the last ten years."

With this philosophy of responsible, impactful management education as a key principle they state that "we believe that the dominant research model in business schools must evolve quickly. We must augment the 'great divide' between academic excellence in research and its practical application" they suggest that "we need faculty members to be engaged in and, most importantly, be rewarded for path-breaking multidisciplinary research, applied collaborative research projects as well as innovation in teaching, engagement in society and communities." Simply put, it must provide rigorous, responsible and impactful research which is relevant for all stakeholders.

Ginneberge's paper examines the business school practice linkages through EFMD's experiences with its Excellence in Practice awards. What is unique about Jan's paper is that it chronicles the evolution of EFMD's Excellence in Practice (EiP) awards and identifies the changing character of the outstanding award projects over the 15-year journey of meaningful, positive impact growth for practitioner and other stakeholder audiences. The paper suggests that there have been at least three distinct phases in the journey towards practical impact, namely: the period from 2007-2013 when the era of customised executive education in business schools, occasionally in partnership with business consultants, led to award-winning projects in such areas as organisational development and change, human capital, strategic leadership and strategy implementation processes; on the other hand, outstanding projects in the 2013-2019 period where business schools focused on building stronger linkages with both their business and governmental audiences. For example, interest in socially responsible management education grew and this encompassed collaborative joint projects and ecosystem developments in areas such as the ESG agenda and sustainability; finally, the 2019-2023/4 period saw an intensification in the number and quality of outstanding collaborative projects in both public and business policy applications. In particular, some joint projects tackled so-called 'grand challenges' in areas such as UN sustainable development goals (SDGs) and issues of inequality and social and financial inclusion.

Ginneberge's concluding observations are well-formed. He points particularly to the advent of "complex partnerships and associated design heterogeneity" and the "growth of a high-touch technology-enabled and enhanced development journey". More 'wicked' complex development problems will be the currency of future development projects in practice.

Following this review, we present twelve papers from well-known authors and schools which we have categorised into three clusters, namely, business schools as purposive organisations; building research ecosystems harnessing the power of partnerships and multi-disciplinary frameworks; and tackling complex problems of societal impact.

In the first cluster, business schools leverage their skills and capabilities to address important managerial issues such as organisational purpose, leadership and organisational development and change. These may occur through executive education activities and requests for joint corporate and business school action learning and management projects. In the second cluster, business schools are attempting to build research ecosystems harnessing the power of partnerships between business schools as well as with business, government departments, etc., to generate collective know-how, joint research activities and co-produce impactful insights and outcomes. In the third cluster, more complex ('wicked') socio-economic problems are examined which require tri-sector collaboration (i.e. business, government and civil society) to develop longer-term ecosystems to achieve meaningful long-run societal impact.

CLUSTER 1

Concepts of the purposeful business school

Roy Suddaby's paper on 'management education with purpose' argues that management is a 'syncretic profession, "... our research must balance both descriptions of the way the world is, and aspirational visions of the way the world ought to be. Yes, our research must be rigorously scientific, however it must also rest on aspirational values and virtues that define what we study ...". Using research examples, drawn from the Gustavson School of Business in Victoria, Canada, which contains a single department of different management disciplines, he examines how values inform the conduct of research that prioritises human, social and environmental factors. The Gustavson School's sense of purpose and research mission drives research and involves four aspirational value commitments, namely: commitments to regenerative sustainability, basic applied *community-based research*, redefining impact and generating wisdom in addition to scientific knowledge. He concludes by stating "more authority arises when technical experts go beyond the way the world is, and begin to use their expertise to articulate a better world."

Johan Roos, the Chief Academic Officer, of Hult International Business School, a private school with a global footprint, argues that it has a different identity in the academic business school landscape. It has a strong practical focus, a commitment to learning and teaching excellence and a distinctive, academic and business culture. Its approach to research and impact focuses on three objectives – to increase output quality, grow institutional reputation and make a difference in society. With its more applied academic orientation it has created an intellectual learning environment with modern infrastructure and a committed, thought leadership-focused, applied faculty. The research is generated by its research structure involving three 'Impact Hubs' – Futures, Sustainability and People – where faculty become involved in community research e.g. Hult's partnership Sustainability Lab with Unilever and its efforts on diabetic care with Novo Nordisk, Diabetes UK and the NHS demonstrate applied meaningful research partnerships. Its development of Lego/Serious Play

demonstrates how its innovative pedagogical research tools have strongly influenced leadership, organisational development and change programmes and initiatives for its stakeholder partners.

Roos concludes with a series of insights from Hult's approach. Notably, "at the core is a commitment to serving the interests of societal stakeholders" and "its interdisciplinary and inclusive research perspective" and commitment to writing an extensive number of applied case studies demonstrates clear involvement and engagement with societal problems albeit with a somewhat more applied and pragmatic style.

The paper by Anand Narasimhan, IMD's Research Dean, complements Manzoni's (2023) IMD paper. It explains how a clear research strategy has emerged, and grown successfully in a very applied private business school which has a crystal clear 'Real Learning, Real Impact' vision.

Its research impact strategy is closely linked to its practical orientation. Its strategy follows a 'From Practice to Research' perspective. This means that IMD faculty and researchers focus on identifying and solving those practical problems that have long-term relevance and value for its clients and stakeholders. In attempting to solve those highly relevant problems, and issues, researchers apply rigorous, research approaches and hence follow a solution pathway which can be described as 'From Relevance, To Rigour' – reversing the rigour to relevance pattern familiar in academic research.

The paper gives examples of IMD's research agenda and portfolio, which includes topics ranging from 'World Competitiveness' to 'Family Business' as well as Business Transformation (including organisational change, people and planet issues and sustainability). This research output is sometimes reported in top academic journals but more frequently in the top, highly-rated practitioner journals, namely Harvard Business Review and MIT's Sloan Management Review (recognised in the FT top research journal list) and as award-winning projects in EFMD's Excellence in Practice (EiP) awards.

IMD's philosophy of research impact can be detected in answers to the following questions: "What if the realm of practice were to ignite fresh research dialogues?" And, if after the subsequent conversations "put purpose at the core of your strategy", then "practitioner articles [and books] can influence the trajectory of academic research."

In conclusion, the paper notes that it "values both business and applied research. The faculty values plurality (and promotes) multidisciplinary collaboration in our thought leadership activities and are conscientious about acknowledging and rewarding our impact on them."

Jon Foster-Pedley, Dean of Henley Africa Business School, discusses how to carve out identity, meaning and purpose for African management education. He carefully addresses how African schools should design management education models that "recognise the potential impact they could have across the entire ecosystem of society .... It is also necessary [for them] to play a more active role in identifying African-facing problems and engaging with all stakeholders to achieve impactful solutions."

He also discusses a number of collaborative research initiatives involving Henley and other African schools. For example, the award-winning research and teaching partnership with GIBS (the Gordon Institute of Business Science, University of Pretoria) on 'African authentic leadership' in Standard Bank, Africa. And, the pathbreaking teaching project using virtual reality (VR) and immersive learning collaborative partnerships to upskill managers at scale across Africa so that they can be exposed to both continent-wide networks and a wide range of alternative business challenges and potential solutions.

He concludes with the hope that continuing tie-ups with both African and foreign schools will enable research on such pressing issues as the strong development of entrepreneurial start-ups in Africa as well as joint programmes on improving exports and foreign trade, which should in turn, lead to very positive economic and societal impacts for the African continent.

CLUSTER 2

Development of Research Ecosystems, Partnerships and Collective Know-How

Soumitra Dutta, Dean at Saïd Business School, Oxford University, carefully outlines the elements of the school's responsible research strategy. He stresses that "responsible research is not only research that investigates social enterprises or issues of sustainability and development. Scholars focusing on all areas of business activity both can and should engage in research that leads to positive impacts for business and thus for society in general." Further, recognising that management and business is essentially an applied discipline, he emphasises that Saïd's research mission is "to produce research of the highest quality that is rigorous, imaginative and meaningfully relevant to, and enhances, business practice," and leverages the strength of all Oxford's colleges and disciplines.

Professor Andrew Stephen, Saïd's Research Dean also reinforces Dutta's proposition of rigorous, high-quality responsible research indicating applications that address large scale problems which "are boundary spanning and future focused", collaborative in research links with both practitioners and scholars in other disciplines (often in Oxford University) and closely linked with the objectives of all teaching and learning programmes at Saïd, including executive education. Examples such as the 'Future of Marketing Initiative', the 'Scenarios Planning Methodology' and the Skoll Entrepreneurship Centre's work illustrate the range, impact and importance of investigating significant societal problems. Indeed, Saïd's conscious effort to develop ecosystems to drive collaboration and wide collective know-how is clearly evident in the work of the Skoll Centre which brings together partners and co-researchers not just from the University of Oxford but also from countries and business schools/research institutes across the world.

Professor Katy Mason, Associate Dean for Research at Lancaster Management School (LUMS), in developing LUMS research strategy was also influenced by the 'responsible management agenda' and recognised that this represented "a real opportunity for business and management schools – not known for their innovative approach to business and management to shift towards something different, bold and significant" Katy wanted to build a responsible management research centre embracing the needs of the environment, the university, LUMS and individual faculty researchers. Through interactions with all constituencies, she anchored the development of a new research strategy involving a clear vision and set of strategic priorities. The agreed LUMS vision was "to have a reputation as a leading international business and management school through a focus on research, education and engagement, anchored around the theme of responsible management. Following a thorough analysis of LUMS resource strengths and distinctive capabilities, five current, and future-oriented research themes for organisations and society were identified including Sustainability, Social Justice, Innovation, Health and Wellbeing, and the Cyber (Digital) Economy. Five strategic priorities requiring collaborative, engaged, interdisciplinary and partnership-oriented research were identified: namely, a focus on RRBM principles; expanding the boundaries of research excellence; stressing impact and engagement as key issues in research; developing interdisciplinary teams, implementing best practice in research evaluation impact and identifying funding sources, government, NGOs, business, etc., to develop impactful, responsible management research projects. Illustrations of impactful research efforts are then given including the creation of research centres as 'hubs' for the LUMS research ecosystem. The example of the LUMS innovation catalyst partnership for the Blackpool Research Initiative demonstrates how a potentially valuable project for a "green growth regional economy" was generated with LUMS, government and business involvement. And LUMS link with the policy think tank – the Work Foundation – is important in understanding, and developing, initiatives for research on the future of work. As Katy indicates with an engaging metaphor (drawn from ice hockey) you need to "skate to where the puck's going next" to anticipate areas in which collective know-how can create meaningful and impactful research programmes and initiatives.

Linda Barrington and Andrew Karolyi, Associate Dean of Strategy and Dean respectively, of the SC Johnson Cornell College of Business, also advocate the case for responsible, rigorous and impactful research through engagement. They cite Hoffman's (2021) book on the engaged scholar to argue that research publication success measured in terms of high-quality citations and rankings "serves the academic institution primarily and falls short of serving the world at large." They emphasise that "responsibility, rigour and impact with relevance constitute the 'trifecta' of intentions to which business higher education researchers must aspire." They describe how cutting-edge, curiosity-driven scholarship (often of a strong disciplinary focus) should interact and engage with the more practical, and urgent, problems facing business and society. They suggest two main channels of communication for building scholarly, engaged research. First, Cornell has, over time, developed a strong and powerful ecosystem of centres, institutes and special programme initiatives for creating advantage through building, and reinforcing, rich industry and societal relationships and partnerships. This is enhanced through strong project-based experiential learning initiatives (e.g. the SMART project) which require all students to undertake, and offer solutions for, community-engaged projects with industry and government partners jointly moderated by Cornell business school faculty. Many of these projects also have an international dimension and a few are examined and explained in the paper.

Barrington and Karolyi demonstrate clearly how researchers have learned not only to explain how their engaged research has benefitted their stakeholders but also students who take a course sequence – the Engaged College initiative – and, thus, have improved their skills in, and deep awareness of, responsible management practices which they eventually carry into their post-college careers. They (the authors) conclude that while Cornell must always uphold the highest quality standards in its research, the relevance of that management research to all practitioners and stakeholders is just as critical as the rigorous nature and credibility of its academic research.

CLUSTER 3

Complex Societal Impact Projects Requiring Tri-Sector Collaboration and Cooperation

Professor Sherif Kamel, has been a pioneering and influential dean at the American University in Cairo, Egypt. The paper catalogues how he designed, and implemented, an entrepreneurial ecosystem for Egypt to encourage growth in a developing economy. He describes it as "an effective and innovative ecosystem that is government-enabled, private sector-led, innovation-driven, youth-empowered and future-oriented."

He notes that "the culture of entrepreneurship should be built bottom-up and top-down simultaneously in order to create a 'buzz' that can provide the required momentum, passion, drive and energy to help society think entrepreneurially." As the educational partner in building this ecosystem Kamel describes how they solved the jigsaw puzzle of building the ecosystem, one step at a time over a period of around ten years. This required meaningful partnerships forged with the private sector, government and civil society organisations, that enabled the creation of a private sector-led Egypt-wide, effective, scalable and entrepreneurial ecosystem which was anchored by AUCE's educational expertise.

Kamel is not resting on his laurels. His ecosystem may indeed be a 'game-changer' for both Middle East and African inclusive and impactful economic development. For example, he has founded an entrepreneurial education alliance in Africa involving business schools such as GIBS and Stellenbosch in South Africa and Lagos Business School in Nigeria to further nurture entrepreneurialism as a growth engine across the African continent.

Two examples, drawn from different regional economic and social development projects in Wales, further illustrate the pursuit of impactful social and economic development projects. Cardiff Business School in Wales has developed a well-earned reputation as a business school stressing the 'public' good – the social as well as economic dividend – and the 'public value' viewpoint (see Kitchener and Ashworth, 2023). It has focused on research issues associated with inclusive socio-economic growth, inequality and disadvantage in organisations and societies.

The first project 'Making Wales an Anti-Racist Organisation' was identified and formulated during the early phase of the COVID-19 pandemic when the devolved Welsh Government and its First Minister, became concerned about the disproportionate impact of the disease on ethnic minorities in Wales further highlighted by clear evidence of institutional racism. Professor Emmanuel Ogbonna, was asked by Wales First Minister and the Minister for Social Justice, to co-chair (with the top civil servant in Wales, the

Permanent Secretary of the Welsh government) and establish a Steering Group to develop a plan, with clear terms of reference, to eradicate institutional racism. Cardiff's Wales Centre for Public Policy provided assistance for the development of the plan which required the committed cooperation of relevant stakeholder groups from business, government, civil society and voluntary organisations. Following extensive debates, and round table meetings examining the viewpoints of all stakeholders, the steering group is now tasked with the implementation phase of the project in which the multiple and competing demands of stakeholders have to be addressed in terms of a balanced and flexible implementation plan.

Ogbonna, in his conclusions, points out that there are many lessons to be learned in developing and implementing plans in this area. First, to encourage, and improve collaborative networks between academics and all multi-sector stakeholders. Second, to expand the 'voices' of these stakeholders and to work more closely with disadvantaged communities. Third, and most importantly, business and management schools must take race seriously and lead the change towards anti-racism in Wales and elsewhere.

Professor Rick Delbridge, also from Cardiff, discusses his research goals and experience in leaving the 'theory cave' (sometimes called the 'iron cage' (Johnson and Starkey, 2023)) of narrow academic research for the richer pastures of impactful and interdisciplinary research approaches. His first challenge, as the Dean of Innovation for Cardiff University, was to build institutional structures within the university – the 'SPARK' initiative - to build a collaborative, interdisciplinary social science and business research park to enable practitioners and multi-disciplinary researchers to work together on projects designed and implemented jointly to ensure both strong problem formulation and impactful outcomes. Not surprisingly, given the layers of bureaucracy and challenges in navigating processes of university decision-making it took nine years to fully complete the research park. As 'SPARK' became close to reality, Rick chose to return to a more academic role and founded the 'Centre for Innovation Policy Research' (CIPR) and now works with a more focused interdisciplinary group of colleagues within SPARK drawn from the schools of business, planning and social sciences to attack policy and societal challenges from multiple perspectives, particularly the influence of geographic and political systems on outcomes. Rick's current work on innovation and policy practice in Wales is discussed in the paper and has focused on identifying new innovation solutions for policy problems in health, sustainability and improving local communities. He has also promoted novel approaches to the growth of commercial opportunities in the Cardiff Capital Region (the

largest cluster in Wales). He also discusses his 'ecosystem-based' conception of place-based innovation policy and outlines a 4Cs model for regional innovation policy. He reflects that in his own journey "I have not abandoned theory so much as more actively sought to have that theory and underpinning conceptual work inform research that is driven by problems and seeks to be more impactful on policy and practice."

Professor Luciano Barin-Cruz and his research colleagues at HEC Montreal, the leading francophone business school in Canada, explain the work of HEC's research ecosystem the Social Impact Hub, IDEOS, and then examine, in detail, one of its projects, SEED (Scaling Entrepreneurship for Economic Development). SEED's aim is to empower through ecosystem network approaches, positive development and social impact in developing countries such as Sri Lanka, Haiti, Tunisia and Colombia. They aim to do this by building a network of international and local promoters of entrepreneurship programmes in order to increase the capacities and capabilities of local programmes and improve the skills of social enterprises (often micro enterprises) and thereby strengthen the managerial competencies of civil society organisations. Put simply, IDEOS wants to leverage its entrepreneurial ecosystem to catalyse academic partnership collaborations between Canada and the Global South and establish meaningful networks (both academic and practitioner) to translate entrepreneurial knowledge for improving the inclusive economic, social and governance growth of developing countries.

The paper explains the SEED project and its methodology which involved understanding the ecosystem, developing local teaching content and training approaches (training the trainers), facilitating the delivery and analysis of the training programme and assessing its value with all the different stakeholders.

The lessons learned from the SEED programme have enabled many local communities to build their entrepreneurial and economic platforms and capabilities on a continuing basis. The academics involved have published papers in academic journals, white papers, reports, etc., in order to share and disseminate the results of their training programmes to a wider audience.

Importantly, the evidence of the social impact of this social innovation ecosystem has spread to its application to vulnerable, as well as underserved, indigenous communities in Canada. This is not surprising since the key success factor in the SEED programme has been the recognition in all developing countries of the importance of community assets, namely, the value of knowledge, skills and social networks as well as the growth of community identity and pride.

Clearly, the projects from Egypt, Wales and Canada and the Global South are fully encompassed within the so-called EDIR (Equality, Diversity, Inclusivity and Respect) and inclusive growth agenda of business schools. Dean Morris Mthombeni's paper addresses one aspect of EDIR, namely, the role and importance of women in the business school sector. It focuses specifically, on the role of the leader, based on experiences in the evolution of GIBS (the Gordon Institute of Business Science) in the University of Pretoria, South Africa.

He first examines the current state of affairs about the contributions of women in business schools on a number of dimensions (and he 'crunches' the numbers in relation to these dimensions) namely: women as employees in business schools – what is their representation in terms of faculty and management positions? Women in the classroom – what is the gender balance in business school classrooms? Women as authors of journal articles and leading textbooks. Further, how often are they the lead authors or protagonists in well-known teaching cases? What is the level of female representation in emerging industries such as digital and computer technology? How often are women identified as leaders in such growth areas?

His view on the wide adoption of EDIR goals in business schools is that, at least, on the principle of gender equity, few business school leaders practice what they preach.

He then reviews GIBS exemplary progress on many of the above dimensions – over the 20 or so years of its existence it has already had one very successful academic team led by a female dean, Nicola Kleyn, and has strong gender representation in terms of faculty, research, faculty management roles and students in the classroom. He is rightly proud of these gains. His concern is that following COVID-19 the evidence shows a measurable loss of female leaders in society. He concludes with the strong and urgent view that "our role as business schools must be to produce a groundswell of female leaders who can fundamentally drive EDIR across society. This, in turn, will lead to greater female ownership and representation underscoring collective commitments to the UN's SDG 5, namely gender equality."

References

Blackburn, R., S. Dibb and I. Tonks (2023) Business and Management Studies in the United Kingdom's 2021 Research Excellence Framework: Implications for Research Quality Assessment. *British Journal of Management* (forthcoming)

Cornuel, E. (2023) Positive Impact: An Important Role for Business School Leadership in a Changing Precarious World in Cornuel *et al.* (2023) o*p cit*, pp.9-12

Cornuel, E., H. Thomas and M. Wood (Eds.) (2023) *Perspectives on the Impact, Mission and Purpose of the Business School*. Abingdon: Routledge

Davies, J., H. Thomas, E. Cornuel and R. Cremer (2023) *Leading a Business School*. Abingdon: Routledge

De Meyer, A. (2021) Does the DNA of Business Schools Need to Change? *Global Focus, 5* (2) pp.28-31

Ginneberge, J. (2023, this volume) The Evolution of EFMD's Excellence in Practice Awards: A Fifteen Year Journey of Supporting Impactful Growth, in Cornuel, E., H. Thomas and M. Wood (Eds.) (2023) *Business School Research: Excellence, Academic Quality and Positive*

Haley, U.V.C. and A. Jack (2023) Measuring Societal Impact in Business and Management Studies: From Challenges to Change. *Sage Business, White Paper*. London: Sage Publications

Hughes, T., D. Webber and N. O'Regan (2019) Achieving Wider Impact in Business and Management: Analysing the Case Studies from REF 2014. *Studies in Higher Education 44* (4) pp. 628-642

Irwin, A (2023) Open up the Business School! From Rigour and Relevance to Purpose, Responsibility and Quality in Cornuel *et al.* (2023) *op cit*, pp.39-44

Johnson, G. and K. Starkey (2023) How Management Academics Have Locked Themselves in an Iron Cage in Cornuel *et al.* (2023) *op cit*, pp.33-39

Kalika, M. (2022) *BSIS: A Decade of Impact*. France: EMS GEODIF

Kalika, M. and E. Cornuel (2023) The Search for Meaning and its Role in Promoting Business Schools' Societal Impact, Cornuel *et al.* (2023) *op cit*, pp.20-25

Kitchener, M. and R. Ashworth (2023) Building Back Better: Purpose-driven Business Schools in Cornuel *et al.* (2023) *op cit*, pp.45-50

Locke, E. and J.C. Spender (2011) *Confronting Manageriality: How the Business Elite and Their Business Schools Threw Our Lives Out of Balance*. London: Zed Books

Meyer, R.E. (2023) in Haley and Jack (2023) *op cit*, pp.5-6

Pidd, M. and J, Broadbent (2015) Business and Management Studies in the 2014 Research and Excellence Framework. *British Journal of Management, 26* (4), pp.569-581

Thomas, H., A. Wilson and M. Lee (2023) *Creating a New Management University*. Abingdon: Routledge

Tsui, A., M.J. Bitner, S. Netessine (2023) What Topics Should Business School Research Focus on? in Cornuel *et al.* (2023) *op cit*, pp.25-33

About the Author

Howard Thomas is Emeritus Professor at Singapore Management University and Senior Advisor at EFMD Global.

EFMD and Societal Impact

ERIC CORNUEL AND HOWARD THOMAS

Papers on Positive and Societal Impact from an EFMD Perspective

Since its foundation over 50 years ago EFMD has maintained a firm belief in socially responsible management education directed towards the creation of positive, meaningful societal impact.

The values of EFMD are perhaps best exemplified in comments made by Ray van Schaik one of our most respected chairpersons who at that time was President of EFMD. Schaik (1996, p.13) on the occasion of EFMD's 25th anniversary, noted that it has clearly sought to link the corporate and public world and the world of education and hence be a catalyst and a 'broad church' encouraging debate and dialogue between corporations and institutions of management education and learning. Consequently, it has consistently tried to attract a significant proportion of practising managers.

Van Schaik (1996, p.14), further suggested that 'one of the most fundamental properties (of business schools) will be that their students will know how to handle the unexpected, how to handle life'. He went on to add that 'on top of technical skills – which have become a sine qua non ... new managers more than ever should abhor rigid concepts and thrive on the art of improvisation'.

Schaik also clearly specified his vision for the role and purpose of EFMD in the management education environment:

It should endeavour to continue to be a *trait d'union*, a link, between the corporate world and the world of education; it should continue to build and explore a network of personal and business relationships that enables it to contribute to the process of high-quality, practical, 'true to life' education ... and finally, it should continue to cement its relationship with governments and public bodies that are involved in the process of management and education.

The development of the academic, business and government linkages has been a strong influence in the evolution, role and strategic positioning of the business school in the European context. EFMD has constantly focused on linking European educational experience and innovative ideas with meaningful impact on management practice and learning. It has also emphasised an international perspective in building its approaches to the growth of high-quality management education.

As a result, Europeans generally favour socially responsible capitalism acting in concert with all stakeholders over what is sometimes characterised as unbridled shareholder value capitalism. European business, and European management education, has thus developed a clear identity and a balanced relationship with government and society where government is often important in the funding of higher education. In this process, business grows not only economically and technically but also gains social responsibility and legitimacy. And, the European culture and environment encourages greater social empathy and more direct corporate cooperation with government to alleviate poverty and social welfare with an emphasis on inclusive growth and human and economic progress.

DOI: 10.4324/9781003467410-2

Hence, the belief in socially responsible management education is endemic. It has been deeply embedded in its EQUIS accreditation peer review standards for the last ten years and has been enhanced by over 60 impact studies carried out globally in 19 countries by EFMD's Business School Impact System (BSIS). Further, concrete evidence of the practical engagement of business schools has been published in special annual issues of Global Focus (EFMD's magazine). These issues summarise the outstanding evidence of the practical engagement activities of specific business schools who have won EFMD's 'Excellence in Practice (EIP) awards. It is also stressed by agencies such as the GRLI (Globally Responsible Leadership Initiative), EABIS (European Academy for Business in Society, now renamed as Academy Business and Society), PRME (Principles for Responsible Management Education), and RRBM (the Responsible Research in Business and Management Community), which have been carefully nurtured by EFMD in association with the endorsement of the sustainable development goals of the U.N. Global Compact. In particular the RRBM Initiative began with the founder's article (Tsui, 2015) on socially responsible leadership in Global Focus. This led EFMD to support the creation of RRBM with a core 'founding' set of 20 or so scholars. Their overarching aim was to address the two major problems of business school research; namely, its credibility and its practical, societal impact.

It should be pointed out that through a number of EU and EFMD initiatives there is currently a much greater emphasis on cross-European educational networking for the development of interdisciplinarity in teaching and research programmes (e.g. Erasmus) and high-quality faculty development. Thus, the quality, and impact, of European research output is well recognised on the world scene.

In addition, Europeans view formal analytic and strategy models and technical skills as valuable and sensible but also argue that such analytically, and scientifically, rigorous approaches may be too heavily emphasised in current curricula. This, in turn, may sometimes lead to the production of scientific research of little practical managerial relevance.

An emphasis on softer skills, more socially responsible management, and vision and communication skills for engaging employees are viewed as critical and important attributes. Indeed, Europeans believe strongly in a balanced philosophy in management education involving an appropriate mix of course and project work to develop skills of analysis, synthesis and criticism. Through this process, the differentiation between European and other models of management education becomes clear and provides welcome diversity in models and management approaches in management education.

Over the last ten years EFMD has also sponsored a number of research studies on the future of management education (including Thomas et al. (2013) and Carlile et al. (2015)). The initial evidence on directions forward from these research studies was discussed with the EFMD Board and led EFMD to produce and publish a manifesto (based on some of this early research evidence) on its 40th anniversary outlining "The Future of Management Education" (24 January 2012) and reflecting a more European-style of business school which could be achieved by deans adopting five clear principles as follows:

- **Transformational Change**
  Business schools will have to change the way they operate. They should take a multiple stakeholder perspective in the design of their programmes and research activities. Schools should be transformed into moral institutions that perpetuate strong values, a clear vision and open processes in governance and strategic change.
- **A More Holistic Approach to Management Education**
  Business schools should incorporate a more integrated and liberal view of management education in which knowledge of the humanities, culture and history can be integrated into the principles of responsible management and form a framework for cross-disciplinary thinking. This implies that issues of ethics, moral responsibility and sustainability "should be embedded in the core curricula of management education as well as in the broader practices of schools."

- **Sustainability**

  "Sustainability, with its ecological, social and economic dimensions" requires those in management education to "carefully consider cultural and developmental differences when dealing with sustainability issues."

- **Critical Thinking and Whole Person Learning**

  Critical thinking must be designed to emerge from the tension between learning about humanistic principles and the more professional, analytic business subjects, such as accounting, finance and marketing. Students must learn how to absorb skills of both analysis and synthesis but also develop a personal willingness to reflect on issues and incorporate self-criticism into the learning process.

- **Accreditations (such as EFMD Quality Improvement System - EQUIS)**

  Accreditations must be updated to reflect the advent of multiple stakeholder impact perspectives and a more holistic approach to management education. They must also recognise that 75-80% of all business school students are participants in undergraduate programmes. The focus on the MBA by many business schools (largely because of MBA-based reputational media rankings) has diverted attention from undergraduate business education.

Even more recent studies of management education's future added the growing focus on the adoption of technological approaches for online and hybrid teaching models in business schools and more extensive research on digital business models for societal impact.

The Covid pandemic and the Ukraine war threw business schools and management educators into an immediate period of disruptive transformation and change. This disruptive process led to changes in teaching approaches requiring critical development of digital platforms and creating new innovative methods and ideas for research studies and impact goals. It provided a mandate for business schools to generate significant positive impact on societies and ecosystems and learn how to manage them successfully and effectively.

CONCLUSION

We believe that the dominant research model in business schools must evolve quickly. We must augment the 'great divide' between academic excellence in research and its practical application. Otherwise, we may go from a 'publish or perish' to a 'publish and perish' outcome. We need to move towards a more open system instead of an atomised intellectual endeavour that is constrained to fulfilling legitimacy goals in narrow academic circles. It is clear that we need faculty members to be engaged in, and most importantly, be rewarded for path-breaking multidisciplinary research, applied collaborative projects as well as innovation in teaching, engagement in society and communities. We need more engaged professors and scholars (Hoffman, 2021), providing rigorous responsible and impactful research which is relevant for all stakeholders. This is precisely a vision that is supported by EFMD.

Thus, business schools have a critical role to play in 'rewiring' our missions for research relevance, impact and reach, and to be close to the needs and address real issues of society and economy. Being uniquely positioned at the intersection of social science, technology and business, and having a reasonable degree of institutional autonomy, we can contribute immensely to solving global and complex challenges such as climate change, rising inequalities, international isolationism, eroding democratic systems, and the spread of fake news.

Business schools are human institutions embracing humanistic and societal values and management is a creative art and not a deterministic science. We must therefore view management education from a wide range of stakeholder perspectives.

The future identity, image, reputation, value and distinctive differentiation of the business and management school, both as an individual entity as well as its impact and contribution to the success of the societies in which it operates, should be paramount, and the opportunity is clearly apparent in today's environment. This is a journey which EFMD is proud to share globally with our stakeholders in a co-operative and collaborative spirit.

References

Carlile, P. R., S. H. Davidson, K.W. Freeman, H. Thomas and
    N. Venkatraman (2016) *Re-imagining Business Education:
    Insights and Actions from the Business Education Jam*.
    Bingley, UK: Emerald Publishing

Hoffman, A. (2021) *The Engaged Scholar: Expanding the Impact
    of Academic Research in today's world.* Stanford, CA: Stanford
    University Press

Thomas, H., L. Thomas & A. Wilson (2013) *Promises Fulfilled and
    Unfulfilled in Management Education*. Bingley, UK: Emerald
    Publishing

Thomas, H., M. Lee, L. Thomas and A. Wilson (2013) *Securing
    the Future of Management Education*. Bingley, UK: Emerald
    Publishing

Tsui, A. (2015) Re-connecting with the business world: socially
    responsible scholarship. *Global Focus, 9*(1), pp.36-39

Van Schaik, G. (1996) in EFMD *Training the Fire Brigade:
    Preparing for the Unimaginable*. Brussels, Belgium: EFMD
    Publications, pp.13-14

About the Authors

Eric Cornuel is the President of EFMD Global.
*Howard Thomas is Emeritus Professor at Singapore Management University and Senior
Advisor at EFMD Global.*

The Evolution of EFMD's Excellence in Practice Awards: A 15-year Journey of Supporting Impactful Growth

JAN GINNEBERGE

Papers on Positive and Societal Impact from an EFMD Perspective

The Timeline

2007 marked the beginning of the Excellence in Practice journey, which at the beginning had a single winner determined during a workshop held at EFMD's Annual Conference. In 2009, on the occasion of the Brussels Annual Conference, the competition evolved and the jury composition became more elaborate, with sub-juries for each of the four clusters of cases covered. These sub-juries included a diversity of representatives: a provider representative, a corporate representative, a publication representative, and an EFMD representative. The selection of finalists during this year was based on a grid of criteria, making the competition more structured and competitive. The most significant shift occurred in 2010 when the competition adopted its current format, featuring multiple categories and multiple winners. This change allowed for the recognition of a broader range of participants within the competition.

As of 2011, the competition became linked to EFMD's Executive Education Conference with case presentations taking place a day before the conference. This further enhanced the visibility and importance of the competition within the sector. Finally, in 2012, the competition was fully integrated into the conference structure, solidifying its exposure at a significant event.

In summary, the competition's timeline showcases its evolution from a single-winner format to a more elaborate and structured competition with multiple categories and strong ties to the Executive Education Conference.

SIGNIFICANT CONTRIBUTION TO KNOWLEDGE CREATION IN THE SECTOR

The EFMD Excellence in Practice Awards has established a valuable library of best practices since its inception in 2007 (Global Focus, 2010-2022). Over the years, a total of 526 cases have been received, showcasing a wealth of knowledge and expertise in the field of executive development.

The competition's contributions are marked not only by the quantity but also by the diversity of submissions. The cases come from a wide variety of sources, reflecting both global reach (Western Europe, Russia, the Middle East, Africa, India, South-East Asia, China, Australia, South and Central America, the United States, and Canada) and client diversity, encompassing companies, governmental organisations, social profit organisations, and networks. The range of suppliers is equally diverse, with submissions coming from in-house Learning and Development departments, business schools, and alternative providers, contributing to the growing diversity of the partnerships. Many of these projects demonstrated remarkable ambition, with a significant focus on ethical, community, and corporate social responsibility (CSR) initiatives.

This diversity enriched the jury's debates and offered a privileged view of trends in Learning and Development practices. A jury overseeing the competition evolved over the years, reflecting a commitment to professionalising the approach. Notably, practitioners with expertise in the field have become an integral part of the jury composition. This inclusion ensures that the evaluation process benefits from real-world insights and practical knowledge. Furthermore, the competition has been providing feedback to winners since 2009, offering valuable insights for continuous improvement. Starting from 2011, this feedback has been extended to all authors. In summary, the competition's jury

DOI: 10.4324/9781003467410-3

Annual Research Volume 2 – Papers on Positive and Societal Impact from an EFMD Perspective

The Evolution of EFMD's Excellence in Practice Awards: A 15-year Journey of Supporting Impactful Growth
Jan Ginneberge
....

has embraced professionalism by including practitioners and has established a feedback mechanism that promotes ongoing growth and excellence among both winners and submitting partnerships.

The impact of this competition extends beyond the entries themselves. The winning cases, dating from 2015 to 2023, have been available on the EFMD website, with a total of 122 documents accessible online. Additionally, articles in EFMD's Global Focus have been featuring the competition's content since 2008, with a dedicated annual Global Focus supplement featuring edited articles since 2010. As of 2023, 87 articles from this supplement are still available online. Thanks to applicants formalising their experiences and their willingness to share and discuss them on the EFMD website, the Global Focus Supplement, and the Executive Development Conference, an intense exchange amongst practitioners has been made possible.

The Excellence in Practice cases also highlighted the integrator role of in-house Learning and Development departments, emphasising their alignment with multiple internal stakeholders and the deployment of various development approaches. The recognised projects and interventions excelled in the dual challenge of partnering with the business to address key challenges and collaborating with an ecosystem of suppliers to provide solutions that met expectations.

By 2013, companies had been facing a challenging economic climate for over five years, which increased the risk of reactive rather than proactive measures. This environment limited options for long-term interventions focused on developing organisational capabilities and culture. HR development faced scrutiny and efficiency targets, often prioritising the support of existing services with reduced resources over proactive analysis and issue framing. However, the cases in the Excellence in Practice Award competition showcased creativity and adaptability in coping with these pressures and trends, including new formats of risk sharing, mutual commitment, and inventive partnership constructions.

In summary, the 2008 financial crisis prompted a re-evaluation of Learning and Development investments, ultimately highlighting the value and impact that well-structured Learning and Development initiatives could bring. These years marked a period of transformation and adaptation for Learning and Development organisations, where they evolved to become essential contributors to business success and demonstrated their ability to thrive in challenging economic climates. It shifted the perception of Learning and Development from being a cost to being an impactful creator of value.

BRINGING AN INVESTMENT PERSPECTIVE TO LEARNING AND DEVELOPMENT

The 2008 financial crisis had a profound impact on corporations, leading to significant restructuring efforts. One consequence of this crisis was the limitation or even halting of Learning and Development initiatives. This shift led to the requirement for a sound learning business case for each Learning and Development project, emphasising alignment with strategic priorities and ensuring impact. EFMD's Excellence in Practice Award aimed to spotlight these practices and their role in creating impactful Learning and Development interventions, supporting the credibility and professionalism of the wider development ecosystem.

Annual Research Volume 2 – Papers on Positive and Societal Impact from an EFMD Perspective

The Evolution of EFMD's Excellence in Practice Awards: A 15-year Journey of Supporting Impactful Growth
Jan Ginneberge
....

AIMING FOR IMPACT

The Excellence in Practice (EiP) framework prioritises impact as a critical factor for award selection. This is determined by assessing quantitative and qualitative indicators of impact used by the corporate Learning and Development organisation. The actual changes caused by the Learning and Development initiative are considered, as well as the ultimate impact on the company's business, finances, customers or its products and/or services. The perceived impact by owners and stakeholders is also taken into account.

In the past, investing in incumbent executives might have been viewed as a matter of conviction or belief, but Learning and Development projects now explicitly mention the organisational agenda. Objectives frequently centre around leadership, talent, or professional development, serving as catalysts for organisational change that extends beyond the individual participant's dimension. Award winners serve as prime examples as they establish development activities aimed at clarifying priorities and boosting organisational growth.

On a personal level, developments may lean towards predefined competencies and profiles, but a growing trend is to embrace an open growth ambition. This approach seeks to tap into each leader's innate potential, reflecting a broader and more flexible perspective on leadership development. An increasing number of projects concentrate on cultural change, with the goal of creating a conducive context that fosters innovation and entrepreneurship. Notably, some cases incorporate societal impact as an integral part of their project purpose and measurement, whether by nature of the project itself or intentionally added to enrich the learning experience.

DEFINING THE CHALLENGE

In order for the Learning and Development initiative to be considered a valuable investment, it is crucial for the project business case to outline the challenge that the client organisation intends to tackle. The effectiveness of the intervention will ultimately depend on how much impact it has on this challenge. To ensure that there is no confusion, the business case should address the following questions: How was the challenge initially identified? Who was responsible for addressing it? What was the connection between this business challenge and the corporate strategy? How was this integrated into HR and business processes? Finally, what was the desired outcome of the Learning and Development initiative as formulated from the outset?

Personal growth agenda

The Excellence in Practice Awards showcase cases that prioritise personal growth, values, and behaviours among managers and leaders. In today's ever-changing and unpredictable world, it is not enough to rely on rigid models or academic theories from textbooks. Instead, it is crucial for managers and leaders to strengthen their personalities, sense of responsibility, and personal capabilities - particularly in the human and emotional aspects. This will enable them to address challenges and scenarios that defy standard templates and grids.

The award-winning cases take a dual perspective, and consider both organisational and participant viewpoints. They aim to achieve cross-functional and cultural impact, reflecting the aspiration to foster an environment of growth and development. This systems approach recognises the interconnectedness of various factors and highlights the need for holistic solutions to navigate the complexities of today's business environment.

Organisational and business transformation

The focus on Learning and Development as an investment has undergone a significant shift. It now explicitly references both business and organisational aims when developing cohorts of individuals. This shift has led to multi-level, systemic indications of impact, spanning individual, process, organisational, company portfolio, and business levels.

In many cases, orchestrated programmes were designed to target different populations, often interconnected or building on each other. This holistic approach demonstrated a genuine determination among the award winners to drive transformation in both the organisation and the business while nurturing professionals and executives.

A recurring theme in many cases was the challenge of growth. Learning and Development actively embraced this challenge by exploring and paving new pathways for businesses. Talent development award winners recognised a growing need for nurturing 'internal' talent to fill succession or entrepreneurial pipelines. On the other hand, organisational development award winners explicitly referred to organisational turning points, leveraging re-alignment and restructuring efforts to initiate large-scale interventions. These interventions aimed to foster engagement, problem-solving, innovation, and fresh perspectives.

Many projects were deeply embedded in the client's organisational and systemic design. They involved company-wide, multi-layer, intact teams that facilitated cascading ideas and changes throughout the organisation. Beyond this initial layer, numerous cases reported organisational and team impacts. Some referred to these as 'organisational experiments', while others adopted internal consulting formats. Additionally, Learning and Development interventions sometimes resulted in the rollout of leadership frameworks and even performance management systems.

Societal changes

Several initiatives aimed at positioning client organisations within their respective ecosystems were observed in addition to individual and organisational impact indicators. These initiatives included, among others, sustainability reporting by SMEs to align with their B2B supply chains, the redefinition of stakeholder management strategies, and efforts to secure favourable positions in industry rankings.

One of the most notable surprises in this year's collection of cases was the significant increase in submissions addressing Sustainable Development Goal (SDG)-type challenges. The cases received clearly reflected the heightened focus on social and ecological issues, which was triggered by the COVID-19 pandemic's aftermath. This trend wasn't limited to a single cluster, as many cases showcased the intersection of social and ecological concerns with business issues. As someone aptly noted, social and ecological issues are converging with business concerns more than ever before. Thus, alongside the recurrent cases focusing on culture and organisational transformation to support talent retention, enhance client-centricity, foster digital business agility, and promote organisational integration, a diverse array of cases emerged, spotlighting social entrepreneurship, diversity and inclusion, corporate volunteering, stakeholder recognition, sustainability reporting, and other related themes.

MEASUREMENT: LINKING THE IMPACT TO THE CHALLENGE

Over the past 15 years, organisations have become more skilled at measuring their impact. However, there is still room for improvement in this area.

When it comes to measuring the impact of Learning and Development, several effective practices are being shared within the industry. Organisations are increasingly focused on quantifying the influence of Learning and Development on various aspects, such as the self-renewal of a company, the restored confidence of a management group, the successful repositioning of a business portfolio, and the level of integration of successive acquisitions. These measurements include engagement surveys of both employees and external stakeholders, innovation readiness assessments, benchmark assessments of an organisation, behavioural assessments of individuals, impact surveys, career progression indicators, and project outcomes. One innovative case introduced the concept of Social Return on Investment, emphasising the broad-reaching effects of impactful Learning and Development initiatives.

While some cases present compelling quantitative measures of impact, many rely on qualitative measures, often self-reported by participants, with the Net Promoter Score being a persistent trend. Qualitative measures have a less solid claim in evaluating impact compared to those that can link quantitative indicators to the organisational and business claims initially made. Furthermore, the sources of measurement vary, enhancing the strength and validity of the indicators used. Some cases include participants' direct hierarchy, from line managers to directors, while others seek customer feedback. A few cases even employ external providers for impact measurement. The timeline of measurement is equally diverse, ranging from in-programme formative measurements for real-time adjustments to indicators demonstrating impact on behaviours over a range of durations, from within the year to up to a decade of ongoing investments with a focus on both business and people.

The introduction of technology and the active use of peers as feedback and support mechanisms have brought interesting developments. Standard practices now include video-taping and uploading personal projects at the beginning of a programme, progress reporting in between group modules, and webinars held months after the programme's completion.

SOME FINAL COMMENTS ON THE INTERACTIONS BETWEEN RESEARCH AND PRACTICE

Building research from practice

As already indicated above, one of the main contributions of the Excellence in Practice awards to the field of executive development has been to motivate supplier-client partnerships to formalise their projects. And as such it feeds the body of knowledge in general and eventually research in academic-oriented organisations.

Importance of research-inspired practice

When looking at the first five years of the awards, the strong linkage between the executive education consultancy (as well as outside consultancies) activities facilitated customised executive education in areas such as OD, human capital, strategy development, and organisational change. It was also apparent that these endeavours cannot be claimed as an exclusive domain for academic institutions, on the contrary.

In the following five years, the visibility given to a wide variety of projects encouraged several unusual partnerships to come forward and apply. The initial success of applications with a focus on responsible management, and stakeholder management ideas prompted a broader batch of ecosystem development projects, collaboration, and partnerships in areas such as sustainability / ESG, etc., leading to stronger ties across all stakeholders.

In the last five years, these trends strengthened even further, and we have seen an increasing focus on societal challenges such as SDGs, people and the planet, economic growth and inclusion, etc..

A problem-solving perspective to research impact measurement

Professionals across the academic as well as non-academic supplier and client base use a wide body of research to address the challenges at hand. The impact of their projects was measured on the positive evolution of the issues and problems identified. One could see a double route here for measuring the impact of research: where was the research used in projects, and which of these projects were successful? As some of the suppliers are looking for brand recognition of their organisation through the awards, a few are also looking to 'market' their research.

References

Global Focus (2010) Excellence in Practice 2010. Outstanding and impactful partnerships between businesses and educational organisations. *Global Focus, 4*(3)

Global Focus (2011) Excellence in Practice 2011. Outstanding and impactful partnerships between businesses and educational organisations. *Global Focus, 5*(3)

Global Focus (2012) Excellence in Practice 2012. Recognising outstanding Learning and Development partnerships. *Global Focus, 6*(3)

Global Focus (2013) Excellence in Practice 2013. Recognising outstanding Learning and Development partnerships. *Global Focus, 7*(3)

Global Focus (2014) Excellence in Practice 2014. Recognising outstanding Learning and Development partnerships. *Global Focus, 8*(3)

Global Focus (2015) Excellence in Practice 2015. Recognising outstanding Learning and Development partnerships. *Global Focus, 9*(3)

Global Focus (2016) Excellence in Practice 2016. Recognising outstanding Learning and Development partnerships. *Global Focus, 10*(3)

Global Focus (2017) Excellence in Practice 2017. Recognising outstanding Learning and Development partnerships. *Global Focus, 11*(3)

Global Focus (2018) Excellence in Practice 2018. Recognising outstanding Learning and Development partnerships. *Global Focus, 12*(3)

Global Focus (2019) Excellence in Practice 2019. Recognising outstanding Learning and Development partnerships. *Global Focus, 13*(3)

Global Focus (2020) Excellence in Practice 2020. Recognising outstanding Learning and Development partnerships. *Global Focus, 14*(3)

Global Focus (2021) Excellence in Practice 2021. Recognising outstanding Learning and Development partnerships. *Global Focus, 15*(3)

Global Focus (2022) Excellence in Practice 2022. Recognising outstanding Learning and Development partnerships. *Global Focus, 16*(2)

About the Author

Jan is an Executive Advisor and an acknowledged expert in the Learning and Development field. He is also a senior advisor to EFMD's corporate services particularly with respect to the EIP awards programme and the Executive Education conference.

Management Research with Purpose

ROY SUDDABY

Concepts of the Purposeful Business School

Like corporations, business schools have struggled with their sense of purpose. Critics accuse business schools of lacking engagement with practice (Rynes *et al.*, 2001), promoting bad management theory (Ghoshal, 2005), and failing to cultivate an ethos of professionalism in management (Khurana, 2007). Little wonder that leading gurus openly proclaim that management scholarship is troubled (Mintzberg, 2004) and that business schools have lost their way (Bennis and O'Toole, 2005).

Most of the criticisms leveled at business schools derive directly from how we conduct management research. The famous Gordon-Howell Report of 1959 charged business schools with lacking rigorous research and being unscientific (Gordon and Howell, 1959). Today, however, we could as easily argue that business schools are *too* scientific. We produce large volumes of studies that may be statistically significant in a scientific sense, but meaningfully insignificant in a practical sense. Paradoxically, the more scientific our research has become, the less impact it has. Why is this the case? How can we fix it?

The answer to the "why" question rests in the unique knowledge mandate of management as a profession. Professions like medicine or engineering have a scientific knowledge mandate, one that describes the world the way it is. Professions like law, by contrast, have a normative mandate, one that describes the world the way it *ought to be*. Management, however, is a *syncretic profession* (Halliday, 1985), one that occupies an intellectual space between these two ways of knowing. Our research, therefore, should balance both descriptions of the way the world is, and aspirational visions of the way the world ought to be. Yes, our research must be rigorously scientific. However, it must also rest on aspirational values and virtues that define what we study, how it is studied, and why studying it is important. Striking a balance between what is, and what ought to be, is what Thomas Kuhn termed the

'essential tension' in science (Kuhn, 1977). As a syncretic profession, a primary function of our scholarship is to mediate and integrate these two different ways of knowing.

The answer to the 'how' question suggests that business schools must embrace their status as a syncretic profession in their research. Business schools should build their research strategies around a core set of values that encourage researchers to analyse both judgements of fact - the way the world is – and judgements of value – the way the world ought to be. Business schools excel at analysing judgements of fact. They are, however, much less effective at judgements of value as values are less amenable to scientific study. In place of expertise in empiricism, judgements of value require expertise in morality, ethical virtues and an appreciation of how values and facts tend to interpenetrate each other (Suddaby, 2019). If we want to generate research with purpose, management scholars must pay attention to what other professions have known for a long time, i.e. the interaction of technical facts and moral values generates knowledge that will be persuasive to other professions and will grant management the legitimacy, authority and relevance that critics suggest has been lost (Halliday *op cit*).

To illustrate how values can inform and advance management research we examine the research strategy of the Peter B. Gustavson School of Business at the University of Victoria in Canada. The school has a long-standing commitment to the advancement of research that grants priority to human, social and environmental interests. This sense of purpose informs four aspirational value commitments that characterise the research mission of the school; a commitment to regenerative sustainability, a commitment to basic, applied and community-based research, a commitment to redefining impact, and a commitment to generating wisdom in addition to scientific knowledge.

DOI: 10.4324/9781003467410-4

REGENERATIVE SUSTAINABILITY – CREATING PURPOSEFUL RESEARCH

Most business schools acknowledge a commitment to sustainability, which encourages organisations and individuals to reduce human impact on nature. Regenerative sustainability, by contrast, seeks to go beyond minimising human impact by innovative practices designed to *restore and revitalise* the natural and social environment. This approach to sustainability reflects two core values (or pillars) that define the school's purpose – sustainability and innovation. Gustavson's research strategy states, "we embrace research that advances regenerative sustainability that inspires and enables business to transform economies, strengthen communities and revitalise ecosystems."

The commitment to research on regenerative sustainability occurs largely through the Centre for Social and Sustainable Innovation (CSSI). The centre supports faculty, postdoctoral fellows and PhD students engaged in a broad range of projects that seek to innovate regenerative sustainability in the area of climate change, community resilience, indigenous organising and economic reconciliation, immigrant entrepreneurship, regenerative agriculture, food security, and workplace democracy.

An outstanding example of regenerative sustainability research is CSSI Director Natalie Slawinski's decade-long research project on community resilience at Fogo Island on the East Coast of Canada. Natalie uses an engaged research approach to co-create knowledge and help address a societal problem in partnership with Shorefast, a Canadian social enterprise dedicated to building economic and cultural resilience in the community through a variety of charitable programmes and social businesses. Fogo Island is a community off the coast of Newfoundland that suffered decades of economic decline due to the global collapse of cod fishing. Natalie's partnership with Shorefast has generated a number of impact-driven initiatives, most notably the PLACE Dialogues, a yearly workshop that creates tools, resources, and networks designed to advance their community development work.

Faculty member Simon Pek's research exemplifies the school's commitment to regenerative sustainability. Simon is the recipient of $450,000 to support his innovative research on workplace voice and democratic and deliberative forms of organisational governance. Simon takes the objective knowledge from his research and enacts it in practice as the Steering Committee Lead of the Ontario Assembly on Workplace Democracy. Simon also co-founded and serves as a member of the board of directors of Democracy in Practice, a non-profit dedicated to democratic experimentation, innovation, and capacity-building. Simon's research has been recognised by both the University of Victoria, as the inaugural recipient of the UVic President's Chair in Research, and by the Academy of Management as the Western Academy of Management's Ascendant Scholar Award.

Matt Murphy offers a slightly different view of regenerative sustainability in his research. Matt is the principle investigator in a $2,500,000 collaborative grant to promote sustainable communities. This project is an extension of Matt's commitment to programmatic research focused on improving indigenous communities' efforts to protect their rights and fulfil their own visions of sustainable development. One of the many impactful outcomes of this research is the development of a community impact-assessment tool that helps First Nations evaluate and monitor the degree of socio-cultural fit and impact of proposed economic development models.

These projects build on a core commitment to community-based research, which broadens the traditional view of business research that serves the interest of managers to a view that embraces a broader range of stakeholders and a need to understand the impact of managerial practices on the communities and societies in which they operate. The research usefully applies the technical expertise of management scholars to research that holds a value-based purpose – to improve the plight of citizens, workers and communities.

BASIC AND APPLIED RESEARCH – CREATING RELEVANT RESEARCH

Gustavson commits to research that has impact in academia, in the classroom, the boardroom and in global and local communities. As such, the School seeks to generate research that is rigorous and of high academic quality according to our academic peers, but is also pedagogically meaningful to students and educators, and practically relevant to business, practice regulators and stakeholders in business and society. Such research necessarily requires the creation of collaborative partnerships with industry, government and community partners. Below is an illustrative sample of current projects that captures the breadth and depth of the capacity of Gustavson to create research that goes beyond mere statistical significance and adds value to practice through a commitment to research that stands in the service of society.

Faculty members Elango Elangovan and Rick Cotton collaborate with the British Columbia Ministry of Public Safety and the Solicitor General in an action-research project designed to improve the engagement and retention of correctional officers. Their research begins with the observation that most jobs that people do are not easy ones. The work itself can often be an unusual mix of routine activities and stress, anxiety, and uncertainty, the context uninspiring and a bit depressive, the physical environment quite unpleasant and dangerous, and the rewards limited. However, such jobs are also essential and it is an important but difficult challenge to make this work meaningful. Using an action research framework, Elango and Rick created a framework for enhancing the meaningfulness and fit of such jobs. They have provided the Ministry with a set of actionable recommendations that change the design, structure and operationalisation of these jobs. They have also provided mechanisms by which the Ministry can better assess recruitment, engagement, and retention of officers and, in the second phase of this research, will assist the Ministry in implementation.

Another illustration of Gustavon's commitment to research that combines academic research with practical relevance is Basma Majerbi's research on sustainable finance. Basma is a co-investigator in a $1,650,000 grant on coastal climate solutions and an $86,300,000 grant on accelerative community transitions to green energy. This project is part of Basma's ongoing commitment to action-research designed to generate and implement knowledge in projects devoted to positive environmental change. Working with the Centre for Social and Sustainable Innovation, Basma's research was critical in encouraging Gustavson to adopt a carbon offset programme and introduce a carbon neutrality competition in the business school, making Gustavson one of the first carbon neutral business schools in the world.

Notably, both of the projects described above embrace a syncretic model of enacting actionable knowledge. A commitment to syncretic knowledge requires an institutional space for ongoing conversations between the academics who generate foundational knowledge and the varied users or potential users of that knowledge. For most business schools, the institutionalised space for these interactions is often restricted to executive education. While executive education offers a useful starting point for the conversations necessary to create syncretic knowledge, the conversations are often limited to narrow and instrumental topics. This context lacks the opportunity for broad-ranging collaborative discussions on more normative issues that combine academic knowledge and managerial practice to address some of the more challenging problems in society.

STRUCTURE AND MEASUREMENT – CREATING IMPACTFUL RESEARCH

Perhaps the biggest challenge in re-imagining research in a business school is to enact a system that encourages research that goes beyond the academic standard of 'scientific significance'. Gustavson has approached this issue as a tripartite problem of organisational structure, performance measurement, and organisational culture. We address each of these in turn.

Structure

One of the largest impediments to producing knowledge with impact arises from the, often arbitrary, division of managerial issues into the disciplinary subject areas that define most business schools. While the knowledge produced within the departments of finance, marketing, operations, and so on is often impressive, business problems in practice rarely arise as a narrow issue of finance, marketing or operations. Instead, business problems tend to arise as thorny knots of issues that touch on several disciplinary areas. The division of business schools into discrete subject areas is a challenge to creating knowledge that has relevance to managerial practice or policy. Additionally, the departmental structure of business schools creates a form of internal competition for resources that, depending on the reward structure of the school, may discourage multidisciplinary collaboration within the school.

To address this challenge Gustavson has adopted a very flat organisational structure without formal departments. All faculty report directly to the Dean. Researchers are organised around clusters defined by empirical contexts (i.e. health services, indigenous sustainability, immigrant entrepreneurship, sustainable finance) informed by prevailing theoretical puzzles (how do we create regenerative sustainability, what is the relationship between collective memory and reconciliation, how can efficiency and innovation co-exist).

Gustavson has also created a structural element of the school designed to re-imagine the definition of research impact. The Research Impact Team is a group of research faculty and administrators tasked with the responsibility of facilitating impactful research in the school. The team rests on the philosophy that all foundational research should have demonstrable impact in the academic community, in the classroom, and the community. Community, itself, is broken into sub-communities such as government/policy makers, managers, the communities and the public or broader media. The team facilitates this flow of knowledge in many ways. Like most other business schools the team assists faculty in accessing research grants and related resources required for conducting high quality research. Beyond this, however, the Research Impact Team focuses researchers' attention on what to do with their foundational scholarship after publication in a management journal in order to increase impact in pedagogy and real world applications.

For example, the team helps researchers trace the impact of their scholarship in the classroom, both within Gustavson and beyond, using Altimetric tools to determine which publications appear in the syllabi of instructors in business schools around the world, in government white papers, in media posts and so on. The Impact Team also helps management faculty identify the potential impact of their research in addressing real-world problems by educating faculty about the United Nations Sustainability Goals (SDGs) and encouraging faculty to see how their research might contribute to these categories of potential impact. The team also encourages faculty to supplement the quantitative illustrations of their impact (i.e. number of publications, journal rank, number of citations etc.) with qualitative descriptions and contextual detail of the impact of their research in the classroom and the community. To facilitate the use of qualitative data in the faculty review process, the

Impact Team customised the Faculty Activity Database to incorporate qualitative descriptions of research impact and to provide additional commentary that will contextualise the quantitative data typically used in faculty evaluations. The philosophy of performance measurement is elaborated in the following section.

Performance Measurement

Many business schools have research cultures built on a tournament model (Connelly *et al.*, 2014) in which individual researchers compete for incentives that correlate weakly with relevant or desirable knowledge outcomes. While a bit of competition in research may not be a bad thing, unchecked competition has perverse results particularly when attached to incentives. For example, in research performance reviews many business schools discount papers authored by multiple individuals by dividing the contribution of a single publication by the number of authors. This form of rewarding research discourages collaborative research and provides a serious disincentive to large-scale research projects. Even when business schools allocate a full incentive to multiple authors, the tournament reward structure used by most business schools discourages internal collaboration as two authors from the same institution are effectively competing for resource allocations from the same pot. Because purpose-driven research is complex and requires larger teams of researchers, business schools must build a culture and an incentive system that rewards collaboration, both internally and with external partners.

An extension of the tournament model of performance measurement is the application of highly rigid assessment tools. Often these assessment tools rely exclusively on journal lists that rank journals based on their citation impact. Researchers are, then assessed on the number of papers published in high-ranking journals and the number of citations they receive in these journals. This creates an incestuous system of academics rewarding themselves for talking to themselves, and provides little or no incentive for researchers to take their research into the classroom or the community (the problems with journal lists in management faculty evaluation are well documented, for excellent summaries see Wilson and Thomas, 2012). More critically, the traditional model of performance measurement encourages faculty evaluation committees to ignore the substantive content of publications and use the rank of the journal, in which the publication occurs as a proxy.

Gustavson has created a performance measurement system designed to counteract the pernicious effects of traditional faculty evaluation processes. Foremost, the formal faculty evaluation policy provides a clear commitment to evaluation based on the quality of the individual faculty member's publications, rather than the quantity or the placement of the article. While Gustavson still uses a journal list to contextualise evaluations, Gustavson eschews narrowly defined, static, and discipline-based lists that many schools consider 'elite' simply because of the difficulty of the review process (the UT Dallas list is perhaps the best example of this). Instead, Gustavson relies on the Academic Journal Guide (AJG) for its breadth of disciplinary scope and the regularity by which it is updated and revised. Even the AJG, however, has blind spots in its coverage. For example, it does not rank the journal *Nature*, which is widely recognised as the world's leading multidisciplinary science journal and a journal in which Gustavson faculty have published. To address this, the Faculty Evaluation Policy reinforces Gustavson's commitment to using the journal list merely as a source of contextual information – i.e. a guide - rather than a determinant of evaluation.

Most traditional faculty evaluation systems in business schools do not differentiate in the type of research undertaken by faculty. As a result, traditional evaluation systems tend to privilege research that is done quickly over research that takes time. This approach to evaluation explains why management research tends to prefer laboratory work to ethnographic study, pre-existing data sets to customised data sets and quantitative research to qualitative research. As a result, very little management research occurs *in situ*. Even less research in management uses action research or natural experiments. Gustavson, by contrast, is highly committed to community-based research. The University of Victoria is a global leader in community-based research. The collective agreement of the university contains provisions designed to address these issues by ensuring that evaluation committees take into consideration the time and effort involved in establishing research relationships and trust with local communities and requires faculty evaluation committees to account for "the development of long-term relationships with communities" (University of Victoria, 2022). Gustavson follows this commitment and, as can be seen by the examples of research noted above, is deeply engaged in encouraging and properly evaluating community-based research.

Culture

The intent of the structural aspects of Gustavson is to encourage syncretism in research. Structure alone, however, is not enough. To achieve its intended outcomes, Gustavson embeds the structure in a culture that facilitates the intended outcomes – collaborations across subject areas within and beyond the business school, community-engaged research and actionable research. To facilitate fluid conversations across boundaries, all faculty – across disciplinary groups, both research and teaching stream

faculty – are encouraged to attend any formal research presentations or job talks. To encourage innovative collaborations, Gustavson encourages regular informal lunches each week (What's Up Wednesdays) where faculty gather to eat lunch and enjoy free-ranging, unstructured conversations about the progress of their current or prospective research projects. Not only do What's Up Wednesdays nurture potential collaborations, they inspire conversations about additional practices that Gustavson might experiment with to improve the quality and creativity of research. Most critically, these conversations occur in a collegial context and tone, without the formality, structure or unfortunate ego posturing so common to formal paper presentations.

The research culture of Gustavson also encourages innovation in research. Since its founding, Gustavson has pioneered new subject areas of research and pedagogy long before the topics enter the mainstream of research agendas in management schools in North America or Europe. Gustavson was one of the first business schools in North America to adopt formal research and teaching programmes in entrepreneurship, for example. Former Gustavson faculty member Ron K. Mitchell was a pioneer of stakeholder theory with a powerfully impactful model of stakeholder salience published with colleagues in 1997 (Mitchell *et al.*, 1997). Gustavson was an early adopter of sustainability research with a focus on managing the impact of climate change and Gustavson faculty member Monika Winn was a founding member of the Organisations and the Natural Environment division of the Academy of Management. Currently, Gustavson is deeply engaged in programmatic research on indigenous entrepreneurship, organisation and practices of economic reconciliation.

To achieve this level of innovation in research requires a culture that encourages risk-taking. What may appear to be risky in terms of research, however, is really just a shift in identifying how business academics should motivate their research. Traditional business schools motivate their research by identifying gaps in existing theory or empirics. Unfortunately, this 'gap-spotting' approach to research encourages a high degree of path dependence in which new researchers lean heavily on prior research in defining legitimate subjects for research (Alvesson and Sandberg, 2013). Gap spotting encourages academics to talk to each other and ignore phenomena in the world. The syncretic approach to knowledge generation adopted by Gustavson reverses this process and encourages faculty and PhD students to motivate their research not by what prior researchers have said, but rather by an interesting phenomenon with impact on practice. While this may appear to be risky, it actually is not. It simply encourages researchers to follow the phenomenon rather than the crowd.

EMBRACING DIFFERENT WAYS OF KNOWING – CREATING WISDOM IN RESEARCH

A recurrent theme in the varied critiques of business schools is the idea that management research has become so obsessed with scientific rigour that it has lost sight of the relevance and utility of research. Correlations are not always helpful in capturing the complex causality that tends to occur in the real world. Similarly, just because the relationship between two variables is statistically significant, does not mean that the relationship is meaningful in terms of policy or management practice. A growing body of management scholarship acknowledges that our single-minded pursuit of efficiency can be counterproductive. Mass-produced clothing may be cheap and efficient, but it damages the environment and diminishes the soul. Science has advanced the human condition in many ways, but it is not the only way of knowing.

In fact, the ancient Greeks did not see scientific empiricism as the only path to knowledge. The ancients identified five key "virtues" of thought– episteme (science), technê (craft or practice), phronêsis (practical action), *nous* (common sense) and *sophia* (wisdom). Nor did they see empiricism as the highest form of knowledge. For Aristotle wisdom is a superior form of knowledge because it combines both objective knowledge and normative knowledge. As such, wisdom meets the standard of syncretic knowledge because it uses a standard of knowing that integrates what we know to be true and what we ought to do as a result. This ought to be the standard for business school research. True wisdom provides decision-makers with the ability to make wise decisions exemplified by Solomon's creative solution to two competing claims of motherhood.

Wisdom also requires a degree of epistemic humility - an understanding of the limits to our claims to knowledge. The idea of epistemic humility comes from Socrates who observed that wisdom occurs in appreciating what we do not know. An extension of epistemic humility is acquiring an awareness of the unintended consequences of rational action in complex systems. There are many examples of the lack of epistemic humility in management knowledge. One prominent example is Donald McKenzie's analysis of how financial models created the conditions for the 1987 financial crisis in the US. These models, Mackenzie observed, "did more than analyse markets; it altered them" (Mackenzie, 2006).

Another extension of epistemic humility is developing an appreciation for the knowledge of others. In an effort to achieve this form of epistemic humility, and wisdom in their research, Gustavson has initiated a programme designed to explore indigenous ways of knowing. Like many countries, Canada is struggling to acknowledge and come to terms with its history of colonial injustice toward indigenous peoples. One mechanism for accomplishing this is economic reconciliation – the creation of business models and strategies designed to redress the economic injustices suffered by indigenous people caused by colonisation. Indigenous business models employ a logic of understanding that differs from western knowledge in two significant ways. First, it is more oriented to the community or the collective than to the individual (Kumukcham, 2021). Second, it incorporates the notion of the environment as not simply another stakeholder in indigenous business models, but rather as the primary stakeholder (Gordon, 2018). Gustavson has begun the journey toward embracing indigenous management knowledge by recruiting indigenous scholars and initiating a programme of research built around indigenous ways of knowing. While this initiative is in its early stages, it has produced an impressive body of work in a short time (for illustrative examples see Bastien *et al.*, 2023; Suddaby *et al.*, 2023; Salmon *et al.*, 2022).

Purpose-driven management research is a form of syncretic knowledge – knowledge that not only seeks to objectively analyse the present state of the world, but to then use that knowledge to initiate positive change in the world for the future. The objective of purpose-driven research is not merely objective truth, it seeks to achieve normative wisdom. As such, purpose-driven research, ultimately, is also values-driven research. To accomplish this lofty objective business schools must acknowledge that true wisdom comes not just from the integration of objective and subjective ways of knowing, but also from a core understanding of humanistic values and the prioritisation of those values in our research. More critically, purpose-driven research must place the relevance, impact and value of knowledge above the interests of the researchers or the institutions that perform or fund the research.

This is precisely the form of syncretic knowledge that Gustavson strives to achieve in research. The true secret of embracing syncretic knowledge in management research is that it expands the form of authority that business schools can hold in society. Yes, business school professors have held substantial technical authority on a broad range of subjects. However, too often our technical expertise fails to resonate with those critical outside audiences because it lacks moral expertise (Halliday *op cit*).

Moral authority arises when technical experts go beyond describing the world the way it is, and begin to use their expertise to articulate a better world. In order to accomplish this we must revisit the question of the purpose of our research. Consider how we abandoned the notion of Pareto efficiency when it moved into the business school. We abandoned the ideal of efficiency and replaced it with models designed to subvert it by creating barriers to efficient competition. Management scholarship will acquire the relevance, influence and authority it desires when we embrace a broader understanding of our research purpose and a deeper understanding of our syncretic knowledge mandate.

References

Alvesson, M., & J. Sandberg (2013) Has management studies lost its way? Ideas for more imaginative and innovative research. *Journal of Management Studies, 50*(1) pp.128-152

Bastien, F., D.M. Coraiola and W.M. Foster (2023) Indigenous Peoples and organisation studies. *Organisation Studies, 44*(4) pp.659-675

Bennis, W. G. and J. O'Toole (2005). How business schools have lost their way. *Harvard Business Review, 83*(5) pp.96-104

Connelly, B. L., L. Tihanyi, T.R. Crook and K.A. Gangloff (2014) Tournament theory: Thirty years of contests and competitions. *Journal of Management, 40*(1) pp.16-47

Ghoshal, S. (2005) Bad management theories are destroying good management practices. *Academy of Management Learning & Education, 4*(1) pp.75-91

Gordon, G. J. (2018) Environmental personhood. *Columbia Journal of Environmental Law, 43*, pp.49-91

Gordon, R. A. and J.E. Howell (1959) *Higher Education for Business*. Columbia University Press

Halliday, T. C. (1985) Knowledge Mandates: Collective Influence by Scientific, Normative and Syncretic Professions. *British Journal of Sociology, 36*(3): 421-447

Khurana, R. (2007) *From Higher Aims to Hired Hands: The Social Transformation of American Business Schools and The Unfulfilled Promise of Management as a Profession*. Princeton, NJ: Princeton University Press

Kuhn, T. (1977) *The Essential Tension: Selected Studies in Scientific Tradition and Change*. Chicago: University of Chicago Press

Kumukcham, J. (2021) Community-based Business Model of Indigenous People: Indigenous Entrepreneurship, Innovation and Value Proposition. in Guha, S., Majumdar, S. (eds) *In Search of Business Models in Social Entrepreneurship*, pp. 209-231. Springer, Singapore

MacKenzie, D. (2006) *An Engine, Not a Camera: How Financial Models Shape Markets*. Cambridge, MA: MIT Press

Mintzberg, H. (2004) Managers Not MBSs. *Management Today, 20*(7) pp.10-13

Mitchell, R.K., B.R. Agle and D.J. Wood (1997) Toward a theory of stakeholder identification and salience: Defining the principle of who and what really counts. *Academy of Management Review, 22*(4) pp.853-886

Rynes, S. L., J.M. Bartunek and R.L. Daft (2001) Across the great divide: Knowledge creation and transfer between practitioners and academics. *Academy of Management Journal, 44*(2) pp.340-355

Salmon, E., J.F. Chavez and M. Murphy (2022) New Perspectives and Critical Insights from Indigenous Peoples' Research: A Systematic Review of Indigenous Management and Organisation Literature. Academy of Management Annals

Suddaby, R. (2019) Objectivity and truth: The role of the essay in management scholarship. *Journal of Management Studies, 56*(2) pp.441-447

Suddaby, R., T. Israelsen, F. Bastien, R. Saylors and D. Coraiola (2023) Rhetorical history as institutional work. *Journal of Management Studies, 60*(1) pp.242-278

University of Victoria, Faculty Evaluation Policy 2022-2024, section 25.12 accessed online on June 23, 2023 at https://uvicfa. wpengine.com/wp-content/uploads/2023/02/2022-2025-Collective-Agreement-Working-Copy.pdf

Wilson, D.C. & Thomas, H. (2012). The legitimacy of the business of business schools. What's the future? *Journal of Management Development, 31*(4) pp.368-376

About the Author

Roy Suddaby is the Winspear Chair of Management and Associate Dean of Research at the Peter B. Gustavson School of Business, University of Victoria, Canada.

Impact-Driven Research: The Case of Hult

JOHAN ROOS

Concepts of the Purposeful Business School

Pioneering a Different Approach

Business and management research receives only a small fraction of total academic research funding globally, with most resources going to areas like sciences, engineering, and health (Starkey *et al.*, 2010). Within universities, funding for business and management research often comes from the business school's own budget rather than university-wide research funds. This suggests that neither the research aspiration and outcomes, nor the presumed impact of business school research impress major funders like the European Research Council, the US National Science Foundation, or major donors. In view of this fact, it is high time to try new approaches to business school research.

It is globally acknowledged in our sector that business schools should orient their research more towards addressing major societal challenges, embrace multidisciplinary research tactics, and create value for stakeholders even outside academia. By encouraging faculty members, professional researchers, post-docs, and doctoral candidates to cluster into Impact Labs, the approach by Hult International Business School resonates with these ambitions to have an impact that matters more to society.

Whether it's assisting a humanitarian organisation to develop more inclusive leadership, publishing teaching cases about how to use Artificial Intelligence (AI) in companies or in business education, or using hands-on tools to address stress levels among managers, Hult's research strategy and operational model diverges from orthodoxy that often emphasises the importance of publish or perish regardless of the societal impact. As this article explores, our research model can offer insights into how research in business schools can be framed, supported, rewarded, and generate outcomes that benefit organisations and communities.

THE UNIQUE HULT PERSPECTIVE

As an independent, non-profit institution, Hult International Business School manifests its presence on a global stage, delivering an enriching and multicultural learning journey to a student body of over 4,000 individuals, representing over 140 nationalities. The geographic expanse of our campuses extends from London to Boston, from San Francisco to Dubai, and even into the digital sphere via our online platform. Additionally, during part of the year, we make our presence felt in vital business epicentres such as New York and Singapore.

Hult's reliance on tuition fees for revenue and its informal and historical roots with Arthur D. Little and EF Education First adds a practical and market-oriented layer to its academic culture.[1] Today, Hult represents one of the philanthropical undertakings from the founder of EF, Mr. Bertil Hult. This mixture of academic and business cultures permeates all our operations, influencing branding, marketing, enrolment, analytics, as well as research strategy, faculty recruitment, and performance management.

Our strategic priorities focus on financial stability and growing institutional prestige while also striving to make Hult an appealing destination for professional development, academic exploration, and diverse learning experiences. A board of directors, with extensive experience in education, governance, business, technology, and law, supports this strategy, offering comprehensive guidance to the institution.

With a global team of around 90 full-time faculty members based around different campus locations and bolstered by a considerable number of long-serving adjuncts, Hult ensures students are privy to an eclectic mix of academic and practical knowledge and skills. Aspects such as entrepreneurship, global perspectives, and personal growth are intrinsic to our students' experience and reflected in the institutional approach to research. This orientation is also reflected in the curriculum design. For example, the

DOI: 10.4324/9781003467410-5

Bachelor of Business Administration focuses on human, business, and technical skills alongside disciplinary knowledge as well as global, entrepreneurial, and personal growth mindsets. In 2023, this programme won the MERIT Award for Innovation in Higher Education.

The faculty selection and performance management processes emphasise teaching excellence in traditional disciplines and emerging areas of business education. Faculty are also expected to generate new knowledge that addresses evolving real-world challenges facing organisations and leaders, to drive pedagogic development and innovation, and to contribute to the academic discourse in their disciplines. For example, in 2022-2023, faculty in the field of data analytics and management pursued a year-long research project with a large European insurance company to develop new knowledge about data governance and data custodianship in multinational organisations. Not only do these insights help leaders deal with an emerging key business issue, but the research also generates teaching cases and academic publications.

In summary, Hult carves a unique identity in the academic landscape through its blend of global outlook, practical focus, commitment to learning and teaching excellence, and its mixture of academic and business cultures, which distinguishes itself from many of its peers in the sector.

HULT'S APPROACH TO IMPACTFUL RESEARCH

Research at Hult pursues three key objectives—increase output quality, grow the institutional reputation, and make a difference in society:

1. *Community-building and integration:* We aim to cultivate a concentrated, robust 'intellectual ecosystem' that drives academic curiosity, underpinned by a requisite infrastructure and a critical concentration of intellectual capital.
2. *Augmenting institutional prestige:* Our goal is to enhance Hult's international standing through impactful research output.
3. *Make a difference in society:* We hold the conviction that our research endeavours can catalyse positive transformations for leaders, learners, organisations, and the wider society by delivering novel insights and by improving practices.

As many faculty members have experience in the corporate world, they have the necessary ethos to impart their knowledge and skills in leadership, change management, and other critical business skills. This proximity to practice also flavours their approach to research. They often forge strong relationships with private, public, and third-sector organisations, enabling engagement

in longitudinal research projects with practitioners. An example is a multi-year partnership with Diabetes UK, Novo Nordisk, and NHS diabetes specialists. This collaboration led to a revolutionary approach to diabetes care, earning the 2017 EFMD Excellence in Practice Award.

Another example that bridges theory and practice is the in-depth research on Unilever's Sustainable Living Plan. Faculty members engaged with leaders in Unilever to better understand their strategic choices and what the company did to integrate sustainability principles into its business model. In 2018, a Hult case on Unilever's development won the Ethics and Social Responsibility category of the UK Case Centre.

Collaborative projects with the International Committee of the Red Cross (ICRC) further demonstrate Hult's commitment to socially impactful research. Faculty assisted in the establishment of the Humanitarian Leadership & Management School (HLMS), an initiative that has fostered inclusive and authentic leadership within the ICRC, enabling its leaders to respond more effectively to humanitarian challenges. A case study of this initiative received the 2021 EFMD Excellence in Practice Award, exemplifying the transformative impact of the research.

Doctoral candidates and their faculty supervisors also contribute to our research ecosystem. Hult offers two distinct part-time doctoral programmes; the Doctor of Business Administration (DBA) and the Doctor in Organisational Change (DOC), both accredited by the New England Commission of Higher Education (NECHE) in the US. Both programmes address practical business issues but significantly differ in their philosophical and practical approaches to knowledge acquisition and problem-solving.

The DOC programme employs action research, a method for in-depth self-reflection and learning about practical problems. In short, action research integrates theoretical knowledge and real-world experience through pragmatic application. The link between theory and practice is, by definition, fluid and dynamic. This is ideal for managers seeking to understand complex business problems and to explore their roles in solving them. For example, the Global Head of Risk in a Hong Kong bank used action research to explore higher order change as a 'form of embodied enactive ethics' in the context of shareholder capitalism. Her work resulted in changed banking policy, allowing increased access to banking services.

A second example is the research by a sustainability practitioner in a manufacturing company in Sri Lanka. He used action research to shift the national discourse about sustainability. His work contributed to the cessation of coal power plant construction in Sri Lanka. The Global Head of Organisational Development in the energy sector in Europe also used this method to examine whether a sense of belonging mattered to globally mobile professionals. Her work resulted in an alternative way to consider belonging at work, which enables global professionals to live a healthier and more fulfilled life.

In contrast, based on a different epistemology, the DBA programme helps practicing managers address business problems using statistical methods. In short, methods grounded in positivism emphasise empirical evidence as the source of authoritative knowledge. For example, a DBA candidate, working as a sustainability consultant, used advanced statistical methods to study how companies' adaptive capabilities drive their environmental responsibility and their Sustainability Development Goals (SDG) performance. His research highlighted how managerial capabilities both drive and reduce non-financial performance and organisational accountability.

Another example of insight gained from statistical methods is the research conducted by a medical doctor and expert on digital health strategies and systems. In her research, she explored why patients prefer emergency room visits over primary care for non-emergency medical conditions. This study helped policymakers and health care leaders understand and manage public health care, particularly in the management of hospital emergency rooms. A senior bank manager in the Middle East also illustrates the societal impact of quantitative research. Based on a study of historical data and financial downturns, he explored how policymakers and banks stimulated and encouraged lending to small and medium-sized (SME) companies during financial downturns. His findings have clear implications for the future of lending to SMEs.

These differences illustrate the broad spectrum of research pursued not only by the two doctoral programmes for practicing managers, but also throughout all of Hult.

ORGANISING IMPACTFUL RESEARCH: IMPACT LABS

Unlike most peer institutions, Hult does not organise faculty and research into traditional disciplines, nor into semi-autonomous research centres. Instead, we organise research activities into dynamic 'intellectual ecosystems' that we call Impact Labs. These labs develop not only concepts and theoretical models but also practical solutions applicable to leadership and organisations. This pragmatic approach to research is captured by the term 'Impact Research'.

The Impact Labs serve as a hub for a diverse group of scholars and practitioners to collaborate on solving practical problems faced by managers and institutions. The labs engage a variety of experts: Impact Fellows (internal faculty members), Visiting Fellows (external academic experts), Doctoral Fellows (DBA and DOC candidates), Post-docs (two or three-year appointments), and Research Fellows (two or three-year appointments). The labs also affiliate with distinguished industry experts.

Each lab concentrates on a broad theme that shapes their research projects. For instance, the 'Futures Lab' focuses on the practical challenges of global risk mitigation and future-readiness, aiming to strengthen organisational resilience in an increasingly complex, technology-driven world. Affiliated Fellows study how evolving technologies are transforming societies, businesses, governments, and individuals using behavioural sciences and empirical data. Projects range from the role of AI in companies, neuroscience, foresight, strategy, and disruptive business models, to new organisational models and theories.

The 'Sustainability Lab' focuses on the practical challenges of industrial and societal 'sustainability transitions', aiming to connect practitioners and researchers at the forefront of this field. The UN SDGs represent the road-map and projects, such as, threats to organisations and society from the climate and biodiversity crises to human rights and 'modern slavery' issues.

The 'Leadership Lab' builds on Hult's renowned strengths in leadership development, people management, and organisational change management. The lab combines this with its history of developing innovative management tools, which refer to a broad range of instruments and techniques used to assess, diagnose, strategise, and develop various organisational and team capabilities. They include diagnostic tests, self-evaluations, strategy frameworks, and creative methods that help managers and teams understand their current state, identify areas for improvement, and develop plans to reach desired goals. The tools draw from fields like organisational psychology, leadership theory, and design thinking, and take many forms from surveys to simulations to board games. While diverse in nature, management tools share the purpose of providing structure, insight, and direction to enhance organisational and team effectiveness. Examples of such tools developed by affiliated faculty members include an in-depth leadership experience based on cardio-neuroscience, looking at the role of the heart rate on learning effectiveness zones. Other examples include a simulation of boat-sharing marketing decisions, and a board game for sensitive diversity issues. This lab serves to further develop a variety of tools based on the needs reported by company interventions and executive education, as well as on pedagogical innovations and 'learning-to-learn' practices.

More than a dozen faculty and staff members have been certified in the LEGO® Serious Play© (LSP) method (Roos and Victor, 2018), which is used with students, corporate clients, and among internal staff. LSP is a multi-modal and play-based method helping clients and students to go beyond words and to 'think with their hands'. At Hult it has been used to effectively develop new and shared perspectives and strategies, to solve tricky people issues, to help in crisis management, for 'real-time' change management in corporate engagement, and for enriched hackathons in degree programmes. Such hands-on learning methods bring a wealth of data that can result in scientific publications. Examples include articles on what drives 'change readiness' based on LSP interventions in organisations, and on the connection between heart rates during critical incident simulations and perceived learning.

Hult's impact research generates teaching materials via new tools and publications, as well as through extensive case writing. In 2023 we decided to accelerate the production of peer-reviewed teaching cases, engaging many faculty members in active case writing. Our approach brings faculty colleagues into cohorts during an intensively coached process to develop high-quality cases. This process encourages a rich, diverse, and robust case portfolio on current managerial and business issues. It also imbues a sense of collective ownership and pride among faculty as well as instilling an institutional Hult 'flavour' to the narratives captured in these cases.

Examples of teaching cases produced in 2023 include how Generative AI transforms marketing, the use of AI in ideation and productisation, inventory planning in manufacturing, HR practices for burnout prevention, startup funding in the UK, building trust and convincing customers, handling of difficult conversations among business students, and how to use AI in business teaching. After a peer review and publication, the flow of teaching cases is integrated into undergraduate, postgraduate, doctoral, and executive education programmes, strengthening our research culture. Thus, the Leadership Lab serves as a crucible for the constant evolution of experiential learning tools, ensuring their effectiveness and relevance in addressing important managerial and organisational challenges.

The incentive system for research prioritises output quality over quantity, while ensuring strategic and ethical guardrails. In addition to academic research outputs, Hult values practice-oriented research and pedagogical developments and innovation. The incentive system includes five categories of intellectual contributions: (1) peer-reviewed academic journals, (2) peer-reviewed teaching cases, (3) peer-reviewed conference contributions, and (4) books. The fifth category includes editor-reviewed practice-oriented research output published in recognised media outlets. These can benefit from significant promotion by Hult advertising and marketing. Hult offers one-to-one coaching with faculty members to boost their individual public profiles. Marketing support, such as in blogs, webinars, social media, planned book publishing, and conference activities are all available on a case-by-case basis.

The institution is open to, and supportive of, individual research projects that span a wide spectrum of subjects. However, a significant portion of Hult's resources is explicitly channelled towards reinforcing the Impact Labs. This approach encourages both focus and critical mass to drive impactful outcomes.

In line with the internal Hult mantra of 'only necessary bureaucracy', the administrative system for research has been simplified. This includes an easy-to-use online form for project applications, an internal blind review and regular (monthly) approval process, access to professional research support, and a transparent incentive system for output. The Dean of Research, reporting to the Chief Academic Officer (CAO), is responsible for implementing the research strategy. The CAO reports at every board of director meeting.

INSIGHTS FROM THE HULT APPROACH

A few elements of our impact-driven research approach stand out.

Firstly, at the core is a commitment to serving the interests of many stakeholders: students, faculty, business, government, and civil society. Our research aims to yield tangible benefits for diverse stakeholders beyond academia. A testament to this is the above-mentioned engagement with various institutions, executive education clients, and the organisations employing the part-time doctoral candidates.

Secondly, our approach underscores the benefits of adopting an interdisciplinary and inclusive perspective *by default*. Unlike the constraints of traditional disciplines or reified research centres, the dynamics of the Impact Lab and their projects mirrors the multi-disciplinary nature of the challenges facing leaders, organisations, and society. Our multitudes of philosophies and practice-oriented research spark the innovative thinking needed to address increasingly complex business and societal problems. The Futures Lab's focus on global risk mitigation and future readiness, as well as the Sustainability Lab's work on sustainability transitions, embodies Hult's commitment to tackling critical global issues. Our research also contributes to continuous improvement in leadership and to learning and teaching in our sector, as illustrated by the drive to develop teaching cases and other learning tools within the Leadership Lab.

Thirdly, Hult's market-oriented support infrastructure and performance management systems encourage productivity and drive impact. This sets Hult apart from both the mindset and the operational norms in most traditional academic institutions. Our incentive system favours impact over effort, and reinforces the notion that research at Hult transcends the pursuit of academic rigour at the expense of relevance to organisations and society.

CONCLUSION

Although difficult to generalise, I hope that elements of the Hult approach to research can inspire peer institutions, especially those operating within traditional academic contexts. Adjustments to research strategy, structure,

systems, and even the culture can make a difference for the value created by research—for students, leaders, learners, organisations, and the wider society.

References

Roos, J. and B. Victor (2018) How It All Began: The Origins Of LEGO© Serious Play©. *International Journal of Management and Applied Research, 5* (4) pp.326-343.

Starkey, K., A. Hatchuel and S. Tempest (2010) How much does business school research cost? Stakeholder cost and value in UK business schools. *Journal of Management Development, 29*(1) pp.23-36

Footnote

[1] Established by the Hult family in 1965, EF is the world's largest private language learning company, specialising in educational travel, language training, cultural exchange, and academic degree programmes. In 2003 EF was asked to take over the ADL School of Management in Boston, which was on the verge of bankruptcy. This charitable educational institution was renamed Hult International Business School.

About the Author

Johan Roos is Chief Academic Officer & Professor in Hult. He was previously the Dean of Jönköping International Business School, President of Copenhagen Business School, Dean of MBA Programs at Stockholm School of Economics, and Founding Director of Imagination Lab Foundation. He has also held academic positions at the International Institute for Management Development, Norwegian Business School, and The Wharton School. Professor Roos is Senior Advisor to Drucker Society Europe, Chair of the High Level Scientific Council at Vienna Center for Management Innovation, and board member of Imagination Lab Foundation.

Research Impact at an Unusual Academic Institution: IMD'S Journey

ANAND NARASIMHAN

Concepts of the Purposeful Business School

Is 2030 here already? The influential position paper from the Responsible Research for Business and Management (RRBM) community features a projected future state for research impact within the field of business schools with the end date of the year 2030 (Co-founders of RRBM, 2017). The scenario draws upon a series of principles that demand implementation by diverse stakeholders operating within the business school ecosystem. But what if this future state is already unfolding in the present? In this article, I assert that IMD, where I have served as the Dean of Research for more than a dozen years, meets many of the criteria outlined by RRBM for their 2030 vision and therefore presents an illuminating case study for other business schools striving to generate substantial research impact that benefits all stakeholders.

IMD: AN OVERVIEW

IMD is an independent academic institution—a not-for-profit, standalone business school operated as a foundation with the status of a Swiss University Institute. IMD is triple-accredited, and our MBA, EMBA, and Executive Education programmes are ranked among the top 10 by Bloomberg BusinessWeek, Forbes, The Economist, and the Financial Times.

IMD was created in 1990 from a merger between the International Management Institute, founded by Alcan in 1946, and the Institut pour l'étude des méthodes de direction de l'entreprise, founded by Nestlé in 1957. This is our origin statement and is very consequential to our identity as an unusual academic institution: 'Founded by business executives for business executives, we are an independent academic institution with Swiss roots and global reach. We strive to be the trusted learning partner of choice for ambitious individuals and organisations worldwide.'

Clearly, the research imperatives of an institution founded by and for business executives would differ from those of a conventional business school. IMD boasts a legacy of over 75 years dedicated to the development of executives, a history that has distinctly shaped an ethos of research that is centred around impact. This commitment to impact is captured in our credo: 'Real learning, real impact'. Faculty members drawn to IMD are inherently driven to make a difference in the lives of participants and their organisations, primarily through innovative pedagogy and meticulously crafted programmes. This alignment with our purpose, 'challenging what is and inspiring what could be, we develop leaders who transform organisations and contribute to society', underscores their passion for fostering tangible change.

IMD possesses distinct characteristics that set it apart as an unusual business school (Manzoni, 2022a).

IMD does not compartmentalise faculty into academic departments or disciplinary silos. Instead, all members collectively form a unified faculty body. This lack of boundaries encourages a cross-disciplinary perspective among faculty members, promoting diverse collaboration and innovative thinking.

The faculty titles at IMD are limited to just two categories: Professor and Affiliate Professor. This streamlined structure eliminates hierarchical ranks, fostering an egalitarian culture among faculty members. This simplicity not only symbolises equality but also nurtures an atmosphere of collaboration and mutual respect.

IMD does not rely on a traditional tenure system. Instead, following an adjustment period, faculty members undergo evaluations for suitability and are offered long-term 'open contracts', although without a guarantee of permanent employment. This approach ensures that faculty are consistently motivated to contribute to the best of their abilities with respect to their teaching, research, and service duties, regardless of their duration within the institution.

DOI: 10.4324/9781003467410-6

Annual Research Volume 2 – Concepts of the Purposeful Business School

Research Impact at an Unusual Academic Institution: IMD'S Journey
Anand Narasimhan
....

Unlike conventional business schools, when offering an open contract to a faculty member, IMD places less emphasis on external endorsements, referred to as 'letters' in tenure decisions, and relies more on internal measures of fit. This independence from external pressures grants IMD faculty greater autonomy in their research pursuits.

The faculty compensation system at IMD incorporates a substantial variable component in the form of a bonus, contingent upon the institute generating an operational surplus (which is most years). The largest chunk of the bonus pool, at 40%, is specifically allocated to individuals' research performance. In an environment that provides plenty of opportunities for an individual to increase their compensation through delivering more teaching on programmes, the bonus system signals the importance of research as a contribution.

At IMD, research activities account for approximately 8% of the annual budget. Roughly half of this amount, all of which is sourced from operating revenues, is allocated to support individual faculty research projects, encompassing articles, case studies, books, and pedagogical materials. The remaining 50% is dedicated to our research centres, primarily financed through the utilisation of chair endowment capital.

One notable practice is that every faculty member, without exception, undergoes an annual review conducted by the President and the Dean of Faculty. This meticulous process ensures alignment and fosters a cohesive agenda among faculty members, reinforcing a shared commitment to the institution's goals.

To ensure effective allocation of resources, faculty members are mandated to submit an annual research activity plan as part of their annual review process. These individual plans are then aggregated to determine the required resource allocation. At the conclusion of each year, a comprehensive tabulation of research outputs is compiled. This tabulation plays a pivotal role in determining the research bonus accorded to each faculty member.

Collectively, these attributes ensure that faculty do what they are passionate about, which is to have 'real impact' on IMD's stakeholders—executives, organisations, academics and management educators, policy makers, and shapers of entrepreneurial activity in Switzerland and elsewhere (Manzoni, 2022b). As I show below, at IMD, thought leadership contributions of all kinds are valued for the impact created—practitioner articles, case studies, and books—not just peer-reviewed academic publications.

FROM PRACTICE TO RESEARCH

In recent years, IMD has been the institution with the most published articles in Harvard Business Review and MIT Sloan Management Review (barring the 'editor institutions'), the two practitioner-oriented outlets in the Financial Times influential list of journals comprising their research index. The research content for the articles comes from closeness to practice, but behind the scenes, there has been a considerable effort underway to collectively master the intricacies of breaking into these top journals. Faculty members who achieved success willingly shared their insights with their colleagues, fostering a culture of shared practice that promotes excellence in writing for practitioners.

Budding scholars in management disciplines are advised to be clear about the question, "What conversation are you joining?" (e.g., Huff, 1998). This means reading research literature closely and being aware of which researchers your forthcoming work aligns with. The research literature itself serves as a foundation for further development. But what if the realm of practice were to ignite fresh research dialogues? The IMD article titled 'Put purpose at the core of your strategy' (Malnight, Buche and Dhanaraj, 2019) is consistently referenced in recent research articles, thereby shaping the emerging research domain of corporate purpose within the strategy literature. The origins of this article are deeply rooted in the world of practice, and the tale of how it was crafted serves as a demonstration of how practitioner articles can significantly influence the trajectory of academic research.

Over the years we here at IMD arrived at a significant realisation that there exist two distinct routes to influencing organisations. The initial route, pursued by business schools through their executive education endeavours, entails effecting change by nurturing individual growth. The second route, harnessed by consulting firms, centres on driving extensive transformations at the organisational level. This led us to question whether a middle-ground approach existed—one that encompassed advisory efforts facilitating large-scale transformations, paired with executive education programmes equipping individuals to independently spearhead transformations, thus reducing reliance on consulting firms (refer to Figure 1).

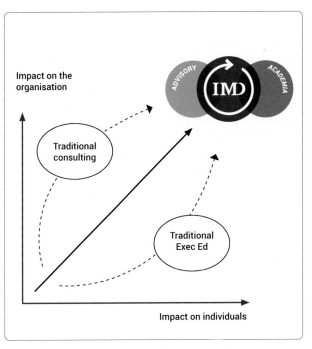

Figure 1 Advisory and Academic path to impact on organisations

It was our colleague Tom Malnight who uncovered the solution through a methodology he termed 'Pathfinder'. Pathfinder revolves around empowering company executives to create opportunities for enduring, sustainable growth. A pivotal facet of Pathfinder entails engaging in targeted discussions with handpicked external companies on specifically identified topics. This approach facilitates the extraction of insights from external sources, fostering innovative ideas and dismantling internal obstacles that hinder growth.

The IMD team used Pathfinder to help our client Mars Petcare with their objective, growing their pet food business significantly. The initiative engaged 20 high-potential executives from different sectors within the company. They collaborated with 30 high-growth companies across diverse industries, as pinpointed by Malnight, for valuable learning experiences. Through the Pathfinder programme, participants identified four key themes with potential for business advantage: addressing broader stakeholder needs, exploring new markets through ecosystems rather than conventional industry definitions, introducing disruptive innovation, and notably, embedding purpose into core strategy. This fourth realisation led Mars executives to understand their mission as more than just boosting pet food sales; they aimed to actively pursue their 'better world for pets' purpose. This clarity prompted Mars Petcare to enter pet health by acquiring veterinary services in the USA and Europe. These acquisitions propelled Mars Petcare to become one of Mars Inc.'s largest and fastest-growing divisions, ultimately elevating the president of the business to the CEO role of the entire company. The programme clearly had a significant impact on both the executives and the organisation.

The Pathfinder initiative was replicated with the Finnish oil-refining firm Neste. In 2009, the company grappled with the dual challenges of low oil prices and restrictive regulations. The CEO of Neste engaged IMD to explore fresh avenues, eventually zeroing in on renewable energy as a promising direction. The company's purpose was defined as 'creating responsible choices every day'. Employing a strikingly similar approach to that applied with Mars Petcare, the executive participants of IMD's programmes had by 2015 helped to establish Neste as the world's largest producer of renewable fuels sourced from recovered cooking oil and comparable forms of residual waste. In the course of this transformation, the company's market valuation surged fivefold. Another remarkable impact narrative.

The IMD team that worked on several Pathfinder programmes wrote up their insights highlighting the importance of purpose in helping organisations redefine their playing field as a means of achieving sustainable business growth. They sought advice from colleagues that were seasoned at publishing in top practitioner journals, and they found success in placing their article in Harvard Business Review. Just as the article was published, the field of strategy had identified purpose as a key topic of future research and so the article became influential in helping researchers shape their ideas. In this manner, the Pathfinder programmes at IMD have made an impact across a diverse spectrum of stakeholders, including executives and their organisations, fellow practitioners, and management scholars.

COMBINING RESEARCH AND TEACHING TO ADDRESS EMERGING CHALLENGES

In 2020, IMD formalised a sustainability strategy from which it was clear that we needed to prioritise research and business education on the topic of sustainability. Two years later, IMD inaugurated a Center for Sustainable and Inclusive Business with the aim of bringing together researchers and practitioners to collaborate on solutions to ensure the transition towards a more sustainable world. IMD's thought leadership on sustainability has grown steadily in all formats, including top-tier journals such as Harvard Business Review, books, and award-winning case studies.

On the education side, we introduced the Leading Sustainable Business Transformation (LSBT) to support senior executives in the challenge of making their organisations more sustainable. Led by Professors Knut Haanaes and James Henderson, the open-enrolment course attracts senior executives from various industries across the world. LSBT addresses the challenge of translating knowledge into action, offering a comprehensive business transformation journey through the lens of sustainability. It includes live case sessions with industry experts, enabling executives to develop smart and sustainable business models to future-proof their organisations and benefit society. The programme also fosters a supportive peer community, promoting a renewed sense of purpose and expertise. Participants engage with cutting-edge research on the interaction between business and sustainability, real-world examples of sustainability transformation, themed masterclasses, and deep dives into current themes, and in discussions to drive their own sustainable business transformation. Business and leadership coaching are provided to enhance the impact of their learning.

The programme's success and impact are measured through tangible outcomes and feedback. Participants in the LSBT programme indicate that the most valuable aspects of the course are the blended learning approach, the supportive community, and the insights gained from industry players. Individual participants benefit from deepening their understanding of sustainability, applying best practices, and developing communication and leadership skills. The programme has already started to make a positive contribution to business and society. The rapid creation of both a centre as well as an executive education programme on the topic of sustainability is an example of IMD's responsiveness to the learning needs of the business community.

WRITING THE CASE FOR IMPACT

At IMD, organisations that serve as our learning partners have always played a central role in faculty members' thought leadership activities (Lorange, 2002). Case studies serve as a crucial medium for bringing intricate business issues into the classroom. Commencing in the early 2000s, IMD faculty members leveraged their strong relationships with executives and organisations within our ecosystem with the aim of developing cases that enabled students to immerse themselves in contemporary management challenges faced by leaders and executives. Notably, case studies delving into Nestle's implementation of an enterprise resource planning system and Nespresso's endeavours to innovate in the coffee market emerged as blockbuster hits in terms of adoption across global business schools, maintaining their status as our top-selling cases to this day.

Beyond their influence on the management education community, the close connections forged with executives and organisations that become subjects of our case studies yield additional forms of impact: our students gain from this network through mentoring, internship opportunities, and placement options. In return, executives are motivated to sustain this association, exemplified by their engagement as executives in residence during career transitions, thus infusing IMD's sphere of influence with their valuable experience and expertise. This reciprocal interaction between the worlds of executives and that of management education aligns well with our mission of cultivating leaders and organisations that effect positive change in society.

We assess the impact of our case study efforts by tracking indicators of dissemination and prestige. In 2022, we distributed close to 220,000 copies of IMD cases to 1,300 institutions in 111 countries, a creditable feat from a small Swiss school. Our case studies and authors consistently win awards in major case competitions, including those by the Case Center and EFMD. Six of our

Annual Research Volume 2 – Concepts of the Purposeful Business School

Research Impact at an Unusual Academic Institution: IMD'S Journey
Anand Narasimhan
....

faculty members were top case writers according to the Case Center, and 12 of our cases made it to their bestsellers list. We communicate our success, celebrate our case writers' achievements publicly, and reward them through variable compensation.

Our recent experience of the case-study 'Angaza: A Silicon Valley Journey', which clinched the Case Center's 2022 Outstanding Case Writer competition, provides a valuable lesson in deepening and broadening impact through case writing. This case narrates the challenges confronted by Lesley Marincola, a Stanford University graduate who developed a solar lamp intended for use in Africa. Unfortunately, the lamp's cost rendered it unaffordable for her target customers, leading Marincola to ponder her next steps. The creators of this case study are Vanina Faber, the holder of the elea Chair for Social Innovation, and research associate Shih-Han Huang, an alumnus of Harvard University and INSEAD, who acquired case-writing skills during their time at IMD.

elea is a Swiss impact investment foundation whose stated purpose is 'to fight absolute poverty with entrepreneurial means, leveraging the opportunities for globalisation'. The foundation proudly sponsors the elea Chair at IMD. Through strategic support and philanthropic investment, the elea foundation champions entrepreneurially led ventures that bring about enduring social impact. When unable to secure venture capital backing for her entrepreneurial endeavour, Marincola sought assistance from elea. With their guidance, she adeptly shifted her focus toward a software-based pay-as-you-go model for smartphones, enabling customers to access the lamp while progressively covering its cost. This pivot allowed her to step away from lamp production, transforming her company, Angaza, into a preferred partner for numerous manufacturers and a range of pay-as-you-go devices. Consequently, Angaza successfully secured "Series A" funding from venture capitalists.

Alongside the IMD case study, the Angaza narrative found its place in a book titled "The elea Way," authored by Farber and Peter Wuffli (2020), a co-founder of the elea Foundation, and published by Routledge. This publication has been warmly embraced by the impact investing community, thanks to the outreach initiatives spearheaded by the IMD elea Social Innovation Center. Furthermore, the book serves as the foundational underpinning for a social innovation programme designed for entrepreneurs, jointly conducted by IMD and the elea Foundation.

Creating and sharing the case study allows IMD to engage with and influence various stakeholders. The field of management education benefits from a well-constructed case that covers topics like social innovation, entrepreneurship, impact investing, and strategic management. At IMD, participants get first-hand exposure to the business challenges related to poverty alleviation. By offering a social innovation programme, IMD contributes to enhancing the skills of entrepreneurs working towards social progress. In the realm of impact investing, the case study serves as a practical example to learn from. Especially for the elea Foundation and other sponsors, the case study becomes a clear representation of the positive outcomes achieved through research funding.

IMPACT BY THE BOOK

Book ideas arise when faculty members' academic knowledge meets the practical experiences of participants. In the introduction to his book on bottom-up change, Strebel (2000) acknowledges, "The genesis of this book occurred during a session managing accelerated change in IMD's programme on Orchestrating Winning Performance. The managers in those sessions argued that the biggest obstacles to faster change are a lack of energy on the frontline and/or a lack of focus at the top among proliferating change projects."

At IMD, book-writing for practitioners is a strong and much-appreciated tradition. For executives and leaders in our programmes, books are valuable both substantively and symbolically. Books encapsulate the essence of a programme, and when participants return to their respective contexts, these books serve as tangible markers of their takeaways. The core content of IMD's highly regarded open-enrolment executive programme, High-Performance Leadership, is grounded in two books: Kohlreiser (2006) and Kohlreiser, Goldsworthy, & Coombe (2012).

Books have been especially useful in engaging the audience of many of IMD's research centres.

The World Competitiveness Center

One of the most eagerly anticipated publications in IMD's calendar is strictly not a book, but a ranking of the competitiveness of nations. The World Competitiveness Yearbook has been keenly scrutinised by governments near and far for over 35 years to make sense of how the ground for national competitiveness shifts from year to year. The rankings have a huge impact on government officials and public policy makers connected to the economic ministries of all the major developed economies. The Center's faculty director and the research team are frequently consulted by various nation-states for advice on how to improve their competitiveness. These activities expand the reach of IMD's impact to beyond the realm of industry and business.

Annual Research Volume 2 – Concepts of the Purposeful Business School

Research Impact at an Unusual Academic Institution: IMD'S Journey
Anand Narasimhan
....

Digital Business Transformation Center

IMD's digital business transformation centre was set up in 2015 with initial funding and support from Cisco. The Center has built up a stakeholder group of chief digital officers and other executives involved in digital transformation of their organisations, and published four books capturing changes in this fast-moving field: Digital Vortex (Wade *et al.*, 2016); Orchestrating Transformation (Wade *et al.*, 2019), ALIEN thinking (Bouquet *et al.*, 2021), and Hacking Digital (Wade *et al.*, 2021). These books are also closely tied to the programme on digital business offered by IMD.

The Global Board Center

IMD was one of the first institutions in the world to offer dedicated programmes for board members. The Board Center counts board members of listed companies, family businesses, private conglomerates, and sovereign wealth funds as its stakeholders. The models and methods of governance discussed in the Center's open-enrolment and custom programmes have been codified in two books: High-Performance Boards (Cossin, 2020) and Inspiring Stewardship (Cossin and Hwee, 2016).

The Global Family Business Center

This IMD centre has been offering programmes for family business owners and executives for over 35 years. Sensing the need for philanthropic families to be helped in their giving activities, centre director and holder of the Debiopharm Chair Peter Vogel co-authored a book (Vogel, Eichenberger & Kurak, 2020) for this important stakeholder community.

As can be seen from these examples, books written by IMD authors impact a wide range of stakeholders – not just students and executive participants in our programmes, but also the constituency that is catered to by each research centre such as board members, family business owners, policymakers, and government officials, chief digital officers, and the like.

NEARING RRBM'S VISION 2030?

To broaden our impact on society at large, IMD has joined forces with the École Polytechnique Fédérale de Lausanne (EPFL) and Haute École Commerce of the University of Lausanne (HEC-UNIL) to create the Enterprise for Society Center (E4S) with the vision of building bridges between academia, business and civil society in order to tackle the great challenges of our time. There is active collaboration in research projects among the three institutions with a view to realising the vision of E4S. The outcome of these activities will result in fulfilling RRBM's principle of service to society.

IMD already fulfils RRBM's remaining principles. The institution values both basic and applied research. The faculty values plurality and multi-disciplinary collaboration. We involve a diverse set of stakeholders in our thought leadership activities and are conscientious about acknowledging and rewarding our impact on them. The scholarly training of IMD faculty ensures that the entire portfolio of our research activities is based on methods of sound quality.

And so, going back to John Elkington's quip at the start, this article seeks to show that there are ways in which business schools can strive to multiply their impact on the business community and society at large. What has hampered efforts thus far can be traced to field-level and organisational incentives that overemphasise peer-reviewed academic articles along with socialisation and development of scholars within relatively insular discipline-based communities of practice. Breaking the barriers to real impact requires schools to take the courageous steps of sincerely valuing all forms of high-quality thought leadership, genuinely encouraging cross-disciplinary collaboration, and actively sensing the needs of the business community that supports their institution and responding to their learning needs.

Annual Research Volume 2 – Concepts of the Purposeful Business School

Research Impact at an Unusual Academic Institution: IMD'S Journey
Anand Narasimhan
....

References

Bouquet, C., J-L. Barsoux and M. Wade (2021) *ALIEN thinking*. New York: Public Affairs

Co-founders of RRBM. (2017, rev. ed., 2020). A vision for responsible research in business and management: Striving for useful and credible knowledge. Position paper, accessible from www.rrbm.network

Cossin, D. (2020) *High performance boards*. London: Wiley

Cossin, D., and O.B. Hwee (2016) *Inspiring stewardship*. London: Wiley

Elkington, J. (2023) Responsibility, resilience, and regeneration… the three R's and the new triple bottom line. *IbyIMD*, September issue

Faber, V. and P. Wuffli (2020) *The elea way: A learning journey toward sustainable impact*. London: Routledge

Huff, A.S. (1998) *Writing for scholarly publication*. Thousand Oaks, CA: Sage

Kohlreiser, G. (2006) *Hostages at the table*. San Francisco: Josey-Bass

Kohlreiser, G., S. Goldsworthy and D. Coombe (2012) *Care to dare: Unleashing astonishing potential through secure base leadership*. San Francisco: Josey Bass

Lorange, P. (2002) *New vision for management education*. Oxford: Elsevier

Malnight, T., I. Buche and C. Dhanaraj (2019) Put purpose at the heart of your strategy. *Harvard Business Review*, September-October, pp.70-79

Manzoni, J-F. (2022a) Leading an (unusual) academic institution through a crisis: A personal reflection. In Cornuel, E. (ed.) *Business school leadership and crisis exit planning*. Cambridge: Cambridge University Press, pp.311-330

Manzoni, J-F. (2022b) Striving for meaningful impact in and through management education: The IMD perspective. *Global Focus Annual Research, 1*, pp.74-80

Strebel, P. (2000) *Focused Energy: Mastering the Bottom-Up Organisation*. London: Wiley

Vogel, P., E. Eichenberger and M. Kurak, (2020) *Family philanthropy navigator*. Lausanne: IMD

Wade, M., J. Loucks, J. Macaulay and A. Nornha (2016) *Digital vortex*. Lausanne: IMD

Wade, M., J. Macaulay, A. Noronha and J. Barber (2019) *Orchestrating transformation*. Lausanne: IMD

Wade, M., D. Bonnet, T. Yokoi and N. Obwegeser (2021) *Hacking Digital*. Lausanne: IMD

About the Author

Anand Narasimhan is Shell Professor Global Leadership and Dean of Research at IMD. He received his doctorate from Vanderbilt University and has previously served at London Business School and Imperial College.

Research and Positive Impact: Henley Business School in the African Context

JONATHAN FOSTER-PEDLEY AND CARA BOUWER

Concepts of the Purposeful Business School

Business does not exist in a vacuum; it is intrinsically linked to the success or failure of the society in which it operates. On a continent like Africa, where social, environmental and historical challenges abound, issues such as inequality, poverty and inclusive growth continue to dominate the context. Yet, African academia continues to follow the line drawn by Western business education models, rather than carving out an African model of management education that addresses the specific economic and social development needs of the continent as a whole.

Books have been written in an attempt to understand the African conundrum, including the 2017 pan-African analysis of the African continent's management education future direction, by Howard Thomas, Michelle Lee, Lynne Thomas and Alexander Wilson (Thomas *et al.*, 2017). The general consensus is that while African institutions of higher learning know they need to embrace their African identity and develop in harmony with the needs of the continent, they have been constrained by internal barriers and the lack of a cohesive approach.

This is understandable given the complexities inherent in the continent. Any discourse around Africa must recognise that our continent comprises 54 unique countries with more than 2,000 living languages (Statista Research Department, 2023) and around 3,000 ethnic groups from the Tuareg of the Sahara Desert to the Maasai of East Africa (Further Africa, 2022). Therefore, when we speak of learning in the African context, of African culture or indigenous knowledge, we are speaking in addition, about learning across colonial borders imposed by the likes of the British, Dutch, French, Germans, Italians and Portuguese; a legacy which may have left a continent divided in itself but still resplendent in wider diversity, culture and context.

Furthermore, breaking down the mental barriers imposed through colonialism is no mean feat. Yet this is increasingly the narrative emanating from Africa itself, enabled by unifying bodies such as the African Union and African Development Bank, and more recently the promise of greater economic and trade cohesion through the continent-wide African Continental Free Trade Area (Thomas, 2022). In the context of business and management education, this role is fulfilled by the Association of African Business Schools (AABS) (AABSchools, n.d.); a conduit for collaboration, impact and – increasingly – as a forum to debate the future relevance of business schools on a continent beset by challenges.

As the first business school in Africa to receive the AABS accreditation, Henley Business School Africa (Henley Africa) has long called for the decolonisation of education in Africa and of helping African institutions, African researchers and African academics to find their own voice. Similarly other institutions, such as the European Foundation for Management Development (EFMD) and the Association to Advance Collegiate Schools of Business as well as African business schools like Lagos Business School in Nigeria and South Africa's Gordon Institute of Business Science (GIBS), UCT Graduate School of Business and Stellenbosch Business School, have also argued along similar lines.

This necessary and ongoing debate does not imply turning away entirely from established models, but rather seeking to offer accessible education that has relevance in the African context and which speaks to the needs of African businesses and the development of the specific leadership skills needed to manage ingrained uncertainty and volatility.

DOI: 10.4324/9781003467410-7

40

Annual Research Volume 2 – Concepts of the Purposeful Business School

Research and Positive Impact: Henley Business School in the African Context
Jonathan Foster-Pedley and Cara Bouwer
·················

PHOTO COURTESY OF HENLEY BUSINESS SCHOOL SOUTH AFRICA

HOW TO FRAME AN AFRICAN BUSINESS SCHOOL MODEL

Henley Africa is by no means alone in seeking to create a more relevant model of business education and leadership development for emerging markets such as Africa. Leading business schools across Africa – including other AABS-accredited institutions and the six members of the newly launched Business Schools for Climate Leadership Africa (BS4CL Africa) initiative (Rabie, 2023) – have begun to collaborate closely on pivotal issues such as the climate crisis, leadership interventions, research and issues of social relevance.

As Sherif Kamel, Dean of AUC School of Business in Egypt, noted at the launch of the BS4CL in January 2023: "Our ultimate goal is for business schools to effectively address climate change issues by integrating timely and critical subjects within the business schools' ecosystem. This encompasses teaching, curriculum, cases, and projects including research endeavours and business development activities, as they help shape the next generation of leaders to impact society" (Rabie, 2023).

This overview should, in fact, underpin more than just our climate change efforts as an African business school community. It highlights the sort of system-wide change needed to have a direct and positive impact on our home continent, and around the world. As argued in a new Henley Africa white paper, 'Climate action: An Existential Priority for African Business Schools' (Foster-Pedley *et al.*, 2023): "Our business schools – regardless of their good reputation – will fail, unless we accept that fundamental changes to the way we do business will, in future, require meaningful changes to how we teach, the voices we echo, how curricula are designed, and how executives go out into the world to create and run organisations."

As things stand, we have to ask if academia in general – and business schools in particular - are up to the task. And if we are honest, no they are not. They need to change, and faster than ever before, given the unexpected disruptions caused by the COVID-19 pandemic and the continuing war in Ukraine, as well as the widening inequality gap between Africa and the rest of the world.

AN EMERGING AFRICAN MODEL

An emerging African business school model holds global relevance not only for emerging economies but for a world grappling to develop the leadership and organisational competencies needed to navigate an unpredictable and changeable environment. The theme of the 2023 EFMD Annual Conference, which explored the role business schools can play in helping organisations and leaders to manage this uncertainty, is testament to the depth of this global challenge.

In Africa, leaders from all spheres of society are confronted on a daily basis with deep-seated challenges. Therefore, if African business schools are to recognise the potential impact they could have across the entire ecosystem of society, it is clear that producing agile leaders is not enough. It is also necessary to play a more active role in identifying African-facing problems and engaging with all stakeholders to advance impactful solutions.

In 2022, Henley Africa released insights from a research project aimed at amplifying the impact of business schools across Africa (Foster-Pedley, 2022). Building on insights generously shared by leading African and international business school experts, we considered the direct (business school environment), social (addressing social problems) and systemic (society as a whole) impact that African business schools should be having. Among the core areas identified was the need to invest more heavily in quality research that is relevant to Africa's needs and which is geared towards solving and contributing to ideas to solve social and environmental issues. In order to get faculty on board, it is important to ensure that Africa-relevant research is promoted and rewarded, so African faculty produce excellent research that enables them to stand toe-to-toe with our international counterparts.

Equally so, it is critical to ensure that action research - which holds such potential to change society for the better - is available widely via open-access platforms and publishers. Without paywalls, there is more scope that such research can step out of the hallowed halls of academia and make impactful difference on the ground. This is, after all, the crux of action research which can be defined as a collaborative "emergent inquiry process in which applied behavioural science knowledge is integrated with existing

Annual Research Volume 2 — Concepts of the Purposeful Business School

Research and Positive Impact: Henley Business School in the African Context
Jonathan Foster-Pedley and Cara Bouwer
....

organisational knowledge and applied to address real organisational issues. It is simultaneously concerned with bringing about change in organisations, in developing self-help competencies in organisational members, and adding to scientific knowledge" (Shani and Coghlan, 2021).

In a 2021 review of applying action research in the business and management context, Abraham Shani and David Coghlan concluded that the process of conductive research with the intention of providing solutions to a problem provided a "potential vehicle for meeting the increasing challenges that systems and organisations faced, but as currently practised and researched in business and management, the potential has barely been tapped" (*ibid*).

To really advance a meaningful action research agenda will, of course, require greater alignment and discussion between stakeholders across society to identify areas requiring focus and research, and which should ideally have the potential to positively impact society or steer innovation and thinking in a new direction.

There are other action areas which also warrant attention:

- *Reinventing the business school curriculum* - It is important to acknowledge the place that indigenous knowledge systems hold in African culture, and how including traditional systems that span health and trade, agriculture and environmental management can offer answers to complex modern-day questions (Ezeanya-Esiobu, 2019). Furthermore, in a world where micro-credentials and online offerings are proliferating, where skills shift in the blink of an eye, and where younger generations are demanding fresh, hands-on approaches to learning, higher education institutions need to offer a range of approaches and touch points that include both theoretical and practical elements. More needs to be done in Africa to embrace vocational and technical education, to harness technology-enabled learning and to shift thinking from a degree-first approach to a stronger appreciation on the acquisition of valued skills via modules or short courses. These days learning is a life-long pursuit, so rather than a straight ladder it should be viewed as a meander through areas of interest and opportunities.

- *Creating pipelines for learning* — At Henley Africa we are developing more short programmes, and we will continue working with our clients to create a pathway to learning as an alternative to the classic university model. Only 6% of South African school starters get a degree within six years of leaving school, compared to 50% in the United Kingdom. In Africa, many talented people go into organisations where they are

trained and become highly capable, but in the process, they miss the chance to get onto the qualifications ladder — which need not be a formal degree, but a certification that carries enough weight to ensure that the holder is able to progress even further in their chosen career. We've created a new pathway of learning that allows executives and managers to get back on the qualification pathway while developing competencies that are immediately helpful to their businesses. This builds up management capabilities, so it is an approach that strengthens African management and personal development.

- *Actively promote collaborations and partnerships* — This has long been a priority for institutions of higher learning, but in the case of Africa this means carefully leveraging both intra-Africa and global relationships, without giving precedence to one over another and with the confidence to promote African ideas on the world stage.

- *Strengthen ties with industry* — This is a critical point on so many levels: as a barometer of the skills needed by businesses now and in the future, as a means of ensuring that programmes are developed to make a discernible impact in the workplace, and a way of ensuring that research is in line with the needs of both the economy and society.

- *Strengthening ties with communities* — It has never been more important for business schools to leverage their trusted position in society by engaging closely with stakeholders across the board. The 2022 Edelman Trust Barometer Special Report, when noting the levels of trust in institutions of higher learning, made the point that learning institutions should build on this trust advantage to make a difference in the world, specifically around issues of climate change (Edelman, 2022). In today's online world there are any number of forums and events that can take place across borders.

- *Improve governance and management of business schools* — Without robust and strategic leadership aligned to the improvement of society as a whole, Africa's business schools will fail to reach their full potential. A critical part of this leadership role must be focused on investing in the development of quality faculty to constantly improve the level of education offered as well as the foresight to incorporate innovative methods and techniques, such as embracing technologies like virtual reality (VR) and packaging research insights in an accessible, online format for busy business leaders.

Annual Research Volume 2 – Concepts of the Purposeful Business School

Research and Positive Impact: Henley Business School in the African Context
Jonathan Foster-Pedley and Cara Bouwer
··················

- **Be prepared to take a more proactive, even activist stance** – The issues of climate, corruption, environment and fair opportunity (either actively or potentially) are so deeply damaging to the present and future, and to the prosperity of businesses, economies and full societies, that business schools need to be prepared to enter into a new territory. It is necessary to exercise our voice, rather than just speech, in our pronouncements and writings.

All of these areas of development should start with a realistic, no-holds-barred assessment of the capacity and existing culture within a business school.

AFRICAN ACADEMICS MUST CONFRONT SOME HARD TRUTHS

At this juncture, African business schools are being challenged to find the right balance between preserving academic freedom and advancing their global standing, and that of their faculty, with the wider imperative to serve growth, prosperity and create employment. A question many African deans are asking themselves is: What is the point of producing journal articles, research and case studies just to secure promotion in an academic system that is failing in its role of producing the skills needed for growth?

This is a particularly pertinent discussion in societies where abstract theories and ideas simply do not get implemented because of a fundamental lack of skills needed to drive adaptation and implementation. Indeed, this is a critical consideration in a country like South Africa that is struggling to produce the sort of talent required to affect the level of change being demanded by the economy and pressing social challenges. As educators, this raises the need to critically question the structure and approach to education in general and to debate the morality and focus of research that does not seek to solve social ills and advance prosperity.

When you start to ask these questions, it becomes clear that the outdated industrial revolution-era system of education is unable to keep pace with the human capital needs of a changing world. Rather than continuing to slowly and incrementally follow an academic model that is effectively a colonial era appendix (Kigotho, 2022), African and other emerging market nations should be advancing an alternative model that works for the needs of their economies and people, rather than one that continues to position research, models and theories from the Global North above those from Africa and the Global South.

While calls to decolonise education have been accelerating in recent years, we have to ask ourselves if this goes far enough (Foster-Pedley, 2020). Greater focus should be given to questioning the structures, habits and orientation of universities in Africa which by their embedded western intellectual biases and values may not act helpfully. Instead of treating the Western model of higher education as a sacred cow, business schools in particular need to find ways of working with technical and vocational models, as well as building greater agility into the system – both of which would extend the reach needed in Africa. Rather than attaching decolonisation solely to issues of pedagogy, African institutions need to revisit our values and determine where our current ethos and perspective is not just out of touch but simply a colonial relic. If so, then we must adapt accordingly.

This will require a mindset shift across the African business school ecosystem, and especially among African academics themselves. To quote African anthropologists Artwell Nhemachena and Munyaradzi Mawere: "Africa cannot afford professors who enjoy burying their heads in the hot sands of the tropics: it is simply too costly for intellectual progress on a continent that has already suffered, for long, the travails of cargo cult[1] mentalities (Nhemachena and Mawere, 2022)."

Getting this right will require a new system, which might include new forms of educational institutions, theory building that is more progressive and inclusive, as well as the uptake of novel and more productive forms of research – such as action research.

Given that Africa still produces less than 1% of the world's research (Duermeijer *et al.*, 2018) - despite being the continent most beset by challenges identified under the United Nations' Sustainable Development Goals (SDGs) (UNDP, 2022) – it could be argued that solution-focused action research holds great potential as an avenue for African academics to shift global perspectives.

Annual Research Volume 2 – Concepts of the Purposeful Business School

Research and Positive Impact: Henley Business School in the African Context
Jonathan Foster-Pedley and Cara Bouwer
....

HENLEY AFRICA: ALIGNING RESEARCH, INSIGHT WITH THE AFRICAN CONTEXT

In recent years, projects that speak to Henley Africa's drive to support a model of African management education have been recognised for their innovation and impact by associations such as the EFMD.

A standout example is the 10-day pan-African leadership programme that was created by Henley Africa and the Gordon Institute of Business Science, another well-respected South Africa-based business school. Created for Africa-wide banking group Standard Bank, as a novel way of enabling executives from across the bank to tap into their leadership potential, the #unTAP strategic leadership programme gathered a diverse group of leaders from various countries in Africa and challenged them to collaborate and stretch themselves. As Henley Africa's Director of Executive Education, Linda Buckley, noted at the time: "The classes were deliberately diverse, a melting pot of culture, creed, race and gender. A lot of the learning shifts actually came from within the groups themselves, we were the alchemy in the process" (EFMD Global, 2020).

Not only did this programme start life by confronting the challenges being faced by the bank, but it also embraced collaboration – both among the programme designers and participants – and reinforced ways in which to work in diverse teams; an increasingly vital business capability in Africa and around the world (Eswaran, 2019).

The #unTAP programme went on to win gold for outstanding case study in the executive development category of the 2020 EFMD Excellence in Practice Awards (EiP).

In 2021, another Standard Bank learning programme, Acceleration, took silver in the talent development category at the EiP. Programme Director Dr Puleng Makhoalibe, who also shepherded the #unTAP programme to success, called Acceleration "a truly African programme uniting leaders to take the bank and the continent forward" (HR Future, n.d.). Makhoalibe unpacked her approach to developing human-centric, creative and life-changing leadership interventions in her recent white paper, 'Using the Project Artistry framework to optimise executive education' (Makhoalibe, 2023).

Our ongoing efforts to create an optimal learning environment for students include actively embracing the potential of new technologies such as virtual reality and immersive learning, which is proving an impactful way to upskill managers at scale across Africa by drawing them into a virtual space in which they can interact and learn from one another, thereby closing geographic barriers to engagement and understanding. Being able to expose African business executives to continent-wide networks and unique business challenges and solutions expands the depth of learning, improves engagement levels and fosters a greater appreciation of the complexity and agility required by executives leading in the African context (Claassen, 2022).

In August this year we formalised the exciting work we have already embarked on in the immersive space under the banner of a new research centre, Henley Explore. Our fifth dedicated research centre, alongside others that focus on international business, reputation, leadership and consumer studies, Henley Explore is headed by our Head of Research, Professor Danie Petzer, and co-director Louise Claassen. Henley Explore strives to provide delegates with truly immersive experiences in an African context using a unique combination of VR films and case studies.

Already, the partnership that Henley Explore co-director Claassen has nurtured with Kenyan production company BlackRhino VR since 2019, has produced four VR films and 10 accompanying case studies. The latest VR film, focusing on South Africa's state-owned rail, port and pipeline company Transnet, is accompanied by three case studies. The VR films produced to date have been successfully used in executive education interventions and as part of Henley Africa's Postgraduate Diploma in Management Practice in Africa (*ibid*), and many of the learnings from this process have been shared in Claassen's 2022 white paper, 'Virtual Reality in Business Education'.

Recognising that accessible research should not only appeal to seasoned academics but to business leaders, executives, trend analysts, policy makers and commentators, our faculty are also collaborating with business to bring complex Africa issues to the fore and spark conversations around potential solutions. In 2023 our research output included insights by Kelly Alexander into the role of business leaders in Africa's renewable energy transition (Alexander, 2023); a case study by Lorenzo Messina exploring the importance of a strong risk culture (Messina, 2022) in the context of South Africa's fight against corruption; and a collaboration between Henley Africa's Petzer and Vickey de Villiers, together with Professor Marianne Matthee from GIBS and Stellenbosch University's Dr Stefanie Kühn, focused on South Africa's fresh fruit industry and how to optimise export performance (Petzer *et al.*, 2023).

Another prime example is Henley Africa Executive Fellow Dr Mélani Prinsloo's forthcoming white paper 'Understanding the land title, tenure tightrope: Is technology the solution to Africa's complex land ownership challenges?' This contribution perfectly illustrates the complexities of shoehorning Western 'best practice' into a complex system without due regard for traditional means of determining land ownership and tenure.

Annual Research Volume 2 – Concepts of the Purposeful Business School

Research and Positive Impact: Henley Business School in the African Context
Jonathan Foster-Pedley and Cara Bouwer
....

IN CONCLUSION

These examples are an appetiser of the level of complexity and relevance which all African business schools should be hoping to achieve. Asking pertinent, context-driven questions that don't brush inconvenient truths under the carpet, can open a wealth of areas for study and examination while also helping to grow and develop Africa for the betterment of all.

The research conducted for Henley Africa's 2022 white paper, 'Amplifying the impact of African business schools', provides some future direction for research output that is more action-orientated, practical and relevant to addressing core issues of development and process across the African continent. Among the input received in compiling this paper was a strong sense that by working closely with a sector or government department to identify issues and blockages upfront, it would be possible to produce research of immediate practical value. Applying this approach across society, government and civil society would create a treasure trove of actionable ideas to help solve social, business and institutional challenges (Foster-Pedley, 2022).

Furthermore, as an immediate compass, African institutions need only look to the SDGs as beacons demanding action and input; the solving of which would make an immediate and profound difference to the lives and prospects of Africans. The priority areas based on an SDG-focused approach, must certainly include youth-related challenges such as entrepreneurial skills, opportunities and funding, as well as ways in which to advance education in line with technology, teaching ethics and building stronger ties with fellow African institutions – as well as global educators – to share outputs. Finding ways to support and accelerate the establishment of start-up companies, created as university spin-offs as a result of research, is another avenue for future development and is something that Stellenbosch University and the University of Cape Town in South Africa do particularly well (Jafta and Uctu, 2013).

Finally, by sharing our reflections on both successes and failures, and learning from other business schools in Africa and across the Global South, it is hoped that this call for a new, democratised and decolonialised African business school model will find fertile ground.

References

AABSchools. (n.d.) *Welcome to AABS: Setting business education standards in Africa*. [Online] Available from https://www.aabschools.com/ [Accessed 15 Aug 2023].

Alexander, K. (2023) *Powering Africa's growth: the renewable energy landscape*. Henley Business School Africa. Available from https://energycentral.com/system/files/ece/nodes/620690/pag.pdf [Accessed 17 Aug 2023]

Claassen, L. (2022) *Virtual reality in business education*. Henley Business School Africa. Available from Henley Business School Africa | Research | The effective use of VR in business school education (henleysa.ac.za) [Accessed 15 Aug 2023].

Duermeijer, C., M. Amir and L. Schoombee (2018, March 22) *Africa generates less than 1% of the world's research; data analytics can change that*. Elsevier Connect. Available from Africa generates less than 1% of the world's research; data analytics can change that (elsevier.com) [Accessed 13 Aug 2023].

Edelman. (2022) *2022 Edelman Trust Barometer Special Report: Trust and Climate Action*. [Online] Available from https://2022 Special Report: Trust and Climate Change [Accessed 16 Aug 2023].

EFMD Global (2020, October 20) *Authentic African leadership requires 'more than a programme'*. Global Focus: The EFMD Business Magazine. [Online] Available from https://www.globalfocusmagazine.com/authentic-african-leadership-requires-more-than-a-programme/ [Accessed 14 Aug 2023].

Eswaran, V. (2019, April 29). *The business case for diversity in the workplace is now overwhelming.* World Economic Forum. [Online] Available from https://www.weforum.org/agenda/2019/04/business-case-for-diversity-in-the-workplace/ [Accessed 13 Aug 2023].

Ezeanya-Esiobu, C. (2019) *Indigenous Knowledge and Curriculum in Africa. In: Indigenous Knowledge and Education in Africa*. Frontiers in African Business Research. Singapore: Springer. Available from https://doi.org/10.1007/978-981-13-6635-2_1 [Accessed 16 Aug 2023].

Foster-Pedley, J., Bouwer, C. and De Villiers, V. (2023) *Climate action: an existential priority for African business schools*. Henley Business School Africa (produced for and on behalf of the Business Schools for Climate Leadership Africa.

Foster-Pedley, J. (2022, June) *Amplifying the impact of African business schools*. Henley Business School Africa. [Online] Available from Revealing research questions the impact of African business schools - Henley Business School South Africa (henleysa.ac.za) [Accessed 14 Aug 2023].

Foster-Pedley, J. (2020, July 2023) *SA higher education doesn't work*. Financial Mail. [Online] Available from https://www.businesslive.co.za/fm/opinion/on-my-mind/2020-07-23-jon-foster-pedley-sa-higher-education-doesnt-work/ [Accessed 20 Aug 2023].

Annual Research Volume 2 – Concepts of the Purposeful Business School

Research and Positive Impact: Henley Business School in the African Context
Jonathan Foster-Pedley and Cara Bouwer
·············

Further Africa. (2022, May 14) *Africa's most popular tribes?* [Online] Available from https://furtherafrica.com/2022/05/14/africas-most-popular-tribes/ [Accessed 15 Aug 2023].

HR Future. (n.d.) *Henley Business School wins Silver in prestigious global awards*. [Online] Available from Henley Business School wins Silver in prestigious global awards - HR Future [Accessed 14 Aug 2023].

Jafta, R. and R. Uctu (2013) *Exploring entrepreneurial activity in Cape Town and Stellenbosch Universities, South Africa*. Industry and Higher Education, 27(2), 117-128. Available from https://doi.org/10.5367/ihe.2013.0143 [Accessed 22 Aug 2023].

Kigotho, W. (2022, September 22). *Decolonial scholarship: Do academics in Africa have clay feet?* University World News: Africa Edition. [Online] Available from Decolonial scholarship: Do academics in Africa have clay feet? (universityworldnews.com) [Accessed 15 Aug 2023].

Makhoalibe, P. (2023). *Using the Project Artistry framework to optimise executive education*. Henley Business School Africa. Available from | Project Artistry framework to optimise executive education (henleysa.ac.za) [Accessed 13 Aug 2023].

Messina, L. (2022). *EOH: corruption, losses, and the impact of a poor risk culture* [Case study]. Paulshof: Henley Business School Africa.

Nhemachena, A. and M. Mawere (2022) *Academics with clay feet? Anthropological perspectives on academic freedom in twenty-first century African universities*. J Afr Am Stud (New Brunsw), 26(2):142-165. doi: 10.1007/s12111-022-09584-4. Epub 2022, June 13 [Accessed 29 Aug 2023].

Petzer, D.J., M. Matthee, S.W. Kühn and V. De Villiers (2023) *South Africa's fresh fruit industry: Optimising export performance and securing sustainable exporter-importer relationships*. Henley Business School Africa. Available from https://content.henleysa.ac.za/white-paper-fresh-fruit-industry [Accessed 17 Aug 2023].

Rabie, N. (2023, January 9) *African business schools' deans launch their climate leadership initiative in AUC School of Business*. [Online] Available from https://blog.efmdglobal.org/2023/01/09/african-business-schools-deans-launch-their-climate-leadership-initiative-at-auc-school-of-business/ [Accessed 12 Aug 2023].

Statista Research Department. (2023, July 18) *Number of languages spoken in Africa 2022, by country*. [Online] Available from https://www.statista.com/statistics/1280625/number-of-living-languages-in-africa-by-country/ [Accessed 14 Aug 2023].

Thomas, D. (2022, May 18) *What you need to know about the African Continental Free Trade Area*. African Business. [Online] Available from https://african.business/2022/05/trade-investment/what-you-need-to-know-about-the-african-continental-free-trade-area [Accessed 13 Aug 2023].

Thomas, H., M. Lee, L. Thomas and A. Wilson (2017) *Africa: The Future of Management Education Volume 2*. Bingley, UK Emerald Publishing

Shani, A.B. and D. Coghlan (2021) *Action research in business and management: A reflective review*. Action Research, 19(3), 518-541. Available from doi: 10.1177/1476750319852147//journals.sagepub.com/doi/pdf/10.1177/1476750319852147 [Accessed 14 Aug 2023].

UNDP. (2022, December 9). *New Africa SDGs report shows slow progress, calls for greater action to meet targets*. [Online] Available from New Africa SDGs report shows slow progress, calls for greater action to meet targets | United Nations Development Programme (undp.org) [Accessed 14 Aug 2023].

Xygalatas, D. (2022, October 20) *What cargo cult rituals reveal about human nature*. Sapiens. [Online] Available from What Cargo Cult Rituals Reveal About Human Nature – SAPIENS [Accessed 15 Aug 2023].

About the Authors

Jonathan Foster-Pedley is Dean and Director of Henley Business School Africa, the only quadruple-internationally-accredited business school in Africa. He is currently chairman of the Association of African Business Schools and the British Chamber of Business for Southern Africa. Jon serves on the board of the Alliance of Management Development Associations in Rising Economies.

Cara Bouwer is an independent writer and researcher.

Developing a Responsible Research Strategy at Saïd Business School

SOUMITRA DUTTA

Research Ecosystems, Partnerships and Collective Know-How

The notions of 'purpose' and 'social responsibility' in business have been gaining increased traction in recent years, in turn raising questions about what business schools should be teaching and researching.

In his famous 1970 *New York Times* essay, Milton Friedman proposed 'there is one and only one social purpose of business... [which is] to increase profits so long as it stays within the rules of the game' (Friedman, 1970), an idea that has formed the basis of business practice, policy, and education ever since – and, in many cases, business research, where areas of inquiry were predicated on an acceptance of the principle of shareholder value.

Since the 2008 global financial crisis, and with growing awareness of the extent of the climate crisis, together with concerns about inequality, exclusion, and other social problems, a number of new ideas have circulated under the umbrella of 'responsible business'.

However, these initiatives can be problematic in two ways.

First, many of these initiatives have been seen as an 'add-on' or a PR exercise, distinct from the main activities of the business, which continues to focus on short-term profit maximisation. 'Corporate social responsibility' has been a particular casualty in this regard.

Second, in formulating and publicising their 'purpose', many companies sound a lot more like charities or non-profit organisations than businesses. In the rejection of the idea that the pursuit of profit should be the sole purpose of business, 'profit' itself has come to be a dirty word. And while most organisations do still seek to deliver profits even while claiming that they are saving the world, a casual observer might reasonably draw the conclusion that the only way to be a responsible business is not to be a business at all.

So, what does this mean for business schools and the development of responsible business research strategies?

I mention the tensions involved in the idea of responsible business particularly because it is important that business schools do not fall into the same trap. 'Responsible' research is not only research that investigates social enterprises or issues of sustainability and development. Scholars focusing on all areas of business activity both can and should engage in research that leads to positive impacts for business and thus for society in general.

For Oxford Saïd, the first step in developing our own responsible research strategy was in recognising that management and business is essentially an applied discipline. Our research mission is: 'to produce research of the highest quality that is rigorous, imaginative and meaningfully relevant to – and enhances – business practice'.

Historically, colleagues across all disciplines have argued for the importance of basic or 'pure' research, driven by a spirit of inquiry and with the aim of increasing the sum of human knowledge. While business and management were establishing themselves as credible disciplines (being relative newcomers to the university curriculum: the majority of business schools were founded only in the last century) it is little surprise that there was an emphasis on theoretical concepts and somewhat abstruse questions. This sort of research was impact-agnostic and tended to support the shareholder-value focus because that was the assumption behind the systems and organisations that were being studied. However, that is changing and is the basis of explicit, useful debates today.

Even so, there is not always a straight line between research and impact; and, if there were, it could raise questions about whether what we were doing could more accurately be described as consultancy. Consultancy projects can be useful in building connections with practitioners and, indeed, in demonstrating the applications of research findings, but combining it directly with research can be a tricky balancing act.

DOI: 10.4324/9781003467410-8

Our research strategy, developed collaboratively by members of our research community, led by the Research Dean, Professor Andrew Stephen, therefore focuses on the core values of high-quality, rigorous, and responsible research, encouraging a wide range of projects and methods that address large scale problems; are boundary-spanning and future-focused; are developed in collaboration with practitioners and with colleagues from other disciplines; and that are directly linked with our teaching on both degree programmes and executive education.

ADDRESSING PROBLEMS

Through research, our scholarly community identifies the most important and interesting challenges facing the world that pertain to business practice and business-related public policies, attempts to make sense of them and proposes innovative, evidence-based ways to tackle them. We encourage our research community to think in terms of tackling big issues and messy problems, going beyond making incremental and purely theoretical contributions that are only of interest to other academics.

A strong example of this is in the cluster of research initiatives under the heading of Responsible Business, many of which were established by (now) Emeritus Professor Colin Mayer CBE, who also led the *Future of the Corporation* programme at the British Academy and has published extensively on the topic of business purpose (Mayer, 2013; 2018). These projects include the **Economics of Mutuality Lab**, which was developed from a five-year research project on Mutuality in Business conducted in partnership with Mars Catalyst, the think tank of Mars Inc., and stimulated by a fundamental question asked by Mars in 2007: 'What is the right level of profit?'

This research programme led to the development of the Economics of Mutuality: a set of new management practices, tools, and metrics to help businesses not only increase financial value, but also improve human capital and community cohesion, and strengthen environmental protection and regeneration. This thinking, together with a set of practical case studies, was published in 2021 by Oxford University Press. *Putting Purpose into Practice: The Economics of Mutuality* (Roche and Mayer, 2021) was made available on an open access basis, reflecting the belief that sharing knowledge drives impact.

In 2020, Mars Catalyst transformed into an independent Economics of Mutuality Foundation, comprising a not-for-profit, public benefit foundation focusing on research, education and advocacy, and a for-profit arm delivering consultancy, executive education and services to business.

The **Oxford Initiative on Rethinking Performance** was initially born out of the Mutuality in Business project, and aims to develop a framework for the measurement and operationalisation of corporate purpose. This initiative has research at its heart, demonstrated by publishing in academic journals and books. It is funded by a consortium of partners, who actively engage with the research team and indeed work with them on specific projects of mutual interest.

The **Enacting Purpose Initiative** is another partnership-based research project, supported by a number of leading universities, corporations and professional service firms, and contributing to the British Academy's work on the *Future of the Corporation*.

The **Skoll Centre for Social Entrepreneurship** was one of Oxford Saïd's first research centres, and continues to conduct innovative research investigating big themes at the nexus of research and practice, as well as to create further impact through education, particularly on the MBA programme. A current study is the **Systems Change Observatory**, which draws on a large sample of ventures affiliated with the Skoll Foundation programmes for a long-term empirical study of systems change efforts in the social impact space, including pathways, challenges and solutions.

Annual Research Volume 2 – Research Ecosystems, Partnerships and Collective Know-How

Developing a Responsible Research Strategy at Saïd Business School
Soumitra Dutta
....

BOUNDARY SPANNING

If business school academics only studied the inner workings of conventional businesses, we would soon run out of things to say. To deliver research with impact we believe it is important to recognise that business thinking and business issues appear not only in established commercial enterprises but also in almost every other type of institution, from health services and other public sector organisations to professional firms, NGOs, social enterprises, and a wide variety of entrepreneurial start-ups. In addition, we recognise the wide variety of new developments and influences that are changing and challenging organisations, including social innovation, artificial intelligence, cyber-crime, engineering and infrastructure development, climate change and the environment. Even within the core business areas of, for example, finance, marketing, and leadership, research at the intersection with these external phenomena yields interesting and meaningful findings that are of immense practical value.

For example, digitisation, artificial intelligence and social media platforms, along with other new technologies, are increasingly overlapping with the traditional work of marketing departments. The **Oxford Future of Marketing Initiative**, which brings together academics and senior executives from some of the world's largest companies, has worked extensively on the new challenges and opportunities arising from this overlap, with three members of faculty incorporating a research spinout, Augmented Intelligence Labs (AIL), in 2020.

The company develops analysis and decision support systems for marketing leaders, creating tools which are integrated into those offered by marketing research companies. Research on modelling multi-relational data (Clarke *et al.*, 2023) has been developed into a tool called Hypertrends, a trend-detection and analysis system that maps complex social connections to understand the flow and significance of ideas, discussion topics and emotions. This analytical capability is being used to underpin the sustainability practice at Kantar, the market data business, and will guide companies' sustainability strategies and investment.

The path from science to impactful business is also trodden by participants in the **Creative Destruction Lab Oxford**, supported by our faculty members focusing on entrepreneurship, as well as by mentors drawn from successful entrepreneurial businesses. Since CDL-Oxford launched in 2019 £1.3bn has been created in equity value along with 716 jobs in businesses working in the areas of AI, climate, fintech, and health.

FUTURE-FOCUSED

A fascinating research collaboration between a number of different University of Oxford departments, led by Oxford Saïd and the Department of Politics and International Relations, is the **Oxford Space Initiative**. As a new, commercial space economy grows alongside the traditional exploration focus of national space agencies, the initiative was created to influence policy for space commerce and governance, aiming to contribute to the development of a responsible and inclusive sector.

Bringing these different academic fields together with governments and young and emerging businesses can allow us to anticipate and mitigate complex future challenges, such as the problem of space debris. This is growing as an issue now, and reflects many much more developed environmental challenges on the ground, but efforts to address it may lead to solutions that enable a 'bad' actor to take out GPS and other broadly used satellites. The Oxford Space Initiative is also an opportunity to study what could be thought of as an 'extreme' context, and certainly a new type of emerging market, raising questions about the role of governments in shaping emerging markets at their inception, and – as hundreds of space agencies are established across the globe in countries such as Rwanda, Egypt, and Azerbaijan – what seems to be a renewed role of government in leading economic development.

In addition, researchers have observed that work on commercial satellite data – that is, building markets for geo-analytics data – may well revolutionise many uses of these data for novel or unexpected purposes, in turn reshaping earth contexts or policy solutions.

INTERDISCIPLINARY

The Oxford Space Initiative is one of many examples of interdisciplinary research engaged in by academics at Saïd Business School. Diversity of thought is the cornerstone of imaginative and innovative research. It also contributes to creating 'responsible' research by discouraging 'groupthink' and drawing on different perspectives to ask critical questions.

Unlike many of our peer business schools, we are an integral part of our parent university. The collegiate structure of the University of Oxford has for centuries fostered interdisciplinary connections. Members of the business school's research community are also affiliated with different colleges of the university, bringing them into contact with scholars from a wide variety of academic backgrounds, with different research interests and levels of expertise and experience.

We recognise that we are fortunate to operate in this rich intellectual environment, and it is part of our research strategy that we actively encourage all members of our research community to make the most of it. This can be through informal means, such as participation in other departments' research seminars or symposia, or something more formal such as collaborating on interdisciplinary research projects. In addition, a number of our faculty members hold joint appointments with other Oxford University departments, creating the conditions for innovative and ambitious work. For example, Felix Reed-Tsochas – whose academic background is in theoretical condensed matter physics – is also a Director of the Complexity Economics Programme at INET Oxford, and a founding Co-Director of the CABDyN Complexity Centre. This interdisciplinary framework forms the basis of research that seeks to develop new approaches for the management of systemic risk (Reed-Tsochas and Johnson).

COLLABORATION AND ENGAGEMENT WITH STAKEHOLDERS

Some of the best – and certainly the most impactful – research ideas come from active engagement with external stakeholders. In the case of business research, this usually means business practitioners and business-related entities (e.g. policymakers, regulators, international organisations). In fact, most of the examples of responsible research projects that I have given above have some element of collaboration with external stakeholders – in some cases, a genuine research partnership.

Other research initiatives such as the **Oxford Future of Marketing Initiative**, the **Oxford Future of Real Estate Initiative** and the **Oxford Initiative on AI x SDGs** are examples of where external corporate funding is being used to directly fund research costs and to enhance the potential for subsequent impact by helping to ensure that the research undertaken is relevant.

LINKS WITH EDUCATION

Research, of course, also drives other activities within the Business School, in particular the provision of quality business education through our MBA and other degree programmes, as well as through executive education.

While influential engagement with non-academic external stakeholders typically occurs through individuals' own networks and via research centres, initiatives or networks that have external stakeholder involvement, executive education and degree programmes (especially those focused on experienced executives such as the Executive MBA and Diplomas) are another viable avenue for research-related external engagement. The management and delivery of executive education in most business schools is a professional job – as it is at Oxford Saïd – but we have long had a policy of ensuring that a member of faculty is appointed as an 'academic director' of every open-enrolment programme (Trevor, 2021).

In addition, some researchers have intentionally engaged with executive education to apply the fruits of their research.

A key example included in REF 2021 is Jonathan Trevor's work on **strategic alignment**. Trevor's research has centred on the principle that organisational performance is secured through an 'enterprise value chain', in which an enterprise's enduring purpose, business strategy, organisational capability, architecture (including organisational structure, culture, processes and people) and management systems should be as closely aligned as possible. This framework provides a valuable system of thought for practitioners to apply to their own setting, regardless of sector. Using a combination of action research, consultancy and executive education as channels for research engagement and impact,

Trevor has worked with senior leadership teams from over 25 global companies (including IBM, Shell and Serco) to help them to align their purpose, strategy and organisational capabilities for improved business performance, agility and resilience.

Also published in REF 2021 was Rafael Ramirez's interdisciplinary research on **Scenario Planning** (SP) to develop the Oxford Scenario Planning Approach (OSPA) (Ramirez, 2021). The OSPA is a distinctive SP methodology that has been influential worldwide across organisations and industry sectors by enabling a shift in the mindset of strategic management from closed to more open and flexible. Approximately 1,000 individuals from several hundred organisations have absorbed this methodology via the Oxford Scenarios Programme, run by our executive education business. As a result of this programme, large companies such as Rolls Royce have changed their approaches to strategic planning; and the programme has also influenced policy and funding decisions within public bodies such as the International Monetary Fund (IMF), the World Economic Forum (WEF), the International Atomic Energy Authority (IAEA), and the National Health Service (NHS), charities such as Diabetes UK and Mercy Corps, and even scientific fields such as gastroenterology and the chemical sciences.

DEVELOPING ECOSYSTEMS

The Skoll Centre for Social Entrepreneurship, which aims 'to equip entrepreneurial leaders for impact within and beyond business', contributes to the fields of social entrepreneurship, social innovation, and systems change. It sees itself as occupying the nexus of research, education, and community, in which the research it catalyses informs its education programmes; insights from the practitioners it works with improve research and teaching; and the community it brings together sparks the collaborations needed to drive systemic change. That is, it has created its own ecosystem that extends beyond the boundaries of the Business School, and indeed the University of Oxford.

Map the System, for example, is a global competition that invites students from universities and higher education institutions to select a social or environmental issue and to research the contextual factors that contribute to it. The Systems Change Accelerator research grants, awarded by the Skoll Centre, invite faculty members at the University of Oxford to put together diverse teams that represent different identities, disciplines, and schools of thought to use research to inform and drive systems change. **The Systems Change Observatory (SCO)** (see earlier Addressing problems section) is a research project that intentionally sets out to build a community of practice and research, drawing together practitioners including funders,

entrepreneurs, Skoll alumni, researchers, and policy consultants. The project is exploring data from a large sample of ventures affiliated with the Skoll Foundation, and draws on insights from organisational design and strategy, institutional and funding contexts, the work of leaders, and broader venture ecosystems. The goal is to generate actionable insights, case studies, and tools in support of systems change, both for practice and policy, looking at different pathways to change and assessing new models (Savaget *et al.*, 2022).

Members of our research community who have been drawn into the Skoll Centre ecosystem continue to publish in established journals. But the outputs of these collaborative, systems-based research projects are just as likely to be a learning tool[1], a map[2] (**Movement of movements** project), or a playbook[3] (**Climate justice playbook**).

These non-traditional academic outputs can occasionally raise questions about the rigour and quality of the research compared with the more familiar publishing approach. This brings us to a final question about how responsible and impact-focused research is assessed and measured.

MEASURING THE IMPACT OF RESPONSIBLE RESEARCH

The measurement of both research quality and impact is a vexed subject. Many (usually very senior) academics worldwide have already spoken out against the publishing treadmill, arguing that it breeds myopia within academia and within disciplinary boundaries. Impact measurement, also, is a challenging task, especially in the short-term – as usually required by funding bodies or governmental assessment exercises – as a true judgement of the value of an intervention cannot usually be made until many years afterwards.

Our answer is to build on the existing metrics of scholarly research by determining KPIs (key performance indicators) relating to the values underpinning our research strategy. Obviously, we continue to encourage our academics to publish in high-quality publications. Research cannot be defined as responsible if it comes at the expense of the careers of members of our research community. However, we also assess, for example, the number of members of our research community conducting interdisciplinary research with colleagues in non-business disciplines – particularly where those collaborations involve future-related topics; the number of scholarly publications that involve relevant external stakeholder groups in some form of collaboration and/or was clearly prompted by a relevant external issue, source or problem; and the number of scholarly publications that have had a demonstrable and documented impact on one or more external stakeholder groups.

Annual Research Volume 2 – Research Ecosystems, Partnerships and Collective Know-How

Developing a Responsible Research Strategy at Saïd Business School
Soumitra Dutta
....

References

Clark G.J., F. Thomaz, A.T. Stephen (2023) Comparing the principal eigenvector of a hypergraph and its shadows. *Linear Algebra and its Applications (673)* pp.46-68

Friedman M. (1970) 'A Friedman Doctrine – The Social Responsibility of Business is to Increase its Profits' *The New York Times*, 13 September 1970

Mayer C. (2013) *Firm Commitment: Why the Corporation is Failing Us and How to Restore Trust in It*. Oxford: Oxford University Press

Mayer C. (2018) *Prosperity: Better Business Makes the Greater Good*. Oxford: Oxford University Press

Ramirez R. (2021) *Building Organisational Resilience Using the Oxford Scenario Planning Approach to Reframe Strategy* REF 2021 Impact Case Study Database

Reed-Tsochas F. and N. Johnson (Series editors) *Complex Systems and Interdisciplinary Science*, World Scientific Publishing

Roche B. and C. Mayer (eds) (2021) *Putting Purpose into Practice: The Economics of Mutuality*. Oxford: Oxford University Press

Savaget, P., M.J. Ventresca, M. Besharov and J. Jacobson (2022) *Unpacking Systems Change Philanthropy: Five Alternative Models*. Skoll Centre Working Paper. Oxford: Skoll Centre for Social Entrepreneurship

Trevor J. (2021) *Improving Organisational Performance Through Strategic Alignment*, REF 2021 Impact Case Study Database

Footnotes

[1] https://www.sbs.ox.ac.uk/sites/default/files/2020-01/movement-of-movements-primer.pdf (ox.ac.uk)

[2] https://www.sbs.ox.ac.uk/sites/default/files/2020-01/influencesg-movement-maps.pdf (ox.ac.uk)

[3] The Climate Justice Playbook for Business: How to Centre Climate Action in Climate Justice (bcorporation.net)

About the Author

Professor Soumitra Dutta is Peter Moores Dean, Saïd Business School, University of Oxford. He is the President of Portulans Institute, Chair of the Board of the Global Business School Network and member of the Global Board of Dassault Systèmes. Professor Dutta is an authority on innovation in the global knowledge economy.

Managing to Make Impactful Business and Management Researchers in the Anthropocene

KATY MASON

Research Ecosystems, Partnerships and Collective Know-How

We are in the Anthropocene – an age of climate emergency, where "climate action failure and extreme weather …[are] the top two global risks" (Hurlbert, 2021). We have failed in our social contract to provide security from disaster and offer the potential transformative change needed to protect our people and planet. The education and research that business and management schools offer requires an urgent response to this climate emergency.

Many are now questioning the meaning and value of business and management schools (Parker, 2018; Wilson and Thomas, 2012), urging deans to take responsibility not only for educating the next generation of environmentally aware business leaders but also for driving research that is likely to generate solutions to redress the fragile balance of the earth through the way we perform our economy. The climate emergency is acting as a market force, changing what students and society expect and demand from our business schools.

A number of different initiatives have been launched to advance what has become known as the responsible management agenda. For example, the Civic University Charter and the Civic Management School agenda have an explicit role in bringing research expertise to bear in the places where our business schools are situated. UN Sustainable Development Goals (SDGs) have focused researchers' attention on an ambitious agenda to solve real-world problems, while the Responsible Research in Business and Management network (RRBM) has established principles of responsible research. The Principles of Management Education network (PRME), calls for the inclusion of this research in our educational programmes.

These Responsible Management movements are a reflection and driver of a broader public debate arguing for significant societal and business practice change, in an attempt to halt the depletion of the planet's ecosystems and to prevent human extinction through restorative action. This represents a real opportunity for business and management schools - not known for their innovative approach to futures - to do something different, bold, and significant.

DEVELOPING A RESEARCH STRATEGY

At Lancaster University Management School (LUMS), our aim has been to nurture a new kind of research culture, and a new kind of business and management researcher, to deliver an ambitious research agenda, designed to deliver real-world positive change (MacIntosh *et al.*, 2017; MacIntosh *et al.*, 2021). We have developed a model (Figure 1) that helps us understand what our researchers will be doing when, and the kinds of resources they need to enable them to deliver. Our research strategy has been developed by taking multiple scales of action into account: the environment, the University, the School, and the individual researcher.

DOI: 10.4324/9781003467410-9

Annual Research Volume 2 – Research Ecosystems, Partnerships and Collective Know-How

Managing to Make Impactful Business and Management Researchers in the Anthropocene
Katy Mason
....

World-leading Engagement
Including:
• Research and Engagement Support
• Engaged Research
• Anticipating future challenges
• Setting field-leading research aganda

World-leading Impact & Reputation
Including:
• Media outputs
• Policy briefings
• Practitioner toolkits

Lancaster University
Management School

Engaged, Impactful Research
[Teams]

World-leading Publication
Including:
• Research journal papers
• Practioner and policy orientated White Papers

World-leading Research Funding
Supporting:
• Discipline-based research
• Multi and interdisciplinary research
• Pathways to impact *designed-in*

World-leading Data & Resource
Including:
• Responsible Research & Innovation/ethics
• Large Data Sets
• Research team: [inter]disciplinary experts and professionals working together

Figure 1 The Engaged, Impactful Research Cycle

The School's vision and shared understanding of the kinds of value we are working to deliver for different stakeholder groups - students, researchers, business practitioners, policymakers and civic communities (*ibid*) - are key to setting priorities and for supporting researchers to design ambitious, meaningful and impactful research.

Lancaster University Management School's (LUMS) vision '*to have a reputation as a leading international business and management school through a focus on research, education and engagement, anchored around the theme of responsible management*', reflects our commitment to rethink the value that business and management schools can deliver for society. In a full-spectrum business and management school such as LUMS, *responsible management* means doing research that has a positive impact on society, the economy and the environment. To build our unique version of *responsible management*, we have been working to generate a deeper understanding of our core capabilities, putting this at the heart of our research strategy development.

In general, an organisation's superior performance can be explained by the distinctiveness of its capabilities and resources (i.e., physical, financial, human) (Barney *et al.*, 2001; Wernerfelt, 1984). The most important resources business schools have, are their people. Understanding the way LUMS manages relationships between people, their adaptability, their innovation capacity, their relationships with students, research funders, practitioners and policymakers, and what works in delivering the LUMS vision, has been central to the development of our school's research strategy (cf. Siegel and Leih, 2018).

While we continue to maintain our *threshold* capabilities and resources (i.e., those required for LUMS to compete in the HE Business and Management market), our *distinctive* capabilities and resources help us create our unique research community. Distinctive capabilities are those that make what we do *valuable*, *rare*, and *inimitable* (Barney, 1991). We have invested significant time in understanding these so we can then put in place the right *organisational support* to leverage them. This has become the foundation of our work to further strengthen our reputation for world-leading research with our research stakeholders and beneficiaries (i.e., with business and third sector practitioners, policymakers, researchers and students).

To understand our distinctive capabilities and resources, we looked for patterns of research interest and expertise within and across our School's academic departments. Our department-level analysis revealed five or six themes for each department, with some overlaps. Next, we mapped the interests of external stakeholders: government, funding bodies, and communities that we had a long and significant history of research engagement with (for example, LUMS has a very long history of working with small and medium-sized enterprises and family businesses). We paid careful attention to the language and framing of stakeholders' real-world concerns. We mapped these against the UN Sustainable Development Goals, which helped us understand what kinds of phenomena (and by implication, multi- and interdisciplinary research), our researchers wanted to pay attention to. Then, we mapped the capabilities our researchers have and need to have, to deliver impactful research, against a number of frameworks,

Annual Research Volume 2 – Research Ecosystems, Partnerships and Collective Know-How

Managing to Make Impactful Business and Management Researchers in the Anthropocene
Katy Mason
....

including Responsible Business and Management Research principles, the Responsible Research and Innovation framework (Owen *et al.*, 2012) and the AREA Framework[1]. This helped us understand *how* our researchers could deliver research that would really make a difference. By holding these frameworks against our department-level data, we began to understand better where our unique strengths lay. Three substantive themes stood out: *Sustainability in Business; Social Justice at Work, in Organisations and Society; and Innovation in Place*. Our unique skills included engaged, collaborative and action research. This exercise also revealed a number of skills gaps.

We worked to understand the research concerns and strengths of our university, to see where the opportunities for challenge-led interdisciplinary collaborations might be. We wanted to anticipate where LUMS researchers might be able to bring their expertise and capabilities to bear on big ambitious interdisciplinary research projects in the future. Two areas stood out – *Health and Wellbeing at Work, in Organisations and Society*, and the *Cyber Economy*.

Finally, we worked to understand the implication of our university's commitment to the Civic Universities Charter, for our school (cf. Goddard and Vallance, 2011). We identified research and researchers working with local and regional communities, and with communities attached to specific places. By the end of this exercise our broad ambition, remained the same - '*to work through our disciplinary strengths and interdisciplinary communities, to pursue our strategic ambitions to be world-leading in generating outstanding research insights that transform lives, communities, organisations, practices and thinking globally*'. However, now we had a much clearer idea of what we might look like in five years' time, and the kinds of impactful research our researchers were likely to deliver within the broad domains of sustainability, social justice and innovation.

Using this deeper understanding of our capabilities and resources, we identified five strategic priorities. First, we are working to position LUMS as a leading Civic Management School. This means embedding Responsible Research and Innovation principles and EDIR[2] best practice in our research engagements with collaborators, stakeholders and the public. The aim is to generate an inclusive approach to research agenda development and delivery for our regional, national and international stakeholders. This aligns with our *Innovation in Place* theme and is shaping where and how we leverage our research expertise in *Sustainability in Business, Social Justice at Work, in Organisations and Society*.

Second, we are working to push the boundaries of research excellence. This means shaping and delivering world-leading programmes of research by targeting investments in the emerging disciplinary strengths of our departments and interdisciplinary strengths of our research centres. We are providing active career development support, mentoring, individual goals, seed-corn funding, and incentives to support applications for research funding, quality research outputs and long-term career progression.

Third, we are putting impact and engagement at the heart of our research. This means supporting senior researchers in leading *big bold bids* for research funding, with impact at their core. External funding will be critical if our research is to be delivered on the scale and with the impact of our ambition. We are developing structures to support agile, interdisciplinary research platforms, including centres and teams, incorporating academics, research and engagement professionals and external stakeholders to collaborate on and deliver our impactful, future-critical research agenda. Based on our own interdisciplinary research (Mason *et al.*, 2019; Whitham *et al.*, 2019), we have introduced the *Lancaster Innovation Catalyst* as a platform designed to support academics in engaging with external research stakeholders around a specific challenge.

For example, in 2018 we brought together economic geographers, organisation, operations management and design scholars with professional service firms from the law and accounting professional services sectors, to develop an ambitious research agenda to understand and innovate *Next Generation Services* (specifically, professional law and accounting services). The team secured funding and delivered an impactful project using collaborative design methods, ultimately publishing their findings in world-leading journals, including in the *Journal of Operations Management*, how artificial intelligence based systems are used in professional service operations (Spring *et al.*, 2023); and the *Journal of Management Studies* revealing how professionals adapt when AI is introduced to their everyday working lives (Faulconbridge *et al.*, 2023). This network of business

Annual Research Volume 2 – Research Ecosystems, Partnerships and Collective Know-How

Managing to Make Impactful Business and Management Researchers in the Anthropocene
Katy Mason
....

partners and interdisciplinary collaborators and scholars have since secured an additional £2m from the Economic and Social Research Council to further catalyse and accelerate innovation adoption in next generation professional service firms. These kinds of engaged-research teams are assembled by our *'One Lancaster'* research and engagement support team who bring interdisciplinary scholars together with external stakeholders, to develop large, ambitious interdisciplinary research proposals.

Fourth, we are investing in understanding and implementing best practice in impact evaluation and development. We are working across institutional requirements (e.g., reporting for REF, TEF, KEF[3] and HEBCIS[4] and accreditation body requirements) to identify and adopt evaluation best practice and we are using this to generate opportunities that extend the reach and significance of our most impactful research. We are increasingly bringing together experienced researchers with early career researchers, research and engagement professionals, and key external stakeholders to strengthen our external engagement and impact. Large grants provide important opportunities to build these teams and to design-in and secure the resources for important pathways to impact. Our Plastics Packaging in People's Lives (PPiPL) project is such an example, bringing together researchers from organisation studies, consumer behaviour, supply chain management and circular economy to take an end-to-end approach to understanding the production and use of plastics all the way along the food supply chain. Industrial partners are a critical part of this project, and research outputs include policy notes, blogs and articles on the future of recycling, making insights accessible to non-academic research users.

Fifth, and finally, we are working to diversify and grow our research funding. We are investing in professional and academic expertise and working closely with cross-university research institutes to develop grand challenge bids that take advantage of interdisciplinary research funding opportunities and expertise. We have introduced a grant writing programme and are supporting a cohort of a dozen or so researchers each year, from across LUMS, in collectively imagining their research futures, and securing the resources they need to help them achieve, within the context of the school's ambition.

This strategy underpins the school's role in achieving the Lancaster University's strategic goal: to be a 'go to' university for research and teaching that transforms lives, communities, practices and thinking in countries across the globe.

BUILDING NEW SUPPORT STRUCTURES & CAPABILITIES

We recognise that this engaged and impactful research agenda - where larger, interdisciplinary teams come together to address real-world problems, and then seek to publish their findings in world-leading journals - represents a very different way of working for many of our researchers. LUMS, like many other business and management schools around the world, has spent the last 15 years supporting our researchers to publish in elite journals. There are good reasons for doing this. Submitting, getting work reviewed and published in the top two or three journals in your discipline can be an important development process, helping researchers to refine theorising, analysis, and argumentation skills. Such publications can, undoubtedly, lead to new and valuable real-world insights; however, some elite journals have turned their backs on phenomenon-led research where the real-world problem is set up as the driver of the research effort. Rather, these journals privilege theoretical problems, having become the social science equivalent of blue-sky research: scientific research that is curiosity-driven in domains where real-world applications may not be immediately apparent.

In a world where the only thing that matters is the 4* publication, research strategy and resources need to support individual researchers, with narrow discipline-based interests: paying rewards when 4* publications are secured; pump-priming travel, transcription and analysis expenses for research designed for a specific paper in a specific journal.

In a world where real-world research impact matters, research support structures need to be different. To deliver on our ambitious agenda - to generate sustainability solutions for business; deliver social justice at work, in organisations and in society; and to drive innovation in places for socioeconomic flourishing - LUMS has been rethinking how to support complex, multidisciplinary and interdisciplinary research. This kind of research requires significant resources, and agile research teams that can be quickly assembled and pivot to deliver on the demands of external research stakeholders. It needs to be done *with* research stakeholders, not just *for* them (Muff *et al.*, 2013): a new way of working for many researchers. In this new world of collaborative, engaged and impactful research, business schools need to invest in development and training to fill the capability and skills gaps of researchers that have, over many years, learned to work in isolation, focusing on niche and sometimes seemingly obscure theory building. This is not to say that such research is not immensely valuable, rather it recognises that business and management schools are now required to deliver much more than this. Supporting and incentivising engagement with ambitious, impactful research programmes must be done without threatening the world-leading outputs or the blue-sky research that our researchers currently deliver.

Care is needed. As the responsible management agenda has gained momentum, early career researchers have reported feeling confused and torn between crafting quality papers, and doing 'engagement', and 'impact' activities. LUMS has been working to set clearer expectations for individuals and groups of researchers by, first, changing the discourse and, second, putting in place the right support structures to help our researchers succeed. We have begun to talk about the engaged, impactful research cycle (Figure 1). By setting researchers' expectations about being part of (and sometimes leading) a team, working on an ambitious research project or programme, our researchers are beginning to understand that they will not always be writing papers, but rather, playing different roles, at different times, in different teams. This requires individual, supported discussions. We use our annual Professional Development Reviews for this. While departments have been good at supporting quality publications, they have been less hands-on in shaping the development of interdisciplinary programmes of research.

For these reasons, we focus on making use of our long-established departmental structures to provide a strong disciplinary base where research expertise is nurtured, and capabilities developed. This remains central to our success. Much newer are our interdisciplinary research support structures. In 2012, we introduced interdisciplinary research centres and groups as a second element in our research support ecosystem. These structures are more temporary, amorphous, and agile than departments and aim to generate opportunities for researchers to get involved in phenomenon-based and challenge-led research bids and projects. Together with the University's Research Institutes, LUMS Research Centres act as an important part of our research ecosystem.

PHOTO COURTESY LANCASTER UNIVERSITY MANAGEMENT SCHOOL

Working out how to distribute our finite research-support resource across the research ecosystem is never straightforward. Departments generate income through teaching, much of which, in common with many business and management schools, is returned to our university's central management system. Research centres are different. Their income is generated through [inter]disciplinary research bids and funds research projects and programmes. School research resources are otherwise secured through an annual planning process on a 'use-it-or-lose-it' basis. Some of the research budget is distributed back to departments in the form of travel and conference budgets, to research centres and groups via an internal competition. Other funds support grant preparations, writing retreats, network-building events, proof-of-concept studies and such like. Using this resource in ways that most effectively supports our research strategy has taken some experimentation.

Because our research centres and groups are more temporally bound by their nature, knowing which are the right research centres to support, when research centres should be discontinued, and when to support new ones, is always a challenge. Finite resources mean only a limited number of research centres can be supported at any one time. It has taken time for us to understand how to nurture and make use of our research centres with the resources that we have. We have on occasion, been able to bring research centres together, using them as a 'plug and play' model to prepare large funding bid submissions. What has become clear is that supporting researchers in learning how to lead research centres and interdisciplinary research teams is crucial. We have more capabilities development to do here, and this is becoming an important element of the grant writing programme that we developed and launched in 2021. The grant writing programme focuses on helping researchers imagine the type of researcher they want to be and helps them explore and understand how they can access the resources and capabilities required to help them get there. Another increasingly important part of our research ecosystem structure is our Lancaster University Innovation Catalyst. The Lancaster University Innovation Catalyst draws on LUMS's rich history and experience of developing peer learning networks with practitioners, particularly SMEs, and regional public sector bodies such as the Local Enterprise Partnerships and County Councils. Based on our own research (Beech *et al.*, 2022; Mason *et al.*, 2019; Whitham *et al.*, 2019), the Innovation Catalyst is designed to support ambitious business and public sector leaders interested in connecting with academic expertise

Annual Research Volume 2 – Research Ecosystems, Partnerships and Collective Know-How

Managing to Make Impactful Business and Management Researchers in the Anthropocene
Katy Mason
....

and like-minded peers to address a particular challenge: for example, creating a regional food packaging recyclate; or developing an electronics skills development cluster (two impactful projects run by the Innovation Catalyst).

Innovation catalysts typically run over a six-month period and take the form of a facilitated series of investigative and action-focused 'Innovation Collaboratories' that collectively map out a group's goals, challenges, and innovation needs - drawing in the right academic expertise, at the right time (see for example, Figure 2). The aim of the catalyst is to build an ecosystem of businesses, industry experts, academics, public sector bodies and other interested parties to solve both individual and shared challenges. By creating the space to innovate and collaborate, the catalyst is supporting the development of resilient, sustainable innovation ecosystems in specific sectors across the Northwest of England. The Lancaster University Innovation Catalyst is a proven and powerful way of helping individual firms and regional collectives with shared issues to develop effective long-term solutions that capture greater value for them and for the region.

One Innovation Catalyst initiative, known as the *Blackpool Innovation Catalyst* – was reported in a local newspaper, the *Blackpool Gazette*. This timely opportunity has been generated by two significant investments: the planned expansion of the windfarm off the coast of Blackpool, and the 'landing' of the North Atlantic Loop in Blackpool. The North Atlantic Loop is a next generation, subsea fibre cable system delivering a diverse, high-capacity network connection to the USA and Northern Europe, meaning Blackpool is uniquely positioned to take advantage of ultra-fast internet speeds and super low latency, supporting future technologies such as robotics and smart manufacturing, as well as opening new possibilities for an online gaming industry. Funded by the government's Community Renewal Fund, the catalyst brought together academic advisers, senior council officers, financiers and leaders in sustainable digital infrastructure projects, to create a unique proposition for Blackpool, which was unveiled during a special symposium at Blackpool Conference and Exhibition Centre. The key idea is to build a cluster of ethically powered data centres which operate on renewable energy and redistribute excess energy into social

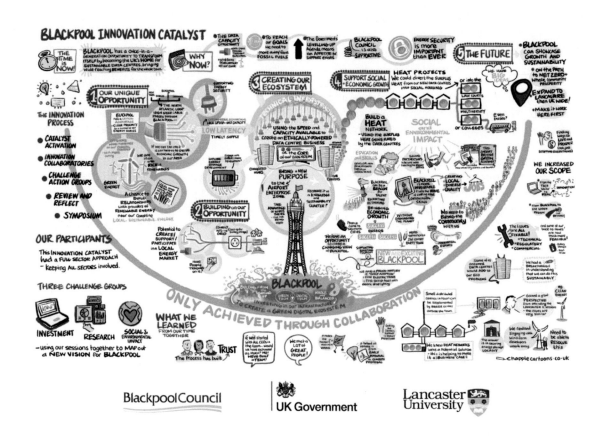

Figure 2 A Co-Produced Conceptualisation and Map of the Blackpool Innovation Catalyst's Goals

Annual Research Volume 2 – Research Ecosystems, Partnerships and Collective Know-How

Managing to Make Impactful Business and Management Researchers in the Anthropocene
Katy Mason
....

heat networks using ground-breaking green technologies; and to use these innovations to catalyse and connect to others. So far, this work has been exploratory. Even so, the ideas created as part of this catalyst could be transformational for Blackpool – not just in creating a thriving digital economy and high-value jobs in the town, but also helping lower income families struggling with energy bills and creating new upskilling and green job opportunities for a green growth regional economy. There is however, much work still to do. In the meantime, we continue to co-develop ideas and practices with keystone actors and communities in Blackpool, so that together, we can make a real difference to our innovative and ambitious communities in this place of astounding natural beauty. We are currently seeking further funding to progress this programme of work.

Our professional research and engagement support teams are helping to make these types of ambitious projects happen, connecting departments, research centres and Lancaster University Innovation Catalysts with keystone actors external to the university, but with a real interest in the concerns at hand. Professional service teams help researchers to navigate the research opportunities landscape, acting as knowledge activists by continuously connecting and choreographing research teams around funding opportunities relevant to the school's expertise and strategic ambition.

Finally, we use our London-based policy think tank, the Work Foundation, as a way of listening to and checking the state of the nation and economy and anticipating future grand challenges. The data the Work Foundation produces using national and regional pulse and rapid response surveys, together with their ongoing conversations with officials, ministers, business and third sector bodies interested in the world of work and the economy, is helping us to become much more anticipatory. As ice hockey legend Wayne Gretzky pointed out, success is often achieved by skating to where the puck is going to be next. Using these insights to shape, review and reflect on our ongoing programmes of research is critical if we are to be truly impactful.

SKATING TO WHERE THE PUCK'S GOING NEXT

The value of business and management research is changing (Davies *et al.*, 2023; Starkey and Thomas, 2022). Three future investments seem critical. First, creating and investing in interdisciplinary challenge-led programmes of research at school level, will help schools build excellence, reputation, and distinctiveness, and will likely have a bigger impact on our society, economy and environment. This is particularly pertinent with the pressures of league tables,

subject QS rankings and research and knowledge exchange quality assessments such as the UK's Research Assessment Framework (REF), the Knowledge Exchange Frameworks (KEF), and to a lesser extent, the Teaching Excellence Framework (TEF), that has put business schools under pressure to be known for something. It is possible that such changes will mark the beginning of the end of academic freedom as we know it. That is for us to decide.

Second, investing in knowledge curation and translation, and making these bodies of work accessible, meaningful and available to research-users will become increasingly important. Third, preparing and developing the capabilities of our researchers to deliver this kind of research, to develop disciplinary excellence and the ability to work in and lead interdisciplinary teams will be critical.

As the consequences of the Anthropocene become more apparent, and work to devise research strategies that develop and direct effective research capabilities and resources for societal, economic, and environmental value, the need for speed will become more apparent too. Rapid change will require collaboration between business schools; regionally, nationally and internationally, as we research new ways to reorganise our economised society and our relationship with our planet (Muff *et al.*, 2013; Parker, 2018).

Business and management schools should strengthen their connection with professional bodies and learned societies. For example, supporting the joint Knowledge Ecosystem initiatives of the Economic and Social Research Council (UK Research and Innovation), the British Academy of Management and Chartered Association of Business Schools which aims to put into practice their shared vision of a business and management-led knowledge ecosystem, directed at delivering a zero-carbon economic recovery. By leading business, science and social science partnerships – supporting engagement across a large community, the initiative aims to deliver productivity, inclusion, sustainability and innovation. Business and management schools can act as a gateway for STEM, humanities and arts faculties wanting to engage in impactful, interdisciplinary programmes of research, and are well placed to orchestrate university-wide engagement and research programmes – even including them in their research strategies.

References

Barney, J., M. Wright and D.J. Ketchen Jr (2001) The resource-based view of the firm: Ten years after 1991. *Journal of management, 27*(6) pp.625-641

Barney, J. B. (1991) Firm Resources and Sustained Competitive Advantage. *Journal of Management, 17*, pp.99-120

Beech, N., K.J. Mason, R. Macintosh and D. Beech (2022) Learning from each other: Why and how business schools need to create a "paradox box" for academic–policy impact. *Academy of Management Learning & Education, 21*(3) pp.487-502

Davies, J., H. Thomas, E. Cornuel and R.D. Cremer (2023) *Leading a Business School*. Abingdon: Routledge

Faulconbridge, J., Spring, M., & Sarwar, A. (2023) How professionals adapt to artificial intelligence: the role of intertwined boundary work. *Journal of Management Studies, 68*, pp.592–618

Goddard, J. and P. Vallance (2011) The civic university and the leadership of place. *Centre for Urban and Regional Development Studies (CURDS) Newcastle University UK.* https://www.regionalstudies.org/wp-content/uploads/2018/07/goddard.pdf

Hurlbert, M. (2021) Transformative Frames for Climate Threat in the Anthropocene. *Frontiers in Sociology, 6*, 728024. https://doi.org/10.3389/fsoc.2021.728024

Macintosh, R., N. Beech, J. Bartunek, K. Mason, B. Cooke and D. Denyer (2017) Impact and Management Research: Exploring Relationships between Temporality, Dialogue, Reflexivity and Praxis. *British Journal of Management, 28*(1). Pp.3-13. 10.1111/1467-8551.12207

Macintosh, R., K. Mason, N. Beech and J. M. Bartunek (2021) *Delivering Impact in Management Research: When Does it Really Happen?* Abingdon: Routledge

Mason, K., M. Friesl and C. Ford (2019) Markets Under the Microscope: Making Scientific Discoveries Valuable through Choreographed Contestations. *Journal of Management Studies, 56*(5) pp.966-999. https://doi.org/10.1111/joms.12426

Muff, K., T. Dyllick, M. Drewell, J. North, P. Shrivastava and J. Haertle (2013) *Management education for the world: A vision for business schools serving people and the planet*. Cheltenham: Edward Elgar Publishing.

Owen, R., P. Macnaghten and J. Stilgoe (2012) Responsible research and innovation: From science in society to science for society, with society. *Science and public policy, 39*(6) pp.751-760

Parker, M. (2018) *Shut down the business school*. Chicago: University of Chicago Press Economics Books

Siegel, D. S. and S. Leih (2018) Strategic management theory and universities: An overview of the Special Issue. *Strategic Organization, 16*(1) pp.6-11

Spring, M., J. Faulconbridge and A. Sarwar (2022). How information technology automates and augments processes: Insights from Artificial-Intelligence-based systems in professional service operations. *Journal of Operations Management, 68*(6-7) pp.592-618

Starkey, K. & H. Thomas (2022) The future of business schools: shut them down or broaden our horizons? In E. Cornuel, H. Thomas and M. Woods *The Value & Purpose of Management Education*. Abingdon: Routledge

Wernerfelt, B. (1984) A Resource-based View of the Firm. *Strategic Management Journal, 5*(2), 171

Whitham, R., Pérez, D., Mason, K. & Ford, C. (2019) Realising the value of open innovation in policy making: Equipping entrepreneurs for valuation work. *The Design Journal, 22*(sup1) pp.189-201

Wilson, D. C. & H. Thomas (2012) The legitimacy of the business of business schools: what's the future? *Journal of Management Development, 31*(4) pp.68-376.

Footnotes

[1] The AREA framework is championed by UKRI's Engineering and Physical Sciences Research Council, and urges researchers to Anticipate research impact on key stakeholder groups; Reflect on the purpose, motivation and potential implications of the research, and to explore the associated uncertainties, areas of ignorance, assumptions, framings, questions, dilemmas and social transformations these may bring; Engage with academic partners to generate a vision of impacts; and to Act in ways that make research processes influential on the direction and trajectory of the research and innovation process itself.

[2] EDIR (Equality Diversity Inclusion & Respect) is an agenda being pursued by the British Academy of Management to reveal challenges and share best practice. For further information see https://www.bam.ac.uk/knowledge-hub/projects/equality-diversity-inclusion-and-respect.html

[3] The UK Government has three quality assessment frameworks in place in its universities: REF – the Research Excellence Framework; TEF – the Teaching Excellence Framework; and KEF the Knowledge Exchange Framework.

[4] HEBCIS: The Higher Education Business and Community Interaction Survey (HE-BCI) is the main vehicle for measuring the volume and direction of interactions between UK HE providers and business and the wider community. The survey collects information on the infrastructure, capacity and strategy of HE providers, and numeric and financial data regarding third-stream activity (that is, activities concerned with the generation, use, application and exploitation of knowledge and other HE provider capabilities outside academic environments, these being distinct from the core activities of teaching and research).

About the Author

Katy Mason is Associate Dean for Research and Professor of Markets and Management at Lancaster University Management School, Lancaster, UK. Katy's research focuses on how managers make and shape markets in relation to innovative technologies, the market devices they use to enrol others and create market boundaries. She is the current President of the British Academy of Management.

Responsible, Rigorous, and Impactful Research Through Engagement

LINDA BARRINGTON AND ANDREW KAROLYI

Research Ecosystems, Partnerships and Collective Know-How

The call for business higher education to be more impactful is growing louder and more articulate. The Principles for Responsible Management Education (PRME) were launched in 2007, the Responsible Research in Business and Management (RRBM) movement formalised in 2016, and the AACSB standards on societal impact for business school accreditation were updated in 2020. These advances, along with the widespread general adoption of the UN Sustainable Development Goals, are indications within just the past decade or so that the paradigm of business higher education is shifting. This is a generational drive with the intention to align business education and research with societal goals, and it is only accelerating. No longer can an institution of business higher education simply focus on shareholder primacy, graduating student pay scales, or elite rankings. More is expected, and more is demanded.

This call for impactful research and education is not new in U.S. business higher education. Agricultural experiment stations attached to land grant universities were established under the Hatch Act in 1887 to "aid in acquiring and diffusing among the people of the United States useful and practical information on subjects connected with agriculture ... and such other research or experiments bearing directly on the agricultural industry of the United States" (Moore, 1988, pp. 164-165). Over 40% of the 1887 workforce was directly employed in agriculture (Lebergott, 1966, Table 2), and approximately 65% of the US population lived in rural areas (U.S. Census, 2004, Table 18). This clarion call of 1887 was not so different than advocating for business colleges today to be ever more relevant to business and society.

What *is* different today? Impactful research and teaching seem to be at odds with what Gerry Johnson and Ken Starkey criticise as the management academy's self-contained research-publication-funding 'iron cage', the unintended result being increasing irrelevance. Andrew Hoffman in *The Engaged Scholar* (2021) similarly argues

that research publishing success serves the academic institution primarily and falls short on serving the world at large. Without questioning the value of sound methodology and evidence-based arguments, today's scholars are adding the value of well-designed and observed experience to the expansion of practical knowledge. This moment in time is the point at which society at large is compelled to strike a balance between the practices we need to trust and keep, and those we need to change.

Responsibility, rigour, and impact with relevance to stakeholders constitute the trifecta of intentions to which business higher education researchers must aspire.

DOI: 10.4324/9781003467410-10

Annual Research Volume 2 – Research Ecosystems, Partnerships and Collective Know-How

Responsible, Rigorous, and Impactful Research Through Engagement
Linda Barrington and Andrew Karolyi
. . . .

A VIRTUOUS CYCLE OF ENGAGEMENT AND RESEARCH

Scholarship with a disciplinary focus at peer-reviewed journals with the highest academic standards will always remain at the core of research that is responsible, rigorous, and impactful. But there is more to be done.

Figure 1 below illustrates how stimulating innovative research can, and often does, start with curiosity-driven scholarship motivated by the value-chain of research in the academy. But when scholars engage with industry and society in real-world challenges, curiosity drives scholarship in turn, and the resulting research feedback loop is more likely to create positive societal effect. This virtuous cycle is maintained when research employs sound methodology, when it adheres to the guiding principles of the open-science movement, and when it follows from evidence-based arguments in the face of real-world advocates and the need for immediacy.

At the Cornell SC Johnson College of Business, we support a two-pronged strategy for building scholarly, engaged research. First, we have an expansive ecosystem of centres, institutes, and special programme initiatives (C&Is) that serve as an engagement channel, leveraging long and deep industry and societal connections. While these C&Is do not always involve students in their many activities, most do. Our second prong, by contrast, puts the student right at the centre of this virtuous engagement cycle through for-credit community-engaged learning projects which include industry partners.

THE ENGAGEMENT CHANNEL OF CENTRES, INSTITUTES, AND PROGRAMME INITIATIVES

Comprised of three separate yet integrated business schools – the Charles H. Dyson School of Applied Economics and Management, the Peter and Stephanie Nolan School of Hotel Administration, and the Samuel Curtis Johnson Graduate School of Management – the Cornell SC Johnson College of Business prides itself on being a place 'where business breadth meets specialised depth'. Our two dozen centres, institutes, and programme initiatives exemplify this, providing an organisational infrastructure for industry and societal engagement[1]. As is typical of most academic centres or institutes at other business schools and colleges, our C&Is host convening events ranging from by-invitation advisory boards and roundtables to large, open conferences. Few of these convenings are solely attended by or targeted to academia; the vast majority are purposefully designed to attract industry or government experts, along with academics, bridging scholarship and decision-making to real world challenges.

In 2022, our C&Is welcomed more than 210 industry leaders and experts in-person, on campus. Annually, they engage 200+ industry executives as members of C&I by-invitation advisory boards or councils.

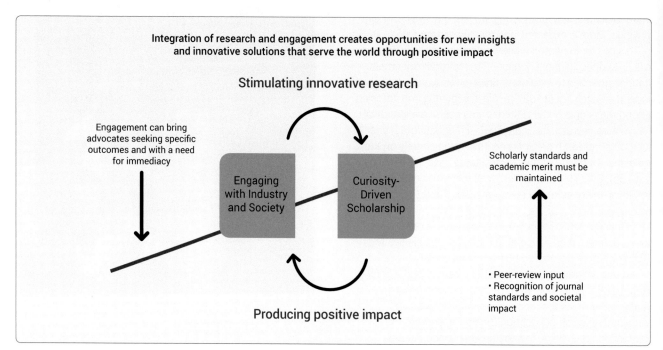

Figure 1 How to Strike the Research Balance in Driving for Impact

How does this ecosystem of C&Is work to create curiosity-driven research that is rigorous and relevant? We regularly canvas our faculty colleagues after one of these conferences or roundtables to remain focused on continuous improvement of format and topics. Following are selected responses from our faculty surveyed about the value of presenting at a C&I roundtable:

Faculty Member 1. "Yes, the experience was super useful! I like how the audience offers industry insights there. ...this paper is currently a working paper. We plan to submit it soon."

Faculty Member 2. "My experience was extremely positive. First of all, there are quite a few corporate decision-makers in the room. I got a few good comments and questions during my presentation. In addition, I have scheduled 4-5 follow-up one-on-one meetings [from which] I have benefited a lot. ...Some were willing to provide me with data for further research if necessary. I especially appreciate the realistic view of the industry. They also show trust and passion for academic research. They are willing to learn from us, which motivates me to do a good job of digging out deeper. They want the research practical and actionable."

Faculty Member 3. "I did find the experience to be highly beneficial and helpful. The participants ... offered me valuable feedback on my research and helped me appreciate how my work could address practical challenges faced by the hospitality sector."

Faculty Member 4. "I received great feedback from the audience, and I was later able to get better data through connections made at the roundtable. The paper will soon be submitted to a journal and hopefully published soon."

Faculty Member 5. "I received good feedback and attendees seemed very willing to help if I needed it. A few months later, I needed data on the topic of the presentation so I asked [to be put] in contact with someone who can help... We're now working with [company] on a research project."

The research presented and referenced in these comments has included publications appearing in peer-reviewed, scholarly business journals, for example, Fuchs *et al.* (2022); Sampson and Shi (2023).

Our colleague Professor Yao Cui reported how his research investigating the heterogeneous treatments of tax policies in the hospitality sharing-economy benefited from such roundtable interactions. In reference to his joint work with Professor Andrew Davis (Cui and Davis, 2022), Cui explained, "I presented my research about the impact of occupancy tax regulation on Airbnb, and the [Centre] board members not only recognised the importance of my findings but also shared their perspectives on how this regulation could affect different segments of hotels. The discussions were thought-provoking and have inspired me to explore related topics for future research. ...Their vast knowledge and intellectual acumen have enriched my perspective on hospitality research."

A sizable number of our C&Is have achieved the level of trust and exchange necessary to support the virtuous cycle of engagement and scholarship described in the faculty comments above. But not all. There are challenges to collaborating closely with employers – academic timelines and rigour, identifying a key organisational contact, gaining the trust of the organisation, negotiating research participation specifics. University research protocols on proprietary data can also present unique challenges. Both the scholars and the industry partners must recognise sufficient benefit for the engagement to be successful and of lasting value (Barrington, 2016). Our longer-running C&Is have established stronger industry and community connections. Building these relationships and shaping the format of convening events to best foster mutually beneficial exchanges take purposeful action, reflection, patience, resources, and a lot of good preparation.

With this large number of C&Is (particularly for a business college), it will not be surprising to learn that we have also been able to benefit from *joint* C&I convening events that bring even wider connections between faculty and the outside world. One example is the Cornell ESG Investing Research Conference that we launched in 2022 and that we plan to continue for years to come. This collaboration takes place between the Centre for Sustainable Global Enterprise and the Parker Centre for Investment Research, along with two college-funded interdisciplinary themes, Investing@ Cornell and Business of Sustainability, which build communities of like-minded faculty colleagues. This conference included speakers representing large asset managers, asset owners, as well as regulatory officials from New York Federal Reserve Bank and the IMF in an active two-day event. The conference attracted groundbreaking research presentations and paired them up with conversations on best practices and policy impacting investment in biodiversity, mitigation and adaptation to climate change, and advancing ESG priorities.

Annual Research Volume 2 – Research Ecosystems, Partnerships and Collective Know-How

Responsible, Rigorous, and Impactful Research Through Engagement
Linda Barrington and Andrew Karolyi
....

A SECOND ENGAGEMENT CHANNEL - COMMUNITY-ENGAGED LEARNING

The second prong of our engaged research strategy is our dynamic and expanding work in community-engaged learning. This primarily entails for-credit course projects which put the student at the centre of the virtuous impact cycle, working with external organisations or businesses to address a real-world challenge. These engagements can stimulate curiosity-driven research on the part of faculty teaching the course as well as the students themselves.

Community-engaged learning (CEL), as applied in our college, seeks to deepen the age-old wisdom that we become expert through experience - that we do, in fact, learn by doing. Students are guided by rigorous academic standards to develop measurable solutions for external organisations, including major multinationals, financial institutions, local not-for-profits, NGOs, or government agencies. As they develop connections through respectful, shared problem-solving, they own and feel agency about the project work they do. Their learning is deepened by the work's usefulness outside the classroom, while simultaneously putting their curricular lessons to the test. To fully fit our college's CEL definition, students deliver a critical reflection whereby they pause and examine how their experience benefited or could better benefit 'stakeholders beyond shareholders'. The reflection, overseen by the instructor of record, allows the student to align the project's work with one or more of the UN's Sustainable Development Goals.

A SMART EXAMPLE

Our college's commitment to connecting students with the real world is well exemplified in the work of the Student Multidisciplinary Applied Research Teams (SMART) programme. For the past two decades, this internationally focused community-engaged learning programme has been pairing teams of graduate and undergraduate students and faculty from within our college and across Cornell University with small and medium enterprises (SMEs) and community organisations in emerging markets and less-developed economies. Many of the projects focus on agriculture, healthcare, the environment, and women's economic development. Course curriculum meets problem-solving as students address specific issues and catalyse inclusive and sustainable development, providing technical and analytical assistance to underserved businesses and communities. SMART experiences promote direct student understanding of the challenges faced by emerging markets and the role of business and business tools in private-and public-sector-led economic development. Since its founding by Professor Ralph Christy in 2004, SMART has led 123 projects, engaging over a thousand students and 101 community partners from 27 countries.

Multiple stakeholders are engaged in these compelling projects. Faculty are in the field with graduate students and undergraduates, who earn experience as research assistants in addition to course credit. SMART is based on a co-learning and co-teaching curriculum and approach, therefore both undergraduates and graduate students participate in all aspects of the project (e.g., team leadership, data collection, analysis, and case writing). The community partner benefits from upskilling as they simultaneously contribute to an academic research project. Assignments are well-defined and structured to provide tangible benefits to the partner and students alike. Pre- and post-sessions reinforce this fieldwork learning, such that SMART projects foster relationships that develop cultural understandings and deepen students' cultural humility and respect.

Many of the SMART projects stem from the research interest, outreach, and teaching of key faculty, who serve as SMART mentors on a voluntary basis. Some SMART projects are pitched by Cornell students or alumni who were previous SMART students themselves. All SMART projects are modelled using an empirical research approach and development theory framework, based on two essential components: (i) formulation of the problem statement encapsulating the community partner's main problem and its effects, and (ii) operationalisation of key variables that allow students to transform abstract concepts into tangible indicators that can be systematically examined and analysed.

Annual Research Volume 2 – Research Ecosystems, Partnerships and Collective Know-How

Responsible, Rigorous, and Impactful Research Through Engagement
Linda Barrington and Andrew Karolyi
....

Consider several recent SMART projects as examples.
The CARL Group, Rwanda. The founder of CARL Group
learned of SMART through a special agribusiness
workshop in South Africa hosted by Professor Christy.
SMART assistance was then requested with various
entrepreneurial development assets supporting the
youth-led company in its production and marketing of
innovative, orange-fleshed sweet potato bread, a nutritious
tool in fighting malnutrition. SMART has collaborated with
the CARL group over the last five years to support both its
product and market development strategies. Most
recently, SMART is supporting the company to identify the
most effective ways to penetrate and grow sales in school
feeding programmes and small retail outlets serving
vulnerable populations. In 2020, SMART helped the
company to standardise its bread production and develop
a nutritional label that led to it receiving the first Rwanda
Standards Board quality certificate. As of January 2023,
their bread remained the only quality-assured bread being
sold in Kigali. The company founder, Regis Umugiraneza,
is looking at how to sustainably grow and expand his
business further, making an even greater impact
addressing vitamin-A deficiency in Rwanda.

E&E Green Farms, Rwanda. Seeking a way to diversify
the family income during the COVID-19 pandemic, Rose
Muhumuza started E&E Greens, a seed production
company that specialises in the production of hybrid
maize seeds, soybean and biofortified seeds that are sold
in both local (farmers, agro-dealers, NGOs, and farmer
cooperatives) and export markets (Tanzania and other
African countries). Ms. Muhumuza was introduced to the
SMART project through another SC Johnson College
programme, the Cornell Hanga Ahazaza project. Funded
by the Mastercard Foundation, Hanga Ahazaza focused
on workforce development in the hospitality and tourism
industry. Ms. Muhumuza successfully completed the
Cornell Hanga Ahazaza certificate programme which
included skill-building in many business basics such as
marketing and customer service. The next step was to
develop a robust marketing and communication strategy.
The SMART programme students and post-doctoral
fellow assisted by conducting market research and
developing a social media plan that included a new
company logo, content, and branding guidelines.

The Humble Store, South Africa. Humble is a start-up
company founded by Kamilah Karaan, in Stellenbosch.
Through an exclusive business agreement with Olyberg
(one of South Africa's leading olive farms), Kamilah
procures fresh harvested olives to develop cosmetic
products (such as soaps and face creams) and ready-
to-consume oils and spiced olives. Kamala collaborated
with SMART to identify a strategic direction that would

help her to realise the founding vision of the company.
Students engaged in every step of the project, including
defining the final deliverables (desired product), and
assisting in meeting organisation, language translation,
and data interpretation.

While focused on international emerging markets, the
SMART programme has also included underserved
economies within the United States. For example, following
UN SDG guidelines, SMART team projects have assessed
ESG dimensions of tourism in New Orleans, Louisiana.

Given that the primary SMART faculty leaders are focused
on entrepreneurship within emerging markets, projects offer
opportunities for students to explore and gain first-hand
experience on such wide-ranging topics as uncertain or limited
market access, inadequate infrastructure, corruption, and
financial capital, and more. The students' immersions in their
partners' communities, helping the businesses to grow and
develop through intensive projects with deadlines, informs
critical reflection of their role. It is this last piece of the puzzle
– the critical reflection – which we believe advances
awareness for every student on stakeholder impact broadly.

TRANSFORMING ENGAGEMENT CHANNEL ACTION INTO KNOWLEDGE CREATION

SMART teams have written and published various case
studies in peer-reviewed journals, such as the *Journal of
Agribusiness in Developing and Emerging Economies*
(JADEE), *Emerald Emerging Markets Case Studies, and
International Food and Agribusiness Management Review.* In
2011, the programme compiled and published a book, *Case
Studies of Emerging Farmers and Agribusinesses in South
Africa* (Mabaya *et al.*, 2011), which has been adopted in
classrooms and executive education programmes. In 2018,
Cornell jointly organised Advanced Agribusiness Workshops
with the Asian Productivity Organisation, and eight of the 12
resulting case studies appeared in the volume *Asian
Agribusiness Management: Case Studies in Growth,*

Annual Research Volume 2 – Research Ecosystems, Partnerships and Collective Know-How

Responsible, Rigorous, and Impactful Research Through Engagement
Linda Barrington and Andrew Karolyi
....

Marketing, and Upgrading Strategies. They were developed for these workshops by graduate students in SMART (Christy *et al.*, 2018).

The research acumen that SMART helps to build brings with it other positive impacts, like improved quality of life, security, health, and income. First, the community benefits from the development of the SMART partner business. Most of our business partners have a significant focus on social impact, such as job creation for women, improved community nutrition, or the provision of markets to smallholder farmers. As SMART teams help business partners to grow and develop, the social impact of these businesses also grows, benefiting the community as a whole. Additionally, many community members interact with our students through interviews, stakeholder meetings, and even simple casual interactions, exposing both the community and our students to diverse cultures, expanding intercultural skills.

From among the thousand Cornell undergraduate and graduate students who have completed a SMART project, programme leaders have been able to track down former students now holding prominent leadership positions within the international development sector and in multilateral and international organisations, such as the United Nations, TechnoServe, Catholic Relief Services, and Botswana Institute for Development. Others are policymakers affiliated with various government agencies (in USA, Netherlands, Mongolia, Botswana). Many are researchers and educators within internationally renowned colleges like Cornell, Stanford, UC Berkeley, Purdue, North Carolina at Chapel Hill, and Peking University.

Faculty play a crucial role in meeting with each potential partner to understand their needs, assess the project's potential benefits, and then guide the student teams. Everyone involved collaborates with partners to build up businesses that expand opportunities for underserved populations. This in-depth understanding and direct oversight feeds curiosity-driven and engaged scholarship.

ALIGNED WITH A LARGER COLLEGE STRATEGY

In addition to the value SMART provides for curiosity-driven research, it has expanded strategic importance to the SC Johnson College. While SMART has existed for decades, in the few years since 2016, our college has adopted a revolutionary Grand Challenge curriculum for the Dyson School and incorporated a full Engaged College Initiative. The Dyson Grand Challenge is a three-part, three-year course sequence embedded into the Dyson curriculum, each course building a foundation for the next and culminating in a team-based capstone project, which aligns with the United Nations Sustainable Development Goals.

The Engaged College Initiative, begun in 2020, aspires to provide every student passing through our college an opportunity for hands-on learning about which they critically reflect. Students examine their own role in the process, observe the changes in their thinking on furthering sustainability and improving diversity, equity, inclusion and belonging, and determine how their work benefited or could benefit stakeholders beyond shareholders[2]. SMART projects offer a key pathway for meeting the Dyson School's unique Grand Challenge graduation requirement and for contributing opportunities for engagement aligned with this new college initiative, as well as stimulating curiosity-driven research.

There is another angle to research and engaged learning – in which what is discussed and taught gets researched. Since 2017, Professor Todd Schmit, faculty director of Cornell's Cooperative Enterprise Program, has included engaged learning projects at the undergraduate and graduate level in his Dyson School Cooperative Business Management courses. On the research benefits for faculty stemming from engaged learning projects, Schmit and co-authors (2022) write how the engaged-learning course projects "allow for pre-testing of industry or firm surveys and applied research methods. They also provide access to firm data not available from other sources." Reports from faculty involved with our centres, institutes, and programme initiatives (including those testimonials above) tell similar stories of the research benefits of engaging with industry.

RESPONSIBLE RESEARCH THROUGH ENGAGEMENT – A PARTING THOUGHT

While we must guard our highest standards of scholarship and academic merit, the relevance of management research to stakeholders is just as critical as rigour and credibility. Each of these –relevance, rigour, and credibility – represent the vital three pillars of the Responsible Research in Business and Management movement (RRBM, Tsui *et al.*, 2022). [In full disclosure, EFMD was a founding sponsor of RRBM and one of the co-authors, Karolyi, currently serves as RRBM's Global Chair.] What we offer here is that the integration of research and engagement creates undeniable opportunities for curiosity-driven scholarship, new insights, and innovative solutions. All of these are imperatives toward rendering positive societal impact. We are, after all, responsible for educating the future scholars and managers who will tackle the incredible grand challenges faced by society and business. Our courage and clear-eyed creativity must be put into action.

Annual Research Volume 2 – Research Ecosystems, Partnerships and Collective Know-How

Responsible, Rigorous, and Impactful Research Through Engagement
Linda Barrington and Andrew Karolyi
....

References

Barrington, L. (2016) Engaging Employers as Stakeholders. In S.M. Bruyere (ed) *Disability and Employer Practices: Research across the Disciplines*, pp.27-56. Ithaca, NY: ILR Press

CEMS Network (2023) Defining Environmental Challenges. EFMD *Global Focus, 1*(17) pp.17-22 https://www.globalfocusmagazine.com/defining-environmental-challenges/

Christy, R. D., J. Bernardo, A. Hampel-Milagrosa, and L. Fu (eds) (2018) *Asian Agribusiness Management: Case Studies in Growth, Marketing, and Upgrading Strategies*. World Scientific Publishing Company. ProQuest Ebook Central. https://ebookcentral-proquest-com.proxy.library.cornell.edu/lib/cornell/detail.action?docID=5511173

Cui, Y. and A.M. Davis (2022) Tax-induced inequalities in the sharing economy. *Management Science, 68*(10) pp.7202-7220

Freeman, R. E. (1984) *Strategic Management: A Stakeholder Approach*. Boston, MA: Pitman

Fuchs, C., U. Kaiser, M. Schreier, S.M.J. van Osselaer (2022) The value of making producers personal. *Journal of Retailing, 98*(3) pp. 486-495 https://www.sciencedirect.com/science/article/pii/S0022435921000658

Hoffman, A. (2021) *The Engaged Scholar: Expanding the impact of Academic Research in Today's World*. Stanford, CA: Stanford University Press

Harrison, H., G. A. Karolyi, and J. A. Scheinkman (2020) Climate Finance. *The Review of Financial Studies, 33*(3) pp.1011–1023. https://doi.org/10.1093/rfs/hhz146

Johnson G. and K. Starkey. How Management Academics Have Locked Themselves in an Iron Cage. *Global Focus Annual Research, 1*(1) pp.33-38. https://www.globalfocusmagazine.com/how-management-academics-have-locked-themselves-in-an-iron-cage/

Lebergott, S. (1966) Labor Force and Employment, 1800–1960. In D.S. Brady (ed) *Output, Employment, and Productivity in the United States after 1800*, pp.117-204. Boston, MA: National Bureau of Economic Research. https://www.nber.org/books-and-chapters/output-employment-and-productivity-united-states-after-1800/labor-force-and-employment-1800-1960

Mabaya, E., K. Tihanyi, M. Karaan and J. Van Rooyen (eds) (2011) Case Studies of Emerging Farmers and Agribusinesses in South Africa. Stellenbosch: African Sun Media. https://scholar.sun.ac.za/items/f0583809-c243-4038-8091-7b619a2eaec1

Moore, G. E. (1988). The Involvement of Experiment Stations in Secondary Agricultural Education, 1887-1917. *Agricultural History, Publicly Sponsored Agricultural Research in the United States: Past, Present, and Future 62* (2) pp.164-176. https://www.jstor.org/stable/3743291

Sampson, R.C. and Y. Shi. (2023) Are U.S. firms becoming more short-term oriented? Evidence of shifting firm time horizons from implied discount rates, 1980-2013. *Strategic Management Journal, 44* (1) pp.231-263. First published online: 26 March 2020. https://onlinelibrary.wiley.com/doi/epdf/10.1002/smj.3158

Schmit, T.M., R. Stamm, and R.M. Severson (2022). Engaged learning: Linking course instruction and extension programming. *Applied Economics Teaching Resources, 4*(2) pp.69-83 https://www.aaea.org/UserFiles/file/AETR_2022_011RV4I2_v4.pdf

Tsui, A.S., M. J. Bitner, S. Netessine. What topics should business school research focus on? *Global Focus Annual Research, 1*(1) pp.25-32 https://www.globalfocusmagazine.com/what-topics-should-business-school-research-focus-on/

U.S. Census Bureau (2004). United States Summary: 2000 Population and Housing Unit Counts, Part 1. PHC-3-1. *2000 Census of Population and Housing, United States*. Washington, DC. https://www.census.gov/library/publications/2003/dec/phc-3.html

Footnotes

[1] https://business.cornell.edu/faculty-research/centers-institutes/

[2] Our consideration of the term 'stakeholder' extends that presented in the classic work, Strategic Management: A Stakeholder Approach (Freeman, 1984). In considering 'stakeholders beyond shareholders', we hope students will further recognise stakeholders as cross-generational, including those affected in the future by today's business accomplishments.

About the Authors

Linda Barrington is Associate Dean of Strategy and Societal Impact at Cornell SC Johnson College of Business, Cornell University.

Andrew Karolyi is the Charles Field Knight Dean at the Cornell SC Johnson College of Business, Cornell University. He also currently serves as the Chair of the Responsible Research in Business & Management (RRBM) organisation and as Vice-Chair of the UN Principles for Responsible Management Education (PRME) initiative.

Barrington and Karolyi would like to thank Mary Lorson at Cornell University for valuable insights and contributions to this article. We are grateful for the valuable comments of editor Howard Thomas. The views expressed in the article are those of the authors; any errors or omissions are their own responsibilities.

The Role of Business Schools in Creating National Entrepreneurial Ecosystems: The Case of Egypt and the AUC School of Business

SHERIF KAMEL

Complex Societal Impact Projects Requiring Tri-Sector Collaboration and Cooperation

Overview

In today's time and age, economies worldwide—and especially in emerging markets—need an effective and innovative entrepreneurial ecosystem that is government-enabled, private-sector-led, innovation-driven, youth-empowered, and future-oriented (Kamel, 2016). Over the last few decades, the acceleration of digital transformation and the gradual move from high-tech to deep-tech through artificial intelligence, robotics, cloud computing, and big data, coupled with an evolving entrepreneurial mindset, has dominated various societies in developed and emerging economies, given the potential opportunities created and the growing global population of digital natives (Schroeder, 2017).

However, innovation-driven entrepreneurship can only address some of the economic and social challenges that have developed over many years, particularly in emerging economies, Egypt included (Kamel, 2021a). There are other essential factors that need to be in place, such as societal readiness, human capital investment, universal infrastructure access and adoption, infostructure, and institutionalised governance, in addition to legal, regulatory and other support environments. They all represent essential building blocks for a tech-enabled entrepreneurial ecosystem to become a catalyst for socioeconomic development and growth (Kamel, 2021b).

Building an entrepreneurial ecosystem requires an all-inclusive approach where different stakeholders in society are engaged, including private enterprises, government, civil society, and other institutions and individuals who can enrich, support and advocate for a national entrepreneurial culture that can help transform economies (Ismail et al., 2019). This includes practitioners, industry experts, business leaders, mentors, investors, innovators, and educators. The culture of entrepreneurship should be built bottom-up and top-down simultaneously to create a buzz that can provide the required momentum, passion, drive, and energy to help society think entrepreneurially rather than focus on starting enterprises across different economic sectors (Schroeder, 2013). It is worth noting that with all the interest and potential *entrepreneurship* has generated, there needs to be a proper word in Arabic for entrepreneurship. The term *Reyadet Al-Aamal*, which is being used to mean 'entrepreneurship', is anything but encouraging the cause; the term does not give any of the excitement or passion associated with what entrepreneurship means or represents.

When building a nationwide entrepreneurial ecosystem, the role of higher education institutions, including business schools, is pivotal. They help shape the leaders, entrepreneurs, change agents, and the movers and shakers of tomorrow. Therefore, business schools must expose their students and learners to a lifelong learning experience that prepares them to compete and excel in a changing, dynamic, competitive, entrepreneurial and innovative global environment. Universities of the future—especially business schools—should be driven by an entrepreneurial mindset.

Entrepreneurship and innovation—with the acceleration of universal access to technology tools and applications, mobility and interconnectivity—represent a unique and much-needed opportunity for emerging economies. However, there is never one size that fits all, and the Middle East Africa (MEA) region is no exception. Societies have similarities and differences, even if they share the same language, culture, values, and history and are located in the same region. Those differences are often between and within countries, such as being open to risk-taking and change and accepting failure as a stepping stone to learn from and build on—something that is often a hurdle for many societies from a cultural perspective. Understanding that failure is an integral element of the entrepreneurial journey is essential for success.

DOI: 10.4324/9781003467410-11

Whether economies are developed or developing, populations are large or small, and resources are abundant or limited, human capital remains one of society's most critical assets. Therefore, for the MEA region, a conducive environment anchored around investing in human capital through education and lifelong learning is a must for entrepreneurship to become the driver and catalyst to rebuild economies based on sustainable foundations (Kamel and Schroeder, 2016).

Youth is a unique opportunity that could and should be captured across MEA (Nazeer, 2017). For example, Egypt's population is more than 104 million, with the vast majority—60%—under 30. It is a young society growing at 2.1% annually. Technological access has rapidly increased over the last decades, with over 72.2% internet and 94% mobile penetration rates, respectively. In 2023, over 25 million students are enrolled in K-12 schools and about 3.6 million in 90 universities and higher education institutions. Such demographics allow for societal transformation. Besides, the intersection of innovation, youth, and entrepreneurship could be a game changer. The same applies to most emerging economies in the MEA region. Universal access to digital platforms—rather than specific segments of society—means unlimited access to knowledge, people, opportunities, ideas, and the world at large.

Furthermore, younger generations have been more eager than ever to be self-employed than the previous generations, who primarily sought opportunities as civil servants. Today, they want to venture into the challenging and exciting business world. With the need to create over 800K jobs annually in Egypt, the path for development and growth can only be made through a scaled-up, agile, competitive, and inclusive private sector-led economy. The bigger the base of innovative entrepreneurs and private enterprises, the more likely an increasing number of startups will prevail (Kane, 2010). Therefore, investing in creating a pool of educated, passionate, technology-savvy, resilient, and innovative entrepreneurs is precisely what emerging economies like Egypt need. It is all about scalability, sustainability and impact.

Following, is the journey of the School of Business of the American University in Cairo (AUC). Since 2010 this has been the primary educational partner of the entrepreneurial ecosystem in Egypt and a key player in the MEA region through its portfolio of entrepreneurship, innovation, inclusive development, responsible business and leadership offerings, to help create the next generation of business leaders, entrepreneurs, policymakers and change agents who can make a difference to society.

AUC SCHOOL OF BUSINESS: THE JOURNEY

The school is an example of many business schools around the world that are constantly searching for opportunities to impact society. While the university was established in 1919, the school's origins date back to 1947, offering undergraduate and graduate degree programmes, executive education and community development activities. However, until mid-2009, *entrepreneurship* was only very casually covered in the curriculum. It featured in one chapter of just one of the textbooks used in teaching one of the undergraduate courses titled *Business and Society*. That had to change and fast. The only other venue where the concept of 'entrepreneurship' was addressed was through a student-led association by the name of the *Entrepreneurs' Society (ES)*—established in 2003—with a mission to promote the entrepreneurial culture among undergraduate students on campus through workshops, business plan and case competitions, training courses, and mentorship sessions in addition to a student magazine—*The Lead*.

In the fall of 2009, the school—established in 1993 and formerly known as the School of Business, Economics and Communication—was restructured to become the School of Business. The new mission statement read *"to develop entrepreneurial and responsible global leaders and professionals to impact society."* The main themes were identified to include (a) entrepreneurship and innovation, (b) responsible business and (c) economic development. Shortly after and following discussions with different stakeholders, the school focused on a specific niche—entrepreneurship and innovation with an eye on the family business. Accordingly, the school embarked on a journey to become the destination for *entrepreneurial education* in Egypt. The objective was to play a leading role in spreading the culture of entrepreneurship on campus and helping build a national entrepreneurial ecosystem.

Such an ambitious objective could not have been realised by introducing new entrepreneurship courses as verticals. Entrepreneurship is a way of thinking, a mindset. Therefore, entrepreneurship had to be well-integrated into the curriculum of academic degrees, executive education programmes, research projects, and community development services where content, case studies, projects, assignments, extracurricular activities, capacity building, internships, Co-Op programmes, as well as awareness and advocacy campaigns through student-led clubs and associations. Taskforces and working groups were formed to design a student-centred learning environment to revisit the pedagogical approach and revamp the curriculum to include critical thinking, complex problem solving, design thinking, communication, leadership, family business, responsible business, civic engagement, governance, and ethics.

THE JIGSAW PUZZLE: BUILDING AN ENTREPRENEURIAL ECOSYSTEM—ONE STEP AT A TIME.

The rationale was to strategically transform the school—and gradually the university—to become more creative, innovative, dynamic, and, most importantly, entrepreneurial. The ultimate objective was to change how students and learners think, generate ideas, perceive opportunities, understand innovation, take risks, develop alternative solutions, and become impact-driven. It is worth noting that while some people claim that entrepreneurship cannot be taught, and others believe that some are born gifted with entrepreneurial skills while others are not, there is no doubt that different skills and capacities can be shaped and improved through awareness, education, customised training, coupled with proper guidance and mentorship.

To kick-start such an ambitious journey, it was essential to realise some quick wins to build momentum. Starting with the introduction of new courses as part of the degree offerings would have required multiple conversations and steps to navigate the lengthy approvals across different university levels, including the department of management, the council of the school of business, the provost council, and the university senate—a process that could take up to a year if not more including the time needed to make changes to the course catalogue and define which students would be allowed to enrol in the courses. Such a path was not perceived as timely or effective. Accordingly, it was decided to proceed with two parallel paths to gain time. The first off-campus by formulating a nationwide community development programme, which can help in expediting and scaling up our advocacy efforts to create an entrepreneurial culture (Kamel, 2021b) and the second on-campus by introducing a minor in entrepreneurship coupled with launching a campus-wide entrepreneurship awareness campaign through public lectures, workshops and seminars.

1. Entrepreneurship and Innovation Program (EIP)

In 2010, based on the findings of a market study on entrepreneurship offerings in the MEA region, the school launched the Entrepreneurship and Innovation Programme (EIP). The objective was to educate, train, and inspire students, learners, and entrepreneurs in the intricacies of entrepreneurship through various seminars, workshops, bootcamps, business plan and case competitions, networking events, and mentorship programmes (Kamel, 2012).

EIP aimed to help spread entrepreneurship to a broader audience and identify promising entrepreneurs, helping them develop innovative ideas, turning them into viable startups, and assisting them in formulating their business plans. From the outset and based on the belief that Cairo is not Egypt and that great ideas do not come from big cities or urban settings only and for equity, diversity and inclusion purposes, all EIP offerings were open to everyone, including students and learners from different universities and entrepreneurs from all over the country (Kamel, 2021b). Some activities were offered online.

It is always about people. Therefore, it was essential to raise the awareness of the entrepreneurs, who varied in their education level, socioeconomic background, age, and gender. This step included the identification of knowledgeable and experienced mentors and coaches to help the entrepreneurs develop their business plans and guide them throughout the learning process. The mentors were instrumental in offering entrepreneurs internship opportunities. Over the years, the growing number of mentors led to the establishment of the *AUC mentors' network*, which included faculty from different disciplines, as well as industry and business experts and leaders—many from the university alumni—who shared their knowledge through one-to-one mentoring sessions as well as workshops, and seminars.

The experience of EIP and working closely with young entrepreneurs highlighted the need for providing in-depth support to early-stage entrepreneurs and startups as they worked through their business modelling and planning, fundraising, and setting up their operations and partnerships. These services are usually best provided to a smaller number of startups through an acceleration or incubation programme. This motivated the school to start planning to establish a campus-wide incubator/accelerator that provides an enabling environment for an interdisciplinary entrepreneurial learning experience (Kamel, 2021a).

EIP stirred a substantial impact, where the flicker of entrepreneurship started glowing, with thousands of Egyptians learning more about entrepreneurship. This was an evolving space, and many local and global organisations became actively involved in different stages in growing the ecosystem, including more than 80 private, government and

Annual Research Volume 2 – Complex Societal Impact Projects Requiring Tri-Sector Collaboration and Cooperation

The Role of Business Schools in Creating National Entrepreneurial Ecosystems: The Case of Egypt and the AUC School of Business
Sherif Kamel

non-governmental organisations such as Flat6Labs, the Global Entrepreneurship Programme, 138 Pyramids, Algebra Capital, the Egyptian American Enterprise Fund, Injaz Egypt, Nahdet El-Mahrousa, Endeavor Egypt, A15, ENACTUS (formerly known as Students for Free Enterprise), Cairo Angels, the American Chamber of Commerce in Egypt, Rise-Up Summit, RISE Egypt, the Technology Innovation and Entrepreneurship Center, and Ashoka. This was a collective effort, and everyone added some value. The interaction, diversity, and networking were essential and represented a real learning experience for all—it was a new space, and everyone was learning on the go (*ibid*).

During 2010-2015, EIP helped gradually position the AUC School of Business as the educational partner to the entrepreneurial ecosystem in Egypt, starting with the exciting buzz about the potential and impact of entrepreneurship launched on campus. However, the school efforts reached beyond the campus, all over Egypt, and into the MEA region. The campus was crowded almost weekly with students, fresh graduates, and promising entrepreneurs with ideas who needed further training and mentoring to move to the next level. The reach of EIP impacted more than 2,600 undergraduate and 1,200 graduate students from different universities in Egypt. Moreover, there were 300+ faculty members and educators trained and more than 4,350 learners from Cairo and many provinces in Egypt, whether in the Delta region or Upper Egypt, including Giza, Mansoura, Ismailia, Assiout, Alexandria, Aswan, as well as from other countries in the MEA region including Lebanon, Morocco, the United Arab Emirates, South Africa, Kenya, Sudan, and Nigeria. EIP raised north of €930K to support entrepreneurs in capacity-building.

PHOTO COURTESY AUC

2. Entrepreneurship and Innovation Council (EIC)

During the early stages of launching EIP, discussions were held with various stakeholders, including faculty, students, alumni, entrepreneurs, business leaders, policymakers, civil society leaders, government officials, and others. In 2010, these discussions led to establishing the Entrepreneurship and Innovation Council (EIC) as an advisory arm for guidance, directions and support. The council provided endorsement and visibility. In addition, it was essential to get insights and perspectives from different players in the entrepreneurial space on priority areas to address them in various ways, including research focus to support the national efforts and impact policy. The EIC members included entrepreneurs, academics, policymakers, non-governmental organisations' representatives, and business leaders from Egypt and elsewhere. The members have been instrumental in facilitating several corporate connections and university partnership agreements with different players in the entrepreneurial space in Egypt, the MEA region, and beyond. The members also served as mentors and judges in competitions and contributed to designing and delivering some EIP activities.

3. Minor in Entrepreneurship

Introducing courses in entrepreneurship was vital in bringing the conversation about its potential impact into the classroom. In 2011, the school was the first in Egypt to introduce a minor in entrepreneurship, which included new courses and seminars in entrepreneurship, principles of entrepreneurial finance, entrepreneurial marketing, entrepreneurship and innovation, developing and launching a new venture, social entrepreneurship, and family business. In parallel, following all the required approvals, the school started integrating entrepreneurship into other accounting, economics and information technology courses. The minor was offered to all undergraduate students, irrespective of their majors. The objective was to maximise the value to the campus-wide student body. By 2013, the enrolment in these courses became the highest on campus. The required buzz and vibe about entrepreneurship—that the school worked so hard to realise—was gradually being heard and diffused among the university community. The lesson learned throughout the process was that *if business schools want to preach entrepreneurship, they should practice it first and push their operations and processes to be more efficient.* No one can create and endorse a mindset they are not practising; it is just like those who talk, push and advocate change but never want to change.

Annual Research Volume 2 – Complex Societal Impact Projects Requiring Tri-Sector Collaboration and Cooperation

The Role of Business Schools in Creating National Entrepreneurial Ecosystems: The Case of Egypt and the AUC School of Business
Sherif Kamel
....

4. Doing Business in Africa and the Middle East

In 2012, the school started introducing one and two-week programmes that promote entrepreneurship through the lens of doing business in Africa or the Middle East. The programme is a hybrid of academic, cultural and social content and activities demonstrating the impact of the local context and values on how business is conducted. It was designed to promote entrepreneurship education and research to help transform economies across the MEA region. The programme was often conducted in collaboration with the University of Stellenbosch in South Africa and offered to students from universities worldwide.

5. El-Khazindar Business Research and Case Center (KCC)

Another essential component of the journey was to engage the school's case-writing platform, El-Khazindar Business Research and Case Center (KCC)—established in 2007. Over the years, KCC has produced over 100 mini and long business cases, mainly entrepreneurial issues, successes, and failures related to emerging markets. In 2011, KCC was getting some global visibility by contributing several cases to Innovations—the quarterly journal published by MIT Press—on the occasion of organising the Global Entrepreneurship Summit.

6. The American Chamber of Commerce in Egypt (AmCham Egypt)

Connecting with the business community and availing opportunities for entrepreneurs through networking and partnerships was an integral part of the school's efforts. Accordingly, following several discussions with the leadership of the American Chamber of Commerce in Egypt—the largest business association in Egypt with over 950 corporate members—an Entrepreneurship and Innovation (EIC) core committee was established in 2010 with links to the EIP operations.

7. The Venture Lab (V-Lab)

One of the significant pieces of the jigsaw puzzle was launched in 2013, the first university-based incubator/accelerator in Egypt—the Venture Lab (V-Lab)—to identify, support, mentor and incubate innovative entrepreneurs while capitalising on the university's intellectual capital, infrastructure and research capacities, and connecting them to the university network of faculty, staff, and alumni. The mission of the V-Lab is to support selected high-growth and innovation-driven startups from across Egypt to commercialise their technologies and business models into successful and sustainable ventures (El-Dahshan et al., 2011). By doing that, the V-Lab aimed to foster a thriving ecosystem of innovation, learning, responsible business and good citizenship.

While university-based incubators were popping up everywhere, in 2013, the V-Lab was the first in the MEA region to be well-integrated into the campus community, interacting with the university constituents and supporting entrepreneurs across society. Besides, while some incubators are limited to specific technologies, and others serve only their students, the V-Lab prides itself on being open to entrepreneurs across the MEA region and supporting different technology platforms and economic sectors since its inception.

The V-Lab was established as an interdisciplinary incubator/accelerator to provide support services for qualifying entrepreneurs and startups according to a set of publicly announced rigorous processes for application and qualification that is based on the novelty of the idea, scalability, commercial potential, team experience and commitment to success. The business model was formulated based on research conducted on university-based incubators in the world, building on their experiences and lessons learned while adapting to local needs, norms and values, as well as ways of doing business to help contribute to economic growth, competitiveness, and job creation, investing in human capital and innovation while providing a learning and research platform for the university community to connect and engage with entrepreneurs.

The V-Lab offers two accelerator programmes. The first is the *Startup Accelerator Programme*, which runs two cycles annually. Each cycle includes around 25 qualified startups selected from a pool of 400 applicants (6%), enabling the V-Lab team to work closely with each startup team of entrepreneurs. Entrepreneurs are offered an intensive acceleration experience for 16 weeks. The programme welcomes entrepreneurs from Egypt and the MEA region, bringing entrepreneurs with diverse backgrounds and experiences to campus and giving them access to university resources, including internet access, library and other facilities, as well as engineering and technical labs free of charge and granting the university students and learners insights into the entrepreneurial world. The programme is about scaling up the added value to as many entrepreneurs as possible. Therefore, startups not qualifying for the acceleration programme are invited to attend an extensive interactive capacity-building programme focusing on business and leadership skills, critical thinking, marketing and communications, among other topics. The programme is designed and delivered by the school faculty, business practitioners, and executives selected from the mentors' network; most offer their services on a *pro bono* basis (Ismail, 2020).

Annual Research Volume 2 – Complex Societal Impact Projects Requiring Tri-Sector Collaboration and Cooperation

The Role of Business Schools in Creating National Entrepreneurial Ecosystems: The Case of Egypt and the AUC School of Business
Sherif Kamel
····················

The programme is composed of two tracks. For each accelerated startup, the V-Lab provides a modest seed fund—the equivalent of €2.8K—unfortunately this was discontinued after the 2016 Egyptian pound devaluation, and a set of services, including a co-working space on campus; bootcamps, and capacity-building courses on a variety of topics, such as idea pitching and fundraising; as well as, mentoring, coaching, access to potential investors, market research, access to faculty, assistance with professional services such as human resources and students' recruitment, communication, and legal support.

7.1 Startup Accelerator

The programme was launched in 2013 to help entrepreneurs make their startups investment-ready, allowing them to tap into the right networks and strategise for scaling and growth. It is a 16-week sector-agnostic programme supporting high-growth and innovation-driven early-stage startups. With the support of the V-Lab corporate partners, the economic sectors and industries covered include healthcare, eCommerce, transportation, artificial intelligence, logistics, mobility, IoT, education, energy, green economy, trade, sustainability, logistics and others.

7.2 Fintech Accelerator

Egypt's population is more than 60% unbanked, especially in remote locations, facing challenges accessing the traditional financial infrastructure. Accordingly, fintech is emerging as a key vertical in Egypt's entrepreneurship ecosystem. The Fintech Accelerator is a 16-week equity-free programme for fintech startups offering specialised business knowledge and technology support, equipping entrepreneurs with business design skills, growth-hacking techniques and investment-readiness support through coaching, mentorship, access to an investment clinic, and peer-to-peer support and networking opportunities through demo days and other events. The programme was launched in 2015 to avail space for early-stage entrepreneurs to help them develop fintech solutions for Egypt and the MEA region to work towards building a more inclusive economy, increase access to information and services, and helping to reduce poverty. The school's partners include local financial regulators and international key players, including one of Egypt's leading private banks (Commercial International Bank), the International Finance Corporation of the World Bank Group, and the global financial enabler Mastercard, offering the participating startups unrivalled access to market insights and exclusive opportunities.

By 2023, the programme has graduated 50 startups and supported over 100 entrepreneurs, representing around 35% of Egypt's fintech startups. The startups that went through the acceleration programme have raised north of €3.3 million, which helped finance their growth and user-base expansions. To date, 80% of the accelerated startups are active. They have financially enabled over 450K users in agriculture, healthcare, payment, remittances, lending, insurance, savings, financial literacy and alternative financing. Most of the user base of these startups are unbanked people who otherwise would have been excluded from these financially enabled services. The programme is increasingly contributing to migrating many from the informal economy.

To demonstrate the programme's impact on the social and financial inclusion fronts, one of the startups accelerated—*Neqabty*''16, provides individuals with healthcare services at discounted prices and facilitates traceable digital payments. Neqabty works with Egypt's Engineers Syndicate to provide services to over 700K members. Neqabty is working with various syndicates and labour unions in Egypt and expanding into Africa to facilitate further access to healthcare services. Another example is *Klickit '18*, which enables online school payments and digital fee collection. In 2021, Klickit partnered with the Ministry of Education and E-Finance (the government's financial network) to launch their electronic payment service enabling parents of students from all public schools to pay the tuition online. Klickit's solution serves more than 55K public schools and 400 private organisations, easing the organisational strain and saving time and effort for millions of people.

PHOTO COURTESY AUC

In 2023, the V-Lab celebrates ten years of operations. During that time, it has accelerated 323 startups and created over 12K direct and indirect jobs. These startups have generated more than €147 million. There was one unicorn exit–SWVL, and more than 3000 capacity-building hours and mentorship, many on a one-to-one basis, were offered. The reach and impact of the V-Lab attracted some of the leading local and global companies to become partners, including SODIC–one of the leading real estate development companies in Egypt, the Arab African International Bank (AAIB) and the Commercial International Bank (CIB)–two of the top private banks in Egypt.

7.3 The Startup Launchpad

The 8-week immersive programme aims to grow Egypt's tech-enabled entrepreneurship ecosystem by equipping idea-stage entrepreneurs with the IT skills and knowledge they need to start a business. With a mission of expanding the number of tech-enabled startups–especially in the MEA region where there is limited access to entrepreneurial education–the programme provides basic ideation and entrepreneurship education to aspiring entrepreneurs. The programme helps entrepreneurs–including women–to effectively develop business ideas and increase their startup's chances of survival and success through extensive capacity-building and coaching. The launchpad has graduated 75 entrepreneurs from 9 provinces[2] in Egypt.

7.4 The Incudev Programme

Many universities, governments, non-governmental organisations, and private enterprises establish accelerators and incubators to serve their societies. In Egypt, the V-Lab partnered with Rowad[3] 2030–one of the projects of Egypt's Ministry of Planning and Economic Development and supported by the Drosos Foundation–to offer capacity-building and mentorship programmes to help establish university-based incubators, accelerators and entrepreneurship centres, both in Egypt and the MEA region.

Through Incudev, the V-Lab works with accelerator/ incubator managers either launching or growing their programmes to design and enhance their business models and processes and build their capacities. The objective is to help them support entrepreneurs and startups in the communities they serve. The programme is also designed to capitalise on the knowledge shared between the participating incubators/ accelerators. Since 2021, Incudev has trained 130 managers in 80 different entrepreneurship centres, incubators and accelerators and supported 44 of the 64 universities (69%) in Egypt in awareness and advocacy about entrepreneurship education, including helping them design their curriculum. Incudev supported more than 1K entrepreneurs across Egypt through free consultations, ideations and hackathons.

To measure its impact, the V-Lab has developed several key performance indicators, including the number of startups accelerated, entrepreneurs mentored, students and learners trained, percentage of startups funded, including the amount of financing that was generated as a result of being incubated at the V-Lab, the mentors' ability to link entrepreneurs with business executives and potential investors, and the number of partnerships created between startups and other organisations whether private or public.

The V-Lab has just completed a regional edition of the Incudev programme, with the participation of 18 programme leaders from 7 MEA countries, including Tunisia, Lebanon, Palestine, United Arab Emirates, Rwanda, South Africa and Kenya. It was an excellent opportunity to start a regional network of professionals interested in building their local ecosystems. The Drosos Foundation supported the programme.

In 2023, the V-Lab was recognised as the Middle East North Africa Top Challenger by UBI Global World Rankings 2021-2022 of business incubators and accelerators. The award is granted to incubators and accelerators that offer exceptional value for their startups and the local ecosystem. In addition, in 2022, the V-Lab was recognised as the Best Accelerator in Africa at the Global Startup Awards Africa summit.

8. Research Focus

In 2015, the focus of a large percentage of the research outcome conducted by the school faculty gradually started to tilt towards entrepreneurship, innovation and family business. This was reflected in the quality and volume of publications. Besides, with an eye on impacting policy by supporting government policymakers and local and international development organisations interested in delivering entrepreneurship programmes, the school–through several of its faculty and staff started to produce the Global Entrepreneurship Monitor–Egypt National Report in 2015. In addition, in 2017, the school started producing the Global Entrepreneurship Monitor–Middle East North Africa Regional Report.

9. Centre for Entrepreneurship and Innovation (CEI)

The journey of EIP–established in 2010–continued to link academia with the business world and advocate for a well-thought-out nationwide entrepreneurial culture. EIP was the first of its kind in the MEA region when it pioneered as a university programme focusing on raising awareness of the role of entrepreneurship in economic development and growth through ideation, innovation and preparing startups in early, venture and late stages of disrupting traditional businesses through technologies and then connecting them with accelerators, incubators and investors.

Annual Research Volume 2 – Complex Societal Impact Projects Requiring Tri-Sector Collaboration and Cooperation

The Role of Business Schools in Creating National Entrepreneurial Ecosystems: The Case of Egypt and the AUC School of Business
Sherif Kamel
....

With the introduction of the United Nations' Sustainable Development Goals and the school's focus on sustainability, governance, responsible business and inclusive development, EIP was restructured in 2015 into a fully-fledged centre and became the Centre for Entrepreneurship and Innovation (CEI). This move helped better address SDG goals and broadened the scope to include cross-cutting themes like gender and climate. Accordingly, CEI diversified its target audience and offered a variety of tailored programmes and services by partnering with different national, regional and international organisations.

In 2020, the CEI introduced a series of community development projects and capacity-building activities to address essential issues such as financial sustainability, youth employment, women's economic empowerment, gender equality, diversity, and inclusion in Egypt, especially in remote locations. These programmes are conducted in collaboration with local and international partners and donor agencies to support economic, social and environmental development and engage a diverse pool of students and learners through entrepreneurship programmes and case competitions—including venture capital, innovative solutions and business plans—hackathons and events. For example, the CEI's International Case Competition—introduced in 2019—focuses on issues related to Egypt's business and entrepreneurship landscape, including consumer behaviour, economic trends, regulatory and policy reforms, technology adoption, and the enabling environment. In 2020, a hackathon was launched to increase the students' experience of working in small groups and sharing their creative skills while exploring innovative solutions to social and economic problems and inspiring a more sustainable, accessible, and resilient future for society. The competition usually attracts around 40 teams annually from around the world. It provides access to internships, scholarships and mentorships.

CEI became a brand in the ecosystem and a go-to reference for stakeholders who seek to engage youth, women, startups, and underserved communities while strengthening the links between industry, business and academia. By 2023, the impact of CEI had reached more than 70K participants in entrepreneurship awareness programmes, around 1K students and learners in competitions, over 500 participants in capacity-building workshops and training programmes, and 2K hours of mentoring sessions. They also forged over 100 partnerships in business, industry, academia, civil society and government.

One of the critical projects of CEI is Rabeha[4]—which aims to support women entrepreneurs as part of society's efforts to reduce the gender gap in the national entrepreneurship ecosystem. The project is part of the framework of the UN Women Egypt-UNIDO Egypt Joint Programme 'Women Economic Empowerment for Inclusive and Sustainable Growth' implemented in partnership with the National Council for Women, the Ministry of Trade and Industry through the Micro, Small and Medium Enterprises Development Agency, and generously supported by Global Affairs Canada. The project—delivered in Arabic—includes training, mentoring and incubation to enhance the skills of women entrepreneurs or women with viable and promising entrepreneurial ideas. Since 2020, CEI has trained over 1,500 women in seven provinces in Egypt.

While capacity-building is essential in entrepreneurship, mentorship is invaluable for entrepreneurs to guide their startup ventures. In 2021, CEI became a certified MIT Venture Mentoring Service (MIT VMS) member with the support of the International Finance Corporation of the World Bank Group. The programme aims to create a community of qualified mentors to guide aspiring and established entrepreneurs in Egypt throughout the startup life cycle. The partnership with the Massachusetts Institute of Technology is vital in supporting CEI to continue to train mentors on the principles and methodology of the MIT VMS model and to expand its mentorship network. CEI has successfully recruited 30 mentors and 15 venture founders and delivered over 20 hours of mentoring.

10. AUC Angels

In 2018, AUC Angels—the first university-based angel investor network in the MEA region—was launched. The objective is to build an angel investment network for AUC alumni and friends, provide a strong pipeline of startups, facilitate deal flow, support innovative startups, secure seed funding and beyond. Since its launch, the network has 60 investors who have supported 26 startups—from a pool of 290 applicants (8.9%)—through a total investment of €1.2 million. Notably, 15 of the 26 startups (58%) received follow-on funding. From a regional perspective, the number of strategic partners in the AUC Angels network has reached 20 across the MEA region.

11. The Family Business Consortium

In 2018, the school convened the first meeting of the *Family Business Consortium*. The founding partners included ESCA Ecole de Management (Morocco), Ajman University (United Arab Emirates), American University of Beirut and Holy Spirit University (Lebanon). The objective was to shed light on family business models, given that they represent 60% of the GDP in Egypt and many countries in the MEA region, ranging from small and medium-sized enterprises to large corporations that operate in different industries and economic sectors. The issues addressed included governance, succession planning, resilience, building trust across generations, and family values and legacies. The consortium intended to use research to impact policy and highlight the importance of family business as a catalyst for enhancing economic growth and societal development across the MEA region. In addition to the consortium, the school introduced several other activities in the family business domain, including introducing academic and executive education courses in 2017 for the first time in the Middle East, launching the family business talks series, developing more than 40 teaching cases—winning two case writing global awards—organising the 2023 edition of #IMovedMyBusinessForward campaign on family business and the first virtual international family business research day in collaboration with the Family Business Centre of the Entrepreneurial School in Austria and ESCA Ecole de Management in Morocco, and gradually becoming a convener for conversations on family business, its future, challenges and opportunities.

12. Bachelor's Degree in Business and Entrepreneurship

In 2021, the school started offering the degree to equip students with the skills and knowledge needed to become *business-ready*, including critical thinking, responsible business, and adaptability to complex situations while unleashing their creativity, innovation, and entrepreneurial thinking to prepare them for running a new business venture and learning the fundamentals of business such as managing people, operations, marketing, finance, business ethics, and more.

CONCLUSION

This was an ecosystem that was created seamlessly and organically. It was not led by any one person or organisation or belonging to any specific entity. It was a mushrooming space where individuals and organisations collaborated and supported each other, yet again, in many ways, they were competing for resources, financial support, and bettering their services and offerings; a classic case of co-opetition. It was a learning experience for all. It was and continues to be fun, like a co-working space for creativity and innovation. The school's efforts started in 2010—when there was no entrepreneurial culture at the school or the university—and were driven by the firm belief that entrepreneurship is essential for the future of Egypt and the MEA region. The partnerships we forged with the private sector, government and civil society organisations were a testament and an endorsement of how far the school was transformed and has become an entrepreneurial powerhouse among business schools in the MEA region that is constantly realising a significant impact on society in Egypt.

AUC School of Business's next journey is to help universities in Egypt and across the MEA region replicate its experience, build on it and help establish their entrepreneurial platforms by systematically investing in lifelong learning, attracting youth, promoting innovation, and creating opportunities to transform lives and livelihoods. Creating a nationwide effective, sustainable, and scalable entrepreneurial ecosystem could be a game-changer for Egypt and the MEA region. However, for a national entrepreneurial culture to thrive, it needs to be private sector-led, supported by talented and well-exposed human capital, a conducive environment and a vibrant society to help build the economy more inclusively and impactfully.

Annual Research Volume 2 – Complex Societal Impact Projects Requiring Tri-Sector Collaboration and Cooperation

The Role of Business Schools in Creating National Entrepreneurial Ecosystems: The Case of Egypt and the AUC School of Business

Sherif Kamel

....

References

El-Dahshan, M., A. Tolba and T. Badreldin (2011) Enabling entrepreneurship in Egypt: toward a sustainable, dynamic model. *Innovations 7*(2) pp.83-106

Ismail, A. (2020) A framework for designing business-acceleration programs: a case study from Egypt. *Entrepreneurship Research Journal 10*(2) pp.1-16

Ismail, A., S. Kamel and K. Wahba (2019) The impact of technology-based incubators in creating a sustainable and scalable startup culture in emerging economies: a system thinking model. *Communications of the IBIMA*, Volume 2019, pp.1-16

Kamel, S. (2012) "Entrepreneurial uprising," *BizEd*, November/ December, pp.46-47

Kamel, S. (2021a) *Leading change in challenging times: lessons of disruption and innovation from Egypt–thoughts, observations, and reflections*. Independently Published. Manufactured by Amazon, ISBN: 9798766291527

Kamel, S. (2021b) The role of digital transformation in development in Egypt. *Journal of Internet and e-Business Studies (JIEBS)*, Article ID 911090, ISSN 2169-0391, pp.1-10

Kamel, S. (2016) Startup. *Global Focus, 10*(3) pp.52-55

Kamel, S., and C. Schroeder (2016) Economic recovery and revitalisation. *Research study*. Working group report of the Middle East strategy task force. Washington DC: The Atlantic Council

Kane, T. (2010) *The importance of startups in job creation and job destruction*. Kauffman Foundation Research Series

Nazeer, T. (2017) MENA's entrepreneurial ecosystem has the potential to flourish. *Forbes Middle East*, 13 August

Schroeder, C. (2013) *Startup rising–the entrepreneurial revolution remaking the Middle East*. New York: Palgrave Macmillan

Schroeder, C. (2017) A different story from the Middle East: Entrepreneurs building an Arab tech economy. *MIT Technology Review*, 3 August

Footnotes

[1] Neqabty is the Arabic word for 'syndicate'

[2] Egypt has 27 governorates

[3] Rowad is the Arabic word for 'pioneers'

[4] Rabeha is the Arabic word for 'a female winner'

About the Author

Kamel is a Professor of Management and Dean of the School of Business at The American University in Cairo. Previously, he served as the university vice president for information management. Kamel is also an Eisenhower Fellow. Before joining the university, he managed the training department of the Cabinet of Egypt Information and Decision Support Center. He is also the Vice-Chair of the board of directors of AACSB International (United States) and Deputy Chair of the Global Alliance in Management Education (France).

Making Wales an Anti-racist Nation: A 'Public Value Mission' in Action

EMMANUEL OGBONNA

Complex Societal Impact Projects Requiring Tri-Sector Collaboration and Cooperation

A common criticism of business and management schools across the world is that they are not sufficiently invested in solving wider societal problems and concerns. A recent example that may be cited by critics to illustrate this is the COVID-19 pandemic. Here, business and management academies were generally slow in joining the debates both on the impacts of the virus and the transformation of post-pandemic societies to account for the failures of embedded structures, systems and processes. Arguably, the gaps left by business and management academies were filled by other disciplines. For example, scholars in healthcare have contributed several academic and practitioner research and lobbying activities through highlighting the health and well-being implications of social, economic and psychological pressures that were induced or exacerbated by the pandemic.

A second and pertinent example in relation to this article is that business and management schools continue to be criticised for not playing an active role in addressing issues of inequality and disadvantage in organisations and societies. However, as many articles in the previous issues of *Global Focus* reveal, many schools of business and management are addressing these criticisms in a variety of ways. Indeed, several schools are working hard to improve their external stakeholder engagement and to emphasise their social dividends and relevance, that which is commonly described as 'public good', or that which is referred to as 'public value' at Cardiff Business School. One example of this public value is the initiative to make Wales anti-racist. This example is significant because it is the first major national-level initiative on anti-racism by a 'Western' government. It is also notable because the design, development and implementation of the plan has been led by research emerging from Cardiff Business School. This plan thus provides a useful context for understanding the potential societal impact of business and management research.

Through a discussion of the recently developed Anti-racist Wales Action Plan (ArWAP), this article discusses the ways in which business and management research can shape the debates and policies that can lead to major societal transformations. The article begins with an overview of the context of racialization in Wales and the UK to illustrate the necessity for change and to highlight the rationale for the adoption of an anti-racist approach rather than the conventional approaches to achieving racial equality. This is followed by a discussion of the process of developing the plan, with insights into the role of business and management research in guiding this process. The article concludes with a discussion of the lessons that business and management schools and their scholars might learn from the ArWAP project in developing meaningful, impactful and societally relevant research.

DOI: 10.4324/9781003467410-12

Annual Research Volume 2 – Complex Societal Impact Projects Requiring Tri-Sector Collaboration and Cooperation

Making Wales an Anti-racist Nation: A 'Public Value Mission' in Action
Emmanuel Ogbonna
....

BACKGROUND TO RACIALIZATION AND RACISM IN WALES AND THE UK

Wales is a nation of 3.1 million people but it remains an integral part of the UK. This means that social issues such as racialization and racism are best understood through the wider UK lens. In this regard, it is useful to note that race relations in the UK have a long history which has been explored from historic, economic, socio-psychological and health angles. A useful point to make in relation to this article is that previous race policies have failed to make a meaningful impact in reducing racial discrimination or in improving the lived experiences of ethnic minorities. The consequences of the failure of these policies can be seen in all areas of the lives of people from ethnic minority backgrounds in the UK. For example, in the labour market, ethnic minorities have consistently been up to twice as likely as their white counterparts to be unemployed since labour market statistics began in the UK. Those who are employed, commonly find that racism follows them through their working lives, with data showing, for example, that the average black doctor earns £10,000 less than their white counterparts and the average black nurse earns £2,700 less. Indeed, evidence from the respected think tank, Resolution Foundation, suggests that ethnic minorities in the UK lose £3.2 billion in annual cost of ethnic pay penalties, while another government sponsored review by Lady McGregor-Smith concluded that the full integration of ethnic minorities in organisations and institutions could add £24 billion a year to the UK economy. The disparities also extend to avoidable mortality, with data suggesting that black women in the UK are up to four times more likely to die in childbirth, and Asian women up to two times more likely to die in childbirth than their white counterparts. In law and order, ethnic minorities are more likely to be jailed for the same crime than their white counterparts, and black people are seven times more likely to die following police restraint than their white counterparts. Further, specific evidence in Wales suggests that while the rate of police stop and search for white people is 8 per 1000 of the population, it is 56 per 1000 for black people and 16 per 1000 for those of Asian backgrounds and 28 per 1000 for people of mixed backgrounds.

Many researchers and commentators have argued that these anomalies represent outcomes in a society wherein racial discrimination is institutionalised. However, the history of this conclusion has been contested for a long time but especially since Lord Macpherson used the term 'institutional racism' to describe the activities of The Metropolitan Police Force in London in the formal inquiry into the death of a young black teenager, Stephen Lawrence, published in 1999. Interestingly, the charge of institutional racism was repeated against the Metropolitan Police Force in another inquiry by Baroness Casey in 2023, in a way suggesting that little has changed since 1999. Indeed, although several reports have highlighted the institutionalised nature of racism, the UK government, leaders of the devolved nations and major institutions have steered away from the social and political ramifications of accepting the charge of institutional racism, with the current UK government being especially hostile to any suggestion of structural racism. This denial of racism is widespread in the UK and is unfortunately profound in business and management schools and the universities that house them. The reluctance to accept the existence of institutional racism is, perhaps, a reflection of the domination of these organisations by white, middle class, middle-aged men who have been the major beneficiaries of racialization. These attributes feed into the elite culture in academic and other professional institutions and such culture is maintained through 'othering', with questions such as 'Where do you come from?', 'Which university did you attend?' often posed in ways that reinforce the outsider status of ethnic minorities. Indeed, rather than look for alternative explanations of success, white business and management academics, like many other white professionals, are more likely to attribute their success entirely to their hard work and they commonly believe that this should be the same for everyone. Unfortunately, this view discounts the racialized anomalies that exist in degree awards, award of doctoral studentships, research funding and in employment and promotion opportunities. It is within this context that the significance of the work in Wales can be understood.

Annual Research Volume 2 – Complex Societal Impact Projects Requiring Tri-Sector Collaboration and Cooperation

Making Wales an Anti-racist Nation: A 'Public Value Mission' in Action
Emmanuel Ogbonna
....

AN ANTI-RACIST PLAN FOR WALES

At the early phase of the COVID-19 pandemic, the First Minister of Wales became concerned about the disproportionate impacts of this disease on ethnic minority groups in Wales. He commissioned a series of investigations into this and one was tasked with exploring the socio-economic explanations of the disproportionate outcomes. I was invited to chair this group and following a three-month investigation, the group published its report which, among other factors, identified institutional racism as contributing to the disproportionate outcomes from the pandemic (Ogbonna, 2020). The finding of institutional racism in relation to a country and not just organisations or institutions was profound and had implications that were widespread. The publication of this report also coincided with the killing of an unarmed black man, George Floyd, by law enforcement officers in USA before a social media-watching world. This brutal murder contributed a powerful worldwide visible manifestation of the potentially deleterious effect of racism.

However, while the acceptance of institutional racism at governmental level in Wales may have been novel, it was by no means surprising to those involved in race work. This is partly because scarcely publicised but important and authoritative social attitude surveys have consistently found that a sizeable proportion of British people have strong racist tendencies. Specifically, successive surveys by the National Centre for Social Research (NatCen) show that racism is more common than people may ordinarily believe in the UK. The most recent survey of British racial attitudes in 2017 revealed that 26% of a representative sample of the British population described themselves as 'very or a little prejudiced' against people of other races. An earlier European Social Survey in 2014 also cited by NatCen found that 18% of British people believed that "some races or ethnic groups are born less intelligent" while 44% believed that "some races or ethnic groups are naturally harder working" (see Kelley *et al.*, 2017). It is thus within the context of research-led investigations of the disproportionate impacts of COVID-19 in Wales, the widespread protests from the killing of George Floyd, and our framing of the findings of wider British racial attitudes that the decision was made in Wales to fast track the race equality strategy that was developed prior to the pandemic.

DEVELOPING THE PLAN

Under the leadership of two of the most powerful people in the Welsh Government (the First Minister and the Minister for Social Justice), a Steering Group was established with the remit of developing a plan that will help to eradicate racism in Wales. I was invited to co-chair this Group alongside the Permanent Secretary of the Welsh Government who is the highest-ranked civil servant in Wales. The early decisions of the Group were potentially significant and provide the best examples of the ways in which research emerging from business and management schools could be deployed to shape external policy development. The Welsh Government wanted the Steering Group to adopt its existing template on race equality (developed prior to the pandemic) in developing the plan. This template was based on the principles of equality of opportunities (EO) and equality, diversity and inclusion (EDI). I argued strongly (with the support of some members of the Steering Group) that EO and EDI approaches were implicated in the perpetuation of racialization in that they have failed to make a meaningful impact on the lives of people from ethnic minority groups. This is because EO and EDI commonly adopt a colour-blind approach in ways that fail to recognise how historic patterns of inequality and power relations combine to skew societal outcomes against ethnic minorities. Further, these approaches tend to advocate solutions which shift the burden of racism to the victims. That is, EO and EDI approaches by implication work on the assumption that there is a 'fair playing field'. This means that anomalies in outcomes are viewed as the results of individual deficiencies. In this regard, the task of organisations is presented as seeking ways of addressing these individual deficiencies (for example through additional training, mentoring, and coaching) rather than fixing the structures of racism which combine to weaken the agency of racial and ethnic minorities.

I drew on existing research on race and racialization to position anti-racism as the only approach that will help to eliminate racism. Indeed, the finding that a sizeable proportion of the British population self-confessed to harbouring negative racial attitudes and the conclusion of the report of the socio-economic sub-group that institutional racism was implicated in the disproportionate outcomes from COVID-19 were instructive in this regard. I drew on my own research to argue that, contrary to the understanding of many, racism is not dichotomous, in that the opposite of racism is not non-racism. Instead, I positioned racism as a continuum wherein the racist individual is at one end, the non-racist is in the middle and the anti-racist is at the other end. Significantly, this understanding suggests that the opposite of racism is anti-racism. This is because while non-racism may be positive in intention, it is passive in action. Further, like all people in society, non-racists are often instilled with racist stereotypes from early ages which they commonly internalise and which can surface in times of anxiety. It is this type of response that gives rise to what is sometimes referred to as 'unconscious bias'. By contrast, anti-racism is a conscious process of actively thinking about and changing the structure, systems, processes and procedures that may give rise to racially differential outcomes. Importantly, these views were confirmed by discussions with the numerous ethnic minority groups that were involved in developing the plan. A critical aspect of the success of the plan is that we were able to convince Welsh Government Ministers on the importance of adopting an anti-racist approach in developing the plan.

A CO-CREATION APPROACH

The approach to developing the plan was collaborative and involved the cooperation of a variety of groups. The Steering Group members recognised the value of evidence-based change from the onset and it commissioned Cardiff Business School's Wales Centre for Public Policy (WCPP) to assist with the plan. The aim was to provide rapid reviews of evidence on the substantive areas of concern. The evidence helped us to isolate the key problems in the individual policy areas, to understand how these have been interpreted and dealt with in the past, and to understand the intersectional implications of the various courses of action that were being explored. This also involved working with leading race and ethnicity practitioners and researchers not just from business and management backgrounds but also from healthcare, education and other policy areas. These experts were invited to attend meetings with Welsh Government policy leads and they participated in the numerous roundtable events that were held to shape the plan.

The Steering Group also involved representatives of key organisations and institutions in Wales such as trade union representatives, local government representatives and the Equality and Human Rights Commission, both in the Steering Group meetings and as part of the special roundtable events. However, the Steering Group placed members of ethnic minority groups in Wales at the centre, as the key stakeholders whose lived experiences of racism were pivotal to the recommendations and approaches adopted in the plan. We believed that it was important to ensure that the Welsh Government policy officials (who were predominantly white) had some understanding of the impacts of the policies they developed on the end users, in this case ethnic minorities. We recruited external members of the ethnic minority groups in Wales and we matched them carefully to work with individual policy leads. They were employed as 'Community Mentors' and among other things, their role was to help the policy leads to understand the dynamics and impacts of racism. We took the view that this was important work and we ensured that the mentors were properly remunerated.

CLOSING THE IMPLEMENTATION GAP

Previous research contributions into the implementation of diversity and inclusion initiatives commonly point to the difficulty that organisations have in controlling the agency of managers who do not always value or identify with the diversity agenda. This reluctance to engage with diversity creates an implementation gap (a gap between what is intended and what is realised). To this end, developing an approach that closes the implementation gap is key to the success of any initiative, and we considered this to be even more important in relation to anti-racism. My research into diversity and inclusion and organisational cultures helped enormously in shaping the approach that was adopted in the plan. For example, we recognised the problematic nature of racialization and the ways in which this increases the difficulties in closing the implementation gap. Theoretically, this problem is linked to culture, which was the topic of my doctoral research and which remained my primary research area. I had spent most of my academic career theorising on culture and culture change and largely positioning my work on the idea that *planned* culture change (change in basic underlying assumptions or what is commonly referred to as 'hearts and minds' change) is difficult to achieve.

Juxtaposing this to our work on anti-racism led to the revisiting of two competing approaches in relation to closing the implementation gap; whether the implementation of the plan should rely on appealing to the goodness of individuals, organisations and institutions to do the right thing and embrace anti-racism (voluntarism), or whether individuals,

Annual Research Volume 2 – Complex Societal Impact Projects Requiring Tri-Sector Collaboration and Cooperation

Making Wales an Anti-racist Nation: A 'Public Value Mission' in Action
Emmanuel Ogbonna
....

organisations and institutions should be made accountable for their actions in allowing racism to thrive and should be nudged to do the right thing (compulsion). We held a series of roundtable events to discuss this and the issue also featured prominently in the public consultation events that were held on the plan. We argued that changing intractable identity issues such as those around racialization requires a different approach to be successful. This is because individual positions on identity (in this case race) tend to be relatively fixed, and such positions commonly require an element of compulsion to shift behaviours while trying to appeal to hearts and minds for sustained long-term change. The supporting argument here is that no similar change in history has been achieved without an element of compulsion. Indeed, it is arguable that slavery would have taken a lot longer to abolish had we waited for slave owners to change their hearts and minds. Similarly, equal pay for men and women may not have been secured in the UK and in other countries around the world if it had been left to the goodness of men to change their hearts and minds to promote organic change. We concluded that changing the visible manifestations of culture (behaviours, structures, systems and processes) could have longer-term ramifications through influencing the ways in which the deeper levels of culture (values, beliefs and assumptions) are interpreted and rationalised.

As the implementation process unfolds, we envisage that there will be challenges in managing the multiple and competing demands of the different stakeholders that are involved (the government, public institutions, businesses, white ethnic group and ethnic minority groups). We anticipate that members of ethnic minority groups who have been burdened by racism for so many generations will be impatient and expect change to be rapid and comprehensive. Conversely, businesses and institutions are likely to be concerned and may even protest against the perceived cost of any changes that will be required. The government is likely to grapple with its own internal culture challenges to ensure that it represents the beacon of good practice that it is encouraging others to emulate, and white society is likely to embrace a mixture of support, fear and anxiety as some may erroneously view this as a zero-sum game that disadvantages them. The success of the implementation group will partly be measured by how well it manages these competing interests and expectations and how quickly some of the important milestones in the plan are achieved.

CONCLUSION

In this concluding section, it is useful to highlight three key lessons that business and management schools may learn from this work. The first is the importance of shaking off the perception of academic hubris that has affected the nature and extent of networking and inter-personal relationships between business and management schools and external stakeholders, especially government agencies and the civil service. Ann S. Tsui has done an excellent job of articulating this problem and ways of improving it in previous issues of *Global Focus* but more work is required to establish the contemporary relevance of our scholarship and to link our work to the concerns of various stakeholders. My experience is that many senior civil servants are interested in collaborating with business and management academies in the same way they work with academies in the sciences and social sciences broadly defined.

The second and related issue is that we have to think about expanding the stakeholders we interact with beyond the traditional groups. Many researchers in business and management schools generate empirical data for their studies from managers and employees. However, in developing this plan, our most important source of data was the local ethnic minority groups. Our interaction with these stakeholders helped us to establish an evidential base and to highlight the importance of local community activism in change in ways that the traditional business and management research focus on formal organisations commonly preclude.

Annual Research Volume 2 – Complex Societal Impact Projects Requiring Tri-Sector Collaboration and Cooperation

Making Wales an Anti-racist Nation: A 'Public Value Mission' in Action
Emmanuel Ogbonna
....

The final lesson is in relation to the potential role of business and management schools in leading the change towards anti-racism. This role arises from the importance of business and management schools in producing students who go on to lead private and public sector organisations and in relation to the research areas and topics we study. Race has for too long been neglected as a topic of research and theorising in business and management. Indeed, Sadhvi Dar and her colleagues recently wrote a powerful piece that characterised the 'business school as racist', an accusation they base on the ways in which business schools commonly uphold and perpetuate 'white supremacy'. Business and management schools will require a radical re-think of their approach to race and racialization to shake off this highly negative image. They should begin by acknowledging the centrality of race and racialization in organising and incorporating this into mainstream theorising in business management. Mainstreaming understanding of racism should go beyond the current focus of research and behavioural scrutiny on ethnic minorities as victims of racism. This should extend to studying and scrutinising the behaviours of white people as those who perpetrate racism, who witness racism, who preside over systems that maintain racism and as those who have the power to effect meaningful change (see also Christian *et al.*, 2019). Similarly, business and management schools should seek to lead the charge on decolonisation by decolonising fully all the courses that are taught in such institutions. This will help to incorporate all cultures, values and histories in knowledge creation and development and encourage students and other learners to see the positive in 'difference' rather than finding this threatening.

Overall, the work we are doing in Wales is still at an early phase and it will take a few years to evaluate the success. However, what is certain is that this work presents an exciting example of the application of public value. Other business and management schools are encouraged to follow the example of Cardiff in extending their public value credentials to issues such as race and ethnicity that are traditionally neglected. In this regard, business and management schools can use their considerable power and influence to give voice to groups that are powerless and to help in promoting fairness and transforming society. The work to make Wales anti-racist is huge and is one that will face many obstacles and challenges. However, it is certain that the Anti-racist Wales initiative has laid the foundation for societal changes that are likely to be profound.

References

Anti-racist Wales Action Plan (www.gov.wales/anti-racist-wales-action-plan)

Blanchard, S. (2018) 'Black doctors are paid nearly £10,000 less than white colleagues as figures reveal the NHS's 'unacceptable barriers for ethnic minorities', https://www.dailymail.co.uk/health/article-6217377/Black-doctors-paid-nearly-10K-white-colleagues.html.

Christian, M., L. Seamster and V. Ray, (2019) 'New directions in critical race theory and sociology: Racism, white supremacy and resistance', *American Behavioural Scientist, 63,* 13, 1731-1740

Dar, S., H. Liu, A.M. Dy and D.N. Brewis (2021) 'The business school is racist: Act up', *Organisation, 28,* 4, 695-706

Kelley, N, O. Khan and S. Sharrock (2017) 'Racial prejudice in Britain today', *NatCen Social Research, London*

Macpherson, W. (1999) The Stephen Lawrence Inquiry, https://www.gov.uk/government/publications/the-stephen-lawrence-inquiry

McGregor-Smith, R. (2017) Race in the Workplace: The McGregor Smith Review, https://www.gov.uk/government/publications/race-in-the-workplace-the-mcgregor-smith-review

Mundasad, S. (2021) 'Black women four times more likely to die in childbirth', https://www.bbc.co.uk/news/health-59248345

Ogbonna, E. (2020) 'First Minister of Wales Black, Asian and minority ethnic COVID-19 socio-economic subgroup report', https://www.gov.wales/black-asian-and-minority-ethnic-covid-19-socioeconomic-subgroup-report

Resolution Foundation (2018). 'The 3.2bn pay penalty facing black and ethnic minority workers', www.resolutionfoundation.org/comment/the-3-2bn-pay-penalty-facing-black-and-ethnic-minority-workers/

The Guardian Newspaper (2023) 'Met police found to be institutionally racist, misogynistic and homophobic, 21 March

Tsui, A. S. (2022) 'Celebrating small wins and calling bold actions' *Global Focus 16*(1) pp. 34-42

About the Author

Emmanuel Ogbonna is Professor of Management and Organisation at Cardiff Business School, Cardiff University. Emmanuel has been elected to the Fellowships of the Academy of Social Sciences, the British Academy of Management, the Chartered Institute of Personnel and Development, and the Learned Society of Wales. He is a Trustee and Vice-Chair of Race Council Cymru.

Leaving the Theory Cave: Forays into Innovation Policy and Practice in Wales

RICK DELBRIDGE

Complex Societal Impact Projects Requiring Tri-Sector Collaboration and Cooperation

The field of management studies routinely finds itself in debates regarding the rigour and relevance of its research (for a brief overview, see Thomas, 2022). These debates have become more prominent and, some might argue, more urgent, as we contemplate wider social and environmental crises and the contribution, or lack thereof, made by the management research community in seeking to respond to these. Such debates have called into question the role of business schools and have also seen many leading academics review their own careers and contemplate whether they might have spent more time engaging with practice and seeking to deliver wider societal impact from their research. In this paper, I will reflect on some personal choices that I have made in the last few years which have indeed seen me depart from what my good friend Nicole Biggart described as the 'theory cave' in her own reflective essay (Biggart, 2016). While almost all of my research has been undertaken in partnership with others, this latest period in my career has seen me working more collaboratively with practitioners and in a more interdisciplinary manner. The emphasis has been on ways of designing and undertaking research that sees partners involved in both the conception and execution of activities. Moreover, there has been an explicit focus on societal challenges with the purpose of influencing policy and practice. In the short paper that follows, I organise a discussion of these activities under three headings: building institutional structures, nurturing partnerships, and a policy and problem focus for research. I then consider some of the implications of these issues for business schools and universities before closing with some more personal reflections.

BUILDING INSTITUTIONAL STRUCTURES

The first component of the developments that I've been involved in over the last decade or so in Cardiff that I want to outline is the work that colleagues and I have undertaken to develop new institutional structures that underpin a more impactful and interdisciplinary approach to research. The most prominent and innovative of these institutional developments has been the creation of sbarc|spark (1), our social science research park building located on the university's innovation campus in Cardiff (for a discussion of the social science park concept, see Price and Delbridge, 2015). From initial conception to promoting the proposal through the labyrinth of sometimes unsupportive and challenging university bureaucracy, the project took nine years to see the completion of the physical space within which I and up to 800 colleagues now work. The motivation for the initiative came both from internal university politics with a desire on the part of myself and other business school and social science colleagues to secure investment in our area of research, and also from a clear commitment to, and recognition of, the value of interdisciplinary work which draws together researchers from multiple disciplines and sees those researchers work intimately with practitioners from the very beginnings of research design. In itself the spark initiative was a response to a growing discourse in science policy around the importance of addressing societal problems or so-called 'grand challenges' in new ways. This discourse provided the basis for our proposal to develop a social science-led research facility which houses applied social science-led research groups alongside other disciplines, external research stakeholders and collaborators from the public, private, and third sectors. Central to the vision for spark was a recognition of the importance of physical spaces that are

DOI: 10.4324/9781003467410-13

Annual Research Volume 2 – Complex Societal Impact Projects Requiring Tri-Sector Collaboration and Cooperation

Leaving the Theory Cave: Forays into Innovation Policy and Practice in Wales
Rick Delbridge
....

designed to encourage creative interaction, promote serendipity and conversations, and encourage the adoption of collaborative approaches to research, which in turn provide novel ways of thinking about what are by now well-established societal challenges.

More fundamentally spark was born of a view that we need to create new spaces, new organisational forms, new ways of producing *practical* knowledge, if we are to address these pressing societal challenges. The social science research park we have constructed in Cardiff is a physical space but also represents an investment in seeking to develop collaborative relations, building the trust and developing the shared understanding needed to work in disruptively innovative ways. Cardiff University, the city of Cardiff and Wales are fertile settings for this initiative since the university has considerable strength and depth in social science research. Researchers have good working relationships with local and national institutions and with Welsh Government, and the nation itself is both home to many of the challenges that society is facing, while being of a scale where pressing societal needs may be addressed through policy development.

Sbarc|spark is now home to 16 research institutes and centres which address a range of issues from sustainability and climate change through children's mental health and public health to education, civil society, the economy and public policy amongst others. Each of these centres has strong social science components but also contains researchers from a wide range of disciplines. For example, the collaboration of computer scientists and social scientists has been very productive in the areas of security, crime and intelligence, and cyber innovation. Alongside the physical spaces, the university has also extended its commitments to innovation and impact through the creation of innovation institutes, two of which are located in the spark building. The university's business engagement and commercialisation teams are also in sbarc|spark. It should be acknowledged that, while sbarc|spark is a space that is manifestly dedicated to novelty, it is governed according to some very traditional metrics by the university administration and there is a danger that these will stifle innovativeness and creativity. I return to these issues in a later section.

Personally, having spent seven years as the university's Dean of Research, Innovation and Enterprise and as the academic lead for the development of spark throughout this period, I took the opportunity to return to a more conventional academic role in the school and university and established a new Centre for Innovation Policy Research with colleagues from the Business School and also the schools of Geography and Planning and Social Sciences (2).

The centre has become my intellectual home, where I am working in a more interdisciplinary and policy-focused way with a particular emphasis on place and the importance of geographic and political systems in understanding how management research can contribute to practical developments in seeking to respond to societal challenges. While, as noted above, science policy discourse has for at least a decade talked the talk of interdisciplinarity and impact, it has to be said that both funders and universities have often failed to show the imagination and ambition needed to do things differently in practice. The physical space of sbarc|spark contributes to these ambitions but it is also important to note the organisational structures that are crucial in facilitating and supporting interdisciplinary research.

NURTURING PARTNERSHIPS

Creating new knowledge across disciplinary boundaries and seeking to deliver practical impact from these insights requires the development of partnerships both within the academy and beyond. The sbarc|spark initiative builds on research that has shown previously the importance of co-location and proximity in facilitating the conversations and the building of the social relationships that can underpin disruptive innovation. My own previous research has emphasised the importance of trust and a sense of shared enterprise in seeking discontinuous innovation (for a summary see Price and Delbridge, 2015). Alongside around 400 researchers when fully occupied, the sbarc|spark building will be home to approximately the same number of people who work in external organisations. These organisations apply to move into the building and we seek to identify those with the most to gain from co-locating with researchers and the most to offer to that community of researchers, both within the building and more widely across the university. To date, space has been highly sought after and we have seen a range of different organisations move in.

In my own case, a large part of my activity in the last few years has been undertaken working alongside my centre colleagues in collaboration with the Cardiff Capital Region (CCR) (3). The CCR is one of our community members in the sbarc|spark building and indeed their offices sit just across the way on the same floor where CIPR is located. The primary area of work that we have collaborated on over the past three years has been in the design and development of a new Local Wealth Building Challenge Fund (4). The challenge fund was developed in part at least as a response to the challenges that had been brought by the COVID-19 pandemic and has focused on seeking to identify new and innovative solutions to problems experienced by the public and third sector in the areas of health and well-being,

Annual Research Volume 2 – Complex Societal Impact Projects Requiring Tri-Sector Collaboration and Cooperation

Leaving the Theory Cave: Forays into Innovation Policy and Practice in Wales
Rick Delbridge
....

sustainability and decarbonisation, and in transforming local communities. The fund was developed as a novel approach, drawing on challenge-led innovation, in seeking to address societal challenges and create new commercial opportunities for businesses within the region and beyond. While drawing on established practices of procuring innovation such as the Small Business Research Initiative (SBRI), the partnership between the university and the Cardiff Capital Region allowed for the development of a bespoke and novel approach. Our intention is both to deliver solutions to individual challenges and also to develop greater capacity and capability for challenge-led innovation in the public sector and more widely in the region.

Building from the initial partnership between the university and the Cardiff Capital Region, the challenge fund then developed further partnerships around specific challenges which allowed the development and delivery of innovative solutions. For example, our first challenge saw us fund two small technology firms who developed virtual reality and immersive technology solutions to the challenge of training medical staff in clinical procedures during the COVID-19 pandemic (5). Delivering this challenge involved us partnering with the local health board and also with Welsh Government's Centre of Excellence in SBRI. Such partnerships are vital in delivering this form of challenge-oriented innovation and have not always been easy to develop, particularly given the major time constraints that practitioners in both the public and private sector have been facing. As the university partner, we have had a role in both the design and delivery of the challenge fund and also in nurturing a community of practice within the region, and building an evidence base on what has worked and not worked in the initiative to date. We have also played a wider role in working alongside senior colleagues in the CCR as they seek to develop their innovation policies and develop inclusive economic growth activities to deliver on their goals under the city deal funding from the UK Government.

A POLICY AND PROBLEM FOCUS FOR RESEARCH

The experience of working with the Cardiff Capital Region brings me to my third point of reflection with regards to how my own research objectives have developed as I ventured beyond the theory cave with interests that were more exclusively focused on generating knowledge and theoretical contributions within the academy. Being able to contribute to policy development both specifically through our work on the challenge fund but more generally as experts, informal advisers, and friends to the senior leaders of the Cardiff Capital Region has provided an energising opportunity to reflect on how the work of management researchers can be incorporated into policies and practices that speak to delivering public value and societal benefit.

Along with outlining empirical evidence and past research findings, academic researchers can contribute through their analytical focus and through 'in-the-moment theorising' of discussions in ways that can help make both the implications and conclusions of these discussions more tangible. For example, in seeking to offer a useful framing for the Cardiff Capital Region's discussions around innovation policy I have coined a 4Cs framework that seeks to both reflect, as well as offer potential guidance on how the policies might be developed into the future. Each of these four Cs have an underpinning in an academic literature ranging across management, organisation and innovation studies, and has also benefited from input from colleagues with far greater knowledge of regional economic development and the governance and politics of such undertakings than I have.

THE 4CS OF REGIONAL INNOVATION POLICY

Clusters: investment in perceived areas of comparative strength is a well-established component of regional innovation policy. Such clusters are typically defined in sectoral or technological terms and are sometimes criticised for being too technology-led and linear. In our discussions with CCR, we have been keen to highlight the unpredictable nature of innovation and to encourage a 'portfolio' approach rather than having all the eggs in a very small number of baskets. We have also stressed that a capacious understanding of innovation and an acknowledgement of the different types of value that may be created is important for policy to deliver on the needs of our citizens.

PHOTO COURTESY DELBRIDGE

Annual Research Volume 2 – Complex Societal Impact Projects Requiring Tri-Sector Collaboration and Cooperation

Leaving the Theory Cave: Forays into Innovation Policy and Practice in Wales
Rick Delbridge
....

Commons: this component emphasises the processes of cooperation and resource pooling which are seen as the initial 'raw material' and 'pre-conditions' of entrepreneurship and innovation (Potts, 2019). The concept of innovation commons is defined as a space for, and a means of, sharing data, information and knowledge in order to facilitate learning and discovery. Key aspects include the openness of data and availability of resources, connectivity and the skills and capabilities needed to mobilise these (6). The commons can be seen as the 'hedge bet' on the basics of future innovation activity from which future clusters may emerge.

There are two further elements that speak to the 'ecosystem' conception of place-based innovation policy.

Catalysts: innovation policies need to ensure that there are a range of ways in which innovation is catalysed and supported. And that this is done in ways that complement and extend the investment in clusters, address local needs and opportunities, and balances risk. The example above of the Local Wealth Building Challenge Fund is such a catalytic intervention. Challenge-oriented innovation is closely associated with the mission approach that has been gaining considerable traction in innovation policy circles, primarily through the advocacy of Mariana Mazzucato (7). Our experience to date suggests that regional interventions maybe better constructed as 'micro-missions' in order to both more accurately reflect the narrower focus of what is currently being undertaken but also to make such initiatives more comprehensible and identifiable for those who are needed to engage and contribute to the endeavour (Henderson, Morgan and Delbridge, 2023). There is thus a balance to be struck between scale of ambition and practical delivery.

The importance of collaboration and partnerships has been outlined above and our first-hand experience in working to deliver on the policy into practice front has underscored this. Consequently, this means that a final key component is the capacity of a region to deliver on its innovation agenda.

Capacity: absorptive capacity has long been acknowledged as a key feature of innovation. Innovation at any level relies on actors' abilities to recognise and apply knowledge in order to produce value. In our work with the CCR, we have sought to develop elements of regional innovative capacity through working with local organisations including local authorities and health boards. These elements include promoting an understanding of innovation practices, encouraging a willingness to experiment and take risks, and, at the most basic level, finding the time and resources needed to engage in innovative activity. These are crucial components in the capacity of a region to be innovative and need to be explicitly recognised in regional innovation policies.

These four elements of innovation policy have also been informing work that colleagues and I have undertaken for the Welsh Government (8) as it has been developing its recently announced new innovation strategy (9) and also for the local authority of Carmarthenshire for whom we produced an innovation report (10) which has been developed into a strategy for the county. We have also recently completed a report for the Innovation Caucus (11) comparing innovation and regional economic growth activity in Cardiff, Glasgow and Manchester city regions. Alongside these reports, I've also been working with the Learned Society of Wales as the President's adviser on research and innovation in order to provide insights that may be of use in the development of the innovation agenda in Wales. The primary mechanism to date has been to draw insight from a variety of sources which are then developed through roundtable discussions with invited fellows from the Learned Society, key stakeholders and external guest speakers. These have then been captured in a series of briefing notes which cover a variety of different subjects with the intention of contributing to the wider debates around how Wales might improve its capacity for innovation and seek to ensure that future activity and policy is informed by lessons from other small and innovative nations (12).

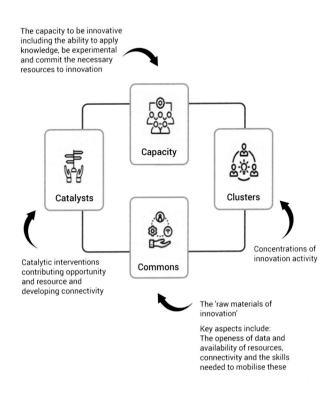

The capacity to be innovative including the ability to apply knowledge, be experimental and commit the necessary resources to innovation

Capacity

Catalysts

Clusters

Commons

Catalytic interventions contributing opportunity and resource and developing connectivity

Concentrations of innovation activity

The 'raw materials of innovation'

Key aspects include: The openess of data and availability of resources, connectivity and the skills needed to mobilise these

Figure 1 The 4 Cs of Innovation Policy

Annual Research Volume 2 – Complex Societal Impact Projects Requiring Tri-Sector Collaboration and Cooperation

Leaving the Theory Cave: Forays into Innovation Policy and Practice in Wales
Rick Delbridge
....

IMPLICATIONS FOR BUSINESS SCHOOLS AND UNIVERSITIES

Previous work has argued that business school scholars have found themselves in a publication imperative 'iron cage' with the result that little academic work has impact on practice (Johnson and Starkey, 2022). If more academics are to engage with the sort of problem and policy-focused research that I have outlined, we will need to see scholars not just leave the theory cave but escape this iron cage. Such endeavour will need the support of senior leaders and it is no coincidence that my 'journey' was undertaken as a senior academic with management responsibility. From such a role, I had more autonomy than most and I was actively involved in seeking to create a more conducive context for such work. Along with the institutional changes described above that have been pursued in Cardiff, we have also developed, over the last few years, a new public value strategy for our business school, which puts research with societal purpose at the heart of the school's activities (see Kitchener and Ashworth, 2022). We have discussed some of the wider institutional challenges that needed to be overcome in navigating this course in detail elsewhere (*ibid*). There has been considerable debate over whether and how business schools need to change if they are to deliver more impactful research. And I will not reiterate these here but suffice to say that without institutional support, the future generations of business school scholars may well find themselves pursuing the impact and societal benefit of their research despite, rather than because of, their institutions (Baudoin *et al.*, 2022).

Beyond business schools, there remains a very important and parallel discussion over universities' role as key local actors in their economic and innovation ecosystems which is perhaps less evident to readers. In our own research (8,11), participants have recognised the important role of universities as 'anchor institutions', sources of continuity, and providers of skills and knowledge as part of a functioning 'triple helix' in collaboration with government and business. Indeed, the sbarc|spark initiative was intended to support such activity and strengthen the university's capacity to act as a 'convenor' for the region and as a collaborator with external partners. But there have also been critics who identify that universities are driven by research and funding priorities and are poor listeners; one comment that resonated was that universities are only interested in research-led innovation, not innovation-led research. As I noted above, sbarc|spark has been integrated into the established university bureaucracy and its conventional performance metrics in ways that might impede rather than encourage innovation and experimentation. While it would be churlish to complain too loudly given the backing that the university has provided to the spark initiative, it is the case that, along with most if not all UK higher education institutions, we have become more centralised and increasingly less agile, innovative and responsive over the time that spark was in gestation. It is vital that resources and decision-making authority are invested in those working closely with practitioners if the potential of universities to deliver on inclusive economic regeneration and innovation is to be realised.

SOME FINAL REFLECTIONS

In some ways these are still fairly early days in my research life beyond the theory cave. And I hope I have conveyed that I have not abandoned theory so much as more actively sought to have that theory and underpinning conceptual work inform research that is driven by problems and seeks to be impactful on policy and practice. From my experiences to date, I would observe that a practical, societal challenge-focus emphasises the value of inter-disciplinarity and the absolute need to work collaboratively. I would also say that experience has shown the tension between seeking to move at pace and the benefits of patience in thinking, planning and building the understanding and relationships that are necessary. Second, I would say that the expertise of management and organisation researchers is potentially valuable (and welcomed) but that we need to be good at listening as well as talking. As my colleagues might attest, there has been some need for this old dog to learn new tricks along the way ... Third, as the latest round of inward-looking management studies debate on the purpose, relevance and rigour swirl, I would say that it seems ever clearer to me that new, innovative and ambitious approaches are needed when it comes to policy (and much more besides), but that policy remains a crucial mechanism through which our research can potentially benefit our citizens. And finally, I will borrow some words from my colleague and friend Alessia Contu (2020) who once concluded her talk on intellectual activism in a session to which I also contributed, thus: "It is hard to do but it is also joyous and hopeful." So, when foraying from the theory cave, travel in hope and I wish you some joy.

References

Baudion, N., S. Carmine, L. Nava, N. Poggioli and O.M. van den Broek (2022) Imagining a place for sustainability management: An early career call for action, *Journal of Management Studies, 60*(3) pp.754-760

Biggart, N. W. (2016) 'Biggart's lament, or getting out of the theory cave', *Journal of Management Studies, 53*(8) pp.138-1387

Contu, A. (2020) 'Answering the crisis with intellectual activism: Making a difference as business school scholars', *Human Relations, 73*(1) pp.737-757

Henderson, D., K. Morgan and R. Delbridge (2023) 'Putting missions in their place: Micro missions and the role of universities in delivering challenge-led innovation', *Regional Studies*, https://doi.org/10.1080/00343404.2023.2176840

Johnson, G. and K. Starkey (2022) 'How management academics have locked themselves in an iron cage', *EFMD Global Focus, Vol 1*. Brussels

Kitchener, M. and R. Delbridge (2020) 'Lessons from creating a business school for public good: Obliquity, waysetting and wayfinding in substantively rational change. *Academy of Management Learning and Education 19* pp.307-322

Kitchener, M. and R. Ashworth (2022) 'Building back better – Purpose-driven business schools', *EFMD Global Focus, Vol 1*. Brussels

Potts, J. (2019) *Innovation Commons: The Origin of Economic Growth*. Oxford University Press

Price, A. and R. Delbridge (2015) *Social Science Parks: Society's New SuperLlabs*. London: Nesta

Thomas, H. (2022) 'Perspectives on the impact, mission and purpose of the business school' *EFMD Global Focus, Vol 1*. Brussels

Weblinks

1. https://www.cardiff.ac.uk/social-science-research-park
2. https://www.cardiff.ac.uk/research/explore/research-units/centre-for-innovation-policy-research
3. https://www.cardiffcapitalregion.wales
4. https://www.challengefund.wales
5. https://www.challengefund.wales/?playlist=9a4a98a&video=b521d5d
6. https://www.learnedsociety.wales/our-publications/innovation-commons-the-raw-materials-of-innovation/
7. https://www.ucl.ac.uk/bartlett/public-purpose/research/mission-oriented-innovation
8. https://businesswales.gov.wales/innovation/sites/innovation/files/documents/MASTER%20COPY%20-%20Scoping%20innovation%20policy%20in%20Wales_final%20report_19th%20May%20final.pdf
9. https://www.gov.wales/innovation-strategy-wales
10. https://www.carmarthenshire.gov.wales/media/1231175/local-innovation-strategy.pdf
11. https://innovationcaucus.co.uk/2023/06/15/regional-economic-growth-through-innovation-policy-and-business-engagement-evidence-from-three-uk-city-regions/
12. https://www.learnedsociety.wales/our-publications/lessons-from-small-innovative-nations/

About the Author

Rick Delbridge is Professor of Organisational Analysis and co-convenor of the Centre for Innovation Policy Research, Cardiff University. While the university's Dean of Research, Innovation and Enterprise, he led the development of sbarc|spark, the social science research park, which opened last year.

Empowering Vulnerable Populations Through Transformative Approaches and Research

LUCIANO BARIN-CRUZ, NADIA PONCE MORALES, KATE PICONE
& LAURENCE BEAUGRAND-CHAMPAGNE

Complex Societal Impact Projects Requiring Tri-Sector Collaboration and Cooperation

Two years ago, HEC Montréal launched the result of numerous consultations that led to updating its mission: to building on our excellence in teaching and research, HEC Montréal is a French-language institution open to the world and solidly rooted in Quebec society, training management leaders who make a responsible contribution to the success of organisations and to sustainable social development. HEC Montréal's renewed mission echoes the willingness of faculty members to rethink business practices to make them more sustainable and more inclusive. The SEED project is a case study within HEC Montréal's research ecosystem led by our Social Impact Hub, IDEOS, that illustrates how rethinking research methods and collaborations across sectors and across cultures can amplify opportunities for the economic empowerment of vulnerable populations.

ABOUT HEC MONTRÉAL'S SOCIAL IMPACT HUB—IDEOS

The mission of IDEOS — *Social Impact Hub at HEC* Montréal is to raise awareness and provide support for the HEC Montréal community, organisations, and entrepreneurs, as well as to disseminate knowledge by placing social impact at the heart of its actions.

IDEOS addresses two main issues that have surfaced from the results of its research and transfer projects, business coaching projects, and collaborations with various stakeholders. These issues include the need to professionalise civil society organisations and social enterprises[1], as well as the need to mainstream social impact into more traditional business models. Both the increasing numbers and diversity of organisations with a social mission, and the inclusion of social and environmental dimensions into for-profit organisations drive IDEOS' activities, which include training, coaching, and research and transfer programmes.

ABOUT THE SEED PROJECT AND ITS METHODOLOGY

Scaling Entrepreneurship for Economic Development (SEED) exemplifies IDEOS' approach and its positive effects. SEED leverages research, as well as local expertise and knowledge, to enhance the capacities of local partners in different countries (Sri Lanka, Haiti, Tunisia and Colombia) supporting micro-enterprises as a key driver for local development. In addition to working with local partners, SEED brings together Desjardins International Development (DID)[2], international funding agencies and three scholars from three partner universities: University of Navarra, University of Alberta, and University of Michigan[3].

The goal of SEED is to create a network of international and local promoters of entrepreneurship programmes, as well as international and local researchers with expertise in entrepreneurial scaling. The purpose of this cross-sector partnership is to lead and mobilise research using field experiments and business cases to create a validated methodology to develop the capacities of local promoters in addressing the barriers often experienced by micro-enterprises. The methodology developed in the context of these field experiments is shared with local promoters in different contexts to multiply its impacts.

Below, the four different phases of the SEED projects will be outlined while detailing the different actions and activities that are undertaken in each specific phase. It is important to note that prior to starting Phase 1, the initial agreement with DID, the local partner institution, the SEED research team, and the international funding agencies involved, has already been approved and agreed upon by the different partners in the project. Likewise, prior to initiating Phase 1, there has been an identification of the target population and the geographic area of the intervention. In this way, the principal elements guiding the start of the project are known to all partners involved.

DOI: 10.4324/9781003467410-14

Annual Research Volume 2 – Complex Societal Impact Projects Requiring Tri-Sector Collaboration and Cooperation

Empowering Vulnerable Populations Through Transformative Approaches and Research
Luciano Barin-Cruz, Nadia Ponce Morales, Kate Picone & Laurence Beaugrand-Champagne

PHASE 1: EXPLORATORY PHASE—UNDERSTANDING THE ECOSYSTEM

Phase 1 is the exploratory research phase. This phase is usually undertaken over a period of approximately two months while collaborating with the international and local partners involved in the project. This phase consists of an extensive literature review, and interviews with key informants, to better comprehend the entrepreneurial ecosystem of the project's target population. The literature review is conducted by the research team, and supported by DID and the local partners, giving access to the most recent documentation and reports about the local entrepreneurial ecosystem. The interviews in this phase are conducted with a variety of stakeholders to obtain a multifaceted perspective of the ecosystem. These interviews are conducted with persons from the target population (for example, women entrepreneurs), as well as other key stakeholders, such as members of the local partner organisation, other entrepreneurship support organisations, regional experts from international or local NGOs, and academics from local universities, etc. The information gathered in Phase 1 from the literature review and stakeholder interviews will aid to identify the barriers and challenges that the target population faces. These preliminary insights on the barriers and gaps in service offerings that have been identified in the ecosystem are compiled and presented by the SEED research team to the partner institutions.

PHASE 2: CO-DEVELOPMENT OF TRAINING CONTENT WITH LOCAL PARTNERS AND TRAINERS

Once all the partners involved in the project have a clear vision of the challenges to be addressed, **Phase 2** commences. This phase is crucial, as it consists of the co-design of the entrepreneurship training programme with local partners and a selection of trainers who will be responsible for delivery. During this four-to-six-month phase, two distinct versions of the training programme are created in an iterative fashion, both of which will be tested with the selected population, allowing comparison of quantitative data collected during the delivery of the training, and qualitative data collected in semi-structured interviews post-delivery. The training of the trainers delivering the programme (ToT) and a pilot are also conducted during this phase. The pilot is used to test the different training programmes with a small group of entrepreneurs to get final feedback before delivery. Sometimes, the research team is present when both the ToT and a pilot are conducted.

PHASE 3: DELIVERY OF TRAINING PROGRAMME AND DATA COLLECTION

Phase 3 consists of the delivery of the training programme which takes place over a period of four-to-eight weeks and applies an experiment approach. During this period, the two distinct training programmes mentioned above are delivered to entrepreneurs randomly distributed in different groups by trainers who have also been randomly assigned. Trainers are usually paired with other trainers or project managers from local promoters who have a deep understanding of the project to secure quality in the delivery. Throughout the delivery, the participants fill out multiple data collection forms, providing the research team with baseline data and information about potential variation on dependent variables. The data from these forms are then used for quantitative analysis to uncover significant patterns in the research variables of interest.

PHASE 4: LEARNING EXPERIENCE WITH PARTNERS

Phase 4 involves conducting semi-structured interviews with an extensive range of stakeholders with different roles within the local entrepreneurial ecosystem. Several weeks after the delivery of the training programme, the research team interviews stakeholders over a period of one to two months. Some interviews take place online to accommodate stakeholders' availability, but most interviews are carried out in person. Once all quantitative and qualitative data is collected, it is analysed by the SEED research team to extract key findings relative to the effects of the programme on different variables of interest. These findings and subsequent recommendations are shared with the project partners. Local entrepreneurship promoters can then apply these recommendations to scale up the training content and format that has been validated through this analysis. Moreover, promoters can consider the evidence-supported success factor in their delivery to the target populations.

Annual Research Volume 2 – Complex Societal Impact Projects Requiring Tri-Sector Collaboration and Cooperation

Empowering Vulnerable Populations Through Transformative Approaches and Research
Luciano Barin-Cruz, Nadia Ponce Morales, Kate Picone & Laurence Beaugrand-Champagne
....

IMPLEMENTATION AND EMPOWERMENT OF ENTREPRENEURS IN MULTIPLE COUNTRIES

Over the last five years, we had the chance to apply this methodology entirely or partially in four different countries: Sri Lanka, Tunisia, Colombia and Haiti. We have implemented all four phases described in the last section in these countries except for Haiti.

In **Sri Lanka**, we collaborated with a local organisation called Sanasa (local financial cooperative) and started developing a case study methodology to understand barriers and opportunities for rural entrepreneurs, especially women. Based on this work, we designed, in collaboration with Sanasa, a field experimental training programme, which we tested among more than 500 entrepreneurs. Our findings allowed Sanasa to test the efficacy of the training before rolling it out to more than 8,000 rural entrepreneurs in Sri Lanka[4].

In **Tunisia**, and in partnership with a local organisation called "Centre Financier aux Entrepreneurs (CFE)", we first undertook an exploratory phase to better understand how formal institutions create opportunities and constraints for women entrepreneurs. We then developed, in collaboration with CFE, a pilot training programme to address some of the limits and opportunities we had observed in the first phase. We deployed a field experiment in three cities to test our two training programmes with 150 women entrepreneurs. Based on our results, the CFE training programme was adapted and replicated in another eight cities in the country, impacting a further 350 women in one year[5].

In **Colombia**, we also started with an exploratory phase and, in collaboration with a local organisation called Finanfuturo, we identified barriers for women's entrepreneurship in the region of Manizales. Based on this, we co-created a training programme with Finanfuturo to improve women entrepreneurs' capacity to innovate, grow their businesses, and enhance their personal empowerment. We followed with a field experiment, testing the trained (treatment) against a control group with more than 150 women entrepreneurs, evaluating the impact of the training on the main dependent variables. The programme is currently in preparation to be scaled up.

In **Haiti**, the project consisted only of the first phase, as the project responded to one specific need of the local organisation: mapping the entrepreneurial ecosystem. In this way, we could better understand the formal institutions in the country promoting or creating barriers for entrepreneurial activity. This project involved 50 local organisations offering entrepreneurship support and 50 entrepreneurs[6]. A follow-up project will be deployed in 2024 to develop a field experiment and test different ways to work on the capacity to innovate entrepreneurs, their growth aspirations, and feelings of empowerment.

These projects have allowed us to implement our mixed-method approach through our four phases methodology. We saw that we could bring our rigorous research-oriented approach to support DID and local organisations in supporting entrepreneurs in marginalised conditions.

THE IMPORTANCE AND IMPACT OF SEED'S METHODOLOGY

The development of these types of projects using this methodological structure is important and pertinent for projects in multiple contexts. Each context exhibits its own unique barriers that inhibit the development of entrepreneurs and the growth of businesses. Thus, using this methodology, it is possible to navigate the idiosyncrasies of each context, tailoring it to the entrepreneurs' realities.

One of the key elements that make this methodology effective is its adaptability. This methodology leaves space for creativity, according to the needs of each project where adaptation is achieved through co-creation with local actors. This co-creation involves both the academic experts in entrepreneurship, as well as the local entrepreneurship promoters who are experts in their local entrepreneurial environment. It is crucial to note as well that using a strategic external partner, such as the SEED research team, composed of researchers based in Canada, the USA, and Europe, and not developing the projects directly with the funding agencies, helps to address power imbalances that can be present in development projects.

Likewise, the Training-of-trainers (ToT) is an important element in enhancing the capacity of local entrepreneurship promoters. This is significant as the local experts are part of the content development process which begins in Phase 2. The trainers are directly involved in the development of the training content and are instrumental in contextualising the contents and adapting them to their entrepreneurial environment. This has proven to be vital in the positive reception of the programmes by the local target population as the content caters to their context. Working with the trainers on the development of the content helps with creating examples tailored to the field, adapting exercises and homework suitable for the target population, as well as best translating the training to the local language or dialect.

Through the training of local experts throughout the whole project process, and specifically in the ToT, the knowledge created stays in-country. In this way, the local partners take ownership of the project throughout the different phases. For each country, once the project ends, it is possible for the local partner to continue delivering the training to a greater number of entrepreneurs in the local context as they have access to all the training materials. Throughout the process, they become the content experts capable of continuing to deliver the programme without further intervention from development entities.

Annual Research Volume 2 — Complex Societal Impact Projects Requiring Tri-Sector Collaboration and Cooperation

Empowering Vulnerable Populations Through Transformative Approaches and Research
Luciano Barin-Cruz, Nadia Ponce Morales, Kate Picone & Laurence Beaugrand-Champagne
··················

In terms of academic impact, SEED allows the research team to work on three main outputs. First, research papers are prepared based on collected data and are submitted to conferences and top-tier journals. The significance of this element lies in the fact that generating and disseminating knowledge is a crucial aspect of a scholar's professional journey. Second, PhD and Masters students participate in the projects, using data to produce their dissertations and having the opportunity of exposure to action research, societal impact, and publication opportunities. Finally, concepts, models, and lessons learned in these projects by scholars participating in the projects are used back in their own universities and integrated in courses and seminars provided to students in the Global North.

TOWARDS A MORE EQUITABLE ACCESS TO EDUCATION AND GREATER ECONOMIC AUTONOMY

Capacity-building is at the heart of the SEED project, which provides various opportunities to build bridges across the development and academic sectors. The approach used in this methodology provides valuable insights into how action research collaborations can be more inclusive, empowering community groups that have traditionally been excluded by conventional top-down training or technical expertise transfer models. By creating a platform for recognising and utilising local expertise and facilitating cross-sectoral, cross-country, and cross-cultural collaboration, the SEED methodology enables the development of local capacity, gradually reducing reliance on external funding and expertise.

It is important to highlight that DID is part of a broader set of international NGOs in Canada that, over the years, have sent abroad thousands of volunteers interested in lending their time and sharing their expertise to support local communities. However, as Tiessen *et al.* (2021) point out, very little research has focused on the complementary contributions of international development volunteers in local community development efforts[7]. In practical terms, given the complexity of the international volunteer sector, few resources are allocated to research efforts that provide evidence to allow for a continuous improvement of capacity-building methodologies and testing new models based on rigorous data and analysis. A direct collaboration between researchers with different areas of expertise provides DID's local partners with access to knowledge and expertise that would be difficult to find, and to fund. Country partners have access to research findings and can provide feedback.

One of the elements that make the SEED project unique is its approach to partnerships across sectors and across the North-South divide. Through a meaningful engagement of communities throughout the project, it provides enabling conditions for new knowledge creation, while also avoiding any imposition of methodologies that may not be appropriate for the cultural context in the countries where the project operates. As explained above, the contents of the training are co-constructed with local partners, allowing for consideration of the multiple realities of target populations who are traditionally excluded from mainstream financial or business incubation services, such as women and youth. These practices allow alternative approaches to capacity development to emerge increasing the agency of local partners, as opposed to considering them as mere beneficiaries of a technical expertise transfer project. The SEED methodology also allows the integration of elements of capacity development that are key for the economic empowerment of vulnerable populations, such as challenging gender norms or deeply ingrained social norms that hinder entrepreneurship. Participants in SEED training and research activities become part of a larger social innovation ecosystem.

This broad social innovation ecosystem spreads to communities in Canada as well. HEC Montréal IDEOS has applied key lessons learned with communities overseas to its collaboration with different partner organisations in Canada that work with underserved communities. One success factor that has been observed in projects supported by the SEED network is the support for identifying community assets, which include knowledge, skills, and social networks, for the benefit of their enterprises, and also for themselves. Constructing training and entrepreneurship incubation programmes and projects collaboratively, with the aim of fostering social capital within communities, has

Annual Research Volume 2 – Complex Societal Impact Projects Requiring Tri-Sector Collaboration and Cooperation

Empowering Vulnerable Populations Through Transformative Approaches and Research
Luciano Barin-Cruz, Nadia Ponce Morales, Kate Picone & Laurence Beaugrand-Champagne
....

proven to be an effective method for empowering individuals from racialized communities or those with a recent history of immigration. Additionally, it generates knowledge on the critical factors that enable the development of a thriving entrepreneurial ecosystem, facilitating the transition from subsistence to market-oriented entrepreneurship. Finally, a very practical but important consideration is the funding structure of the project. The SEED research team does not directly interact with the project funders (in the current case, Global Affairs Canada) responsible for developing the initiatives. DID assumes the responsibility of allocating funding for activities in the countries where it operates, in accordance with its commitments to the funding organisation. This feature helps lessen the power imbalances that result from differences in access to resources between researchers situated in Canada and Europe, and local experts in developing countries. Although this is an element that cannot always be put in place in international development projects, it is important to acknowledge that such programme characteristics can influence the pace at which local partners and communities can build trust and an equal relationship with experts from developed countries.

WHAT TO EXPECT: THE FUTURE OF SEED AND ITS CONTRIBUTION TO THE INTERNATIONAL DEVELOPMENT SECTOR

From a broader perspective, our project contributes to current efforts to challenge international development interventions lacking intersectional analysis that could improve how investments and programmes are designed and targeted. Intersectional analysis and an approach that focuses on capabilities (Sen, 2000) helps develop the creation of opportunities, awareness, and mobilisation for poor, marginalised, and vulnerable people to access skills, resources, and knowledge to participate in their local economic development[8]. Our work addresses both the individual and the collective capabilities that create together an enabling environment for under-represented groups, such as women and youth to thrive.

Our work is particularly relevant in light of the current knowns and unknowns of economic development. We know that even in the best employment situations, population groups that are in a situation of marginalisation face persistent barriers to fully participate in the labour market[9]. We also know that the effects of climate change and of the COVID-19 pandemic have had a disproportionate effect on women and youth, among other vulnerable groups. We also know that unprecedented technological advances, will continue to affect the labour and economic possibilities for populations with unequal access to education and skills development opportunities.

Due to the level of uncertainty linked to market transformations, the international development sector must find new ways of supporting marginalised populations seeking to build sustainable livelihoods. We know that the creation of small and medium-sized businesses by groups such as women and youth can be a powerful solution for self-employment creation while promoting local economic growth. The stimulation of entrepreneurship and an environment that fosters a democratisation of productivity (Thomas & Hedrick-Wong, 2019), that is allowing vulnerable populations access not only to basic inputs, but also to 'enabling inputs' (e.g., financial services) and 'complementary assets' (social capital, knowledge, professional networks, knowledge, and skills networks)[10] should be a key priority for the international development sector and its partners.

Going forward, we envision three main goals for the SEED project to increase its impact.

First, we want SEED to be a laboratory to test and refine a research collaboration approach that surpasses the current divide between those who believe that interventions from the North can solve issues in the South and those who claim that these types of intervention represent new forms of 'colonialism'. We do not claim to transfer knowledge to under-skilled populations, and we want to avoid imposing a specific economic model or ideology on populations in the Global South. We aim at co-creating knowledge with partner communities, local organisations, and partners that can be used both in the South and in the North. At the same time, we recognise that any form of intervention from groups coming from the North (with resources and scientific knowledge) imposes forms of power and can create asymmetric relations. However, we also believe that being conscious and reflective about it, we can create mechanisms to reduce power asymmetries and allow for more truthful collaboration, where each actor can bring their own contribution.

Annual Research Volume 2 – Complex Societal Impact Projects Requiring Tri-Sector Collaboration and Cooperation

Empowering Vulnerable Populations Through Transformative Approaches and Research
Luciano Barin-Cruz, Nadia Ponce Morales, Kate Picone & Laurence Beaugrand-Champagne
....

Second, we want to support entrepreneurs in marginalised conditions to be part of the global movement on socio-ecological transitions. We acknowledge the urgency for action if we want to reverse the current trends contributing to the climate crisis. Local organisations and entrepreneurs are disproportionately impacted by climate change while being able to access fewer resources. We want to contribute to climate justice and support entrepreneurs to adapt or be creators of solutions that will help their regions to mitigate the effects of climate change.

Third, we want to be sure that more students can participate in our projects, both from the North and South. Up until now, we have engaged mostly students from Masters and PhD programmes, usually from universities in the North, with a few exceptions. We see SEED as a platform to train students to conduct meaningful research that can have an impact at multiple levels (practice, research, teaching, societal, etc.). Allowing students from North and South to work in collaboration is a promising avenue to strengthen knowledge circulation and increase the impact of our projects.

The notion of SEED as a laboratory for experimentation with diverse approaches, content, and methodologies points to a promising future where research, teaching, and outreach are integrated and aligned towards achieving tangible impact.

Footnotes

[1] Québec's Social Economy Act adopted in 2013 institutionalises the social economy sector in the province comprised of cooperatives, mutual societies, and enterprising non-profits. For the purposes of this law, a social purpose is a "purpose that is not centred on monetary profit, but on service to members or to the community and is characterised, in particular, by an enterprise's contribution to the well-being of its members or the community and to the creation of sustainable high-quality jobs." Social Economy Act, L.R.Q. (2013). Chapter E-1.1.1, retrieved from https://www.legisquebec.gouv.qc.ca/en/document/cs/E-1.1.1

[2] Founded by the largest cooperative in Canada, Desjardins Group, Desjardins International Development (DID) is an international development organisation based in Canada that helps people take control of their finances and leverage available tools and resources. DID has been offering technical assistance and investment services in the inclusive finance sector for developing countries since 1970. https://www.desjardins.com/qc/en/about-us/community/international-development.html

[3] SEED has been funded in the past by the Social Sciences and Humanities Research Council of Canada (SSHRC) and DID, through the financial contribution by Global Affairs Canada (GAC)

[4] Développement international Desjardins (2021). Conclusion du projet EFECS au Sri Lanka https://www.desjardins.com/qc/fr/nouvelles/integres-chaine-valeur.html

[5] Pôle Ideos (2021). « Présentation du programme de formation Leadership pour les femmes entrepreneures ». [video] https://www.youtube.com/watch?v=BkuupZ9WRAE

[6] SEED Network (2021). Coordinating for Growth & Innovation. Haitian Entrepreneurial Ecosystem. Report presented to Développement international Desjardins. https://ideos.hec.ca/wp-content/uploads/2021/09/2021018_SEED_Haiti_Report_MASTER.FINAL-version-reduite.pdf

[7] Tiessen, R., S. Rao and B.J. Lough (2021) "International Development Volunteering as Transformational Feminist Practice for Gender Equality," *Journal of Developing Societies, 37*(1), pp.30–56. doi: 10.1177/0169796X20972260.

[8] Sen, A, (2000) *Development as Freedom*. New York: Anchor Books

[9] Data from the most recent ILO report on youth employment trends confirms that young people have been disproportionately affected by the economic and employment consequences of the pandemic and that the pace of recovery of youth labour markets in many countries and regions is falling behind that of the labour market for older workers. In the same vein, the UN Department of Social and Economic Affairs, asserts that the pandemic resulted in a disproportionate job loss for informal workers, particularly for women, in 2020. The subsequent recovery from COVID-19 has been driven by informal employment, which has caused a slight increase in the incidence of informality. ILO (2022) Global Employment Trends for Youth 2022. Investing in transforming futures for young people. International Labour Organization; UNDESA (2023) SDG 8. Promote sustained, inclusive and sustainable economic growth, full and productive employment and decent work for all. Progress and Info. https://sdgs.un.org/goals/goal8

[10] Thomas, H. and Y. Hedrick-Wong (2019) *Inclusive Growth: The Global Challenges of Social Inequality and Financial Inclusion*. Bingley, UK: Emerald Publishing

---

About the Authors

Luciano Barin Cruz is a Professor of Management and Sustainability at HEC Montreal. He is the Director of the Sustainability Transition Office and of Ideos, HEC Montréal's Social Impact Hub. His research interests focus on sustainability and social impact.

Nadia Ponce Morales is the Sustainability Coordinator and a part-time lecturer at HEC Montréal. She has close to 20 years of experience as a trainer, facilitator and manager within entrepreneurial and environmental international development programmes focused on women and youth in Canada and 14 African, Asian and Latin American countries.

Kate Picone is a Project Manager at Ideos, specialising in entrepreneurship and social innovation management. She has actively participated in the development of international projects in various countries, including in Africa, Latin America, and the Caribbean, with a focus on supporting vulnerable populations, such as women and rural entrepreneurs.

Laurence Beaugrand-Champagne is the coordinator of Ideos. Laurence develops and implements Ideos' projects and initiatives. In addition, she plays an active role in improving collaboration within the social impact ecosystem at HEC Montréal, as well as within the Montréal ecosystem.

The Female Leader: Experiences from the Gordon Institute of Business Science, South Africa

MORRIS MTHOMBENI

Complex Societal Impact Projects Requiring Tri-Sector Collaboration and Cooperation

Visible and measurable progress in advancing the status and standing of females in business school leadership is crucial to role-modelling effective gender representation. As the higher education eco-system from which leaders in society, business and politics are shaped and informed, walking the talk on the advancement of female leaders must be evident not only in our classrooms but in our organisational practices - anything less is gender-washing.

At the beginning of the year, at the 2023 EFMD Dean's Conference in Madrid, I attended a session entitled 'implementing strategies to attract and retain female talent in business schools'. It was hosted by business school deans who participate in the EQUAL4EUROPE initiative. As the vigorous discussion ensured, with a panel consisting entirely of males, my eyes were opened to the persistent and systemic prejudice plaguing females in academia, especially at leading business schools. These include resistance to cite research by females (citation injustice) (Ennser-Kananen, 2019); lower numbers of female professors and associate professors; heavier female workloads (Doyle & Hind, 1998; Parlak et al., 2021) and the deflating strategies that Dr Sarah Jane Aiston has described as 'internal silencing' (caused by a fear of speaking out) or 'silence by exclusion' (a lack of representation on key decision-making committees and panels) (Aiston, 2019). Macro and 'micro-inequities' (Rowe, 1990) like these have been successfully used to keep females out of the top ranks of many universities and business schools, and further derail the equality, diversity, inclusion and respect (EDIR) goals espoused by business schools. Clearly, and despite making a collective commitment to gender equity as per Sustainable Development Goal (SDG) 5, few business school leaders practice what they preach.

CRUNCHING THE NUMBERS ON FEMALE REPRESENTATION

Recently, the global business school environment has seen a welcome increase in the number of female deans and females occupying senior positions. A development championed, amongst others, by Women in Business Education (WiBE) under the enthusiastic leadership of founder and CEO Lisa Leander, who is among those who correctly point out that the percentage of business schools accredited by the Association to Advance Collegiate Schools of Business (AACSB) is showing a rise in female deans from 17% in 2008 to 25% in 2018 (Leander and Watson, 2021) and edging up to 25.7% in 2020 (Bisoux, 2021). Among this number are a few with whom GIBS is proudly associated: Caroline Roussel of IÉSEG School of Management (France), Wendy Loretto from the University of Edinburgh Business School (Scotland); Vanessa Chang of Curtin University (Australia); Wendy Costen of Smith School of Business at Queens University (Canada) and Catherine Duggan of the University of Cape Town's Graduate School of Business (South Africa).

DOI: 10.4324/9781003467410-15

Annual Research Volume 2 – Complex Societal Impact Projects Requiring Tri-Sector Collaboration and Cooperation

The Female Leader: Experiences from the Gordon Institute of Business Science, South Africa
Morris Mthombeni
···················

Until she stood down in 2020, GIBS was shaped and led by Nicola Kleyn from 2015. This was, in a blow for the number of female deans in Africa, the same year in which the visionary Enase Okonedo moved on. Like Kleyn, Okonedo handed the reins of Nigeria's Lagos Business School to a male colleague. However, it is worth nothing that they both went on to bigger and better things in higher education (Hinson, 2020).

Notwithstanding the usual and expected movements in these demanding positions, the latest figure of 25.7% of female deans is a disappointing achievement for business schools, because it falls short of representing the number of females in the business world, where they made up around 32% of senior management roles in 2021 – a figure which was also the highest to that date (Grant Thornton, 2022), but still far from reflecting the true gender equity long desired. The reasons why more females are not breaking through into top jobs in business schools are systemic and include in-built institutional biases and a less aggressive stance by some female academics when it comes to putting themselves forward for consideration, as well as the fact that many females do not enter academia through standard academic paths; typically acquiring their doctorates later in life (EFMD, 2017). These brakes to progressing up the academic leadership ladder are not dissimilar to those noted as holding females back in the corporate space, from the insidious nature of bias and sex discrimination, to the pressures on females to shoulder the role of carers in society, as well as a lack of choices, networks and mentorship (AAUW, 2016).

PHOTO COURTESY MTHOMBENI

Fortunately, this picture is changing; thanks to hard-fought awareness and active steps to address these challenges. For instance, research from Grant Thornton, released in 2022, painted an encouraging story of growing inclusivity and diversity around the world – particularly with regards to females in leadership positions. The research does, however, highlight a profound difference between regions. While North America had 33% of leadership roles held by females in 2022, in step with the European Union, this figure was higher at 35% in Latin America, 37% in the ASEAN countries of Southeast Asia, and a commendable 40% across Africa (Grant Thornton, 2022).

Effectively, Africa is pulling the global average beyond the key 30% tipping point. As the Grant Thornton researchers noted: "The global increase is largely driven by improvements in Africa and APAC [Asia-Pacific recorded 30% from 23% in 2018]. Africa represents a success story for female leaders, reaching 40% of overall senior roles. This is an increase from 39% in 2021, and a significant step up from 30% in 2018" (*ibid*).

While Africa exceeds the number of human resource directors and chief marketing officers, compared with the other regions studied by Grant Thornton, the continent still has work to do when it comes to boosting the numbers of female chief executives. This fact tells us that businesses themselves, despite a bigger pipeline of female talent to choose from, are still reluctant to achieve effective gender equity at C-suite positions.

OUR APPROACH TO FEMALES-IN-LEADERSHIP

Seeking to be an exemplar, as opposed to being a rationaliser, GIBS is committed to the advancement of females in the workplace, and society as a whole. This commitment resonates deeply across South Africa where the goal of driving racial transformation after the country's painful history of apartheid is written into law and represents a crucial consideration when it comes to achieving ESG targets for businesses. The very process of creating a more just and equitable South Africa as measured by race has, in turn, supported the acceleration of female leaders in corporate roles, government and civil society.

South Africa holds a joint second position with Australia in the Global Government Forum's G20 ranking, just behind Canada, for gender parity in the public service sector (Hunt, 2022). South Africa is now reaching a figure of 48.6% of senior public service positions being held by females – this means the country is just 1.4 percentage points from reaching gender parity in this area. Since the advent of democracy in 1994, South Africa has also seen the number of female Members of Parliament rise from just 2.7% to around 45% (Hunt, 2022), while 32% of Supreme Court of Appeal judges are women, 31% of solicitors and 30% of the country's ambassadors (Gwaelane, 2020).

Annual Research Volume 2 – Complex Societal Impact Projects Requiring Tri-Sector Collaboration and Cooperation

The Female Leader: Experiences from the Gordon Institute of Business Science, South Africa
Morris Mthombeni
....

Yet, in business and despite good progress in the boardrooms and C-suite in general, South Africa boasts only three female CEOs of a top 40 listed company, in spite of an increasing number of women holding senior corporate positions. While this stark discrepancy in top businesses should keep us focused on the job at hand, it is also important to acknowledge that South Africa has done extremely well when it comes to advancing EDIR, particularly of females and previously disadvantaged persons. The GIBS story, in turn, is very much in line with this success in celebration of female leaders.

Breaking this assertion down into numbers, GIBS is proud that its female faculty consists of 19 of the 35 core faculty positions at our business school – or 54%. Our four major research communities are all led by female professors. In the case of the African Markets and Management research community, Helena Barnard, a respected international business scholar, has the reins. Kerrin Myres, who is a shining light in the field of social entrepreneurship, leads Entrepreneurship in Africa. Leadership and Performance in Africa is chaired by irrepressible scholar Caren Scheepers. While Charlene Lew, a rising scholar in decision making, chairs our Ethical Business in Complex Contexts research community, which works closely with the GIBS Centre for Business Ethics (CfBE), which relies on Mollie Painter, an extraordinary professor at GIBS and full professor at Nottingham Trent University in the UK. Many will know Painter for her body of work on business ethics. Some might argue that GIBS is overburdening female faculty, paradoxically curtailing their academic career. The facts tell a different story. These colleagues are among the most productive and esteemed scholars at GIBS.

From knowledge creators and to knowledge disseminators, 78% of GIBS academic programme leads are female (either full, associate or assistant professors) and 50% of our faculty department heads are also female. Females also hold the majority of senior leadership positions in the school, making up 66% of the executive committee and 80% of the board of directors. Once again, they lead while shining as teachers and scholars. GIBS discourages dichotomisation and the act of dividing and polarising, and instead encourages dilemma reconciliation.

GIBS' success, as reflected in the figure below, is a function of safe spaces that are deliberately created for females to thrive. These safe spaces have resulted in healthy demographic outcomes like 54% of faculty, who are female, of which 43% are associate professors, and 57% are full professors. We are proud of the continuous work to earn our reputation as a champion for female leadership in the field of business education. As the Red Queen from Lewis Carroll's Through the Looking-Glass said, "*It takes all the running you can do, to keep in the same place. If you want to get somewhere else, you must run at least twice as fast as that.*"

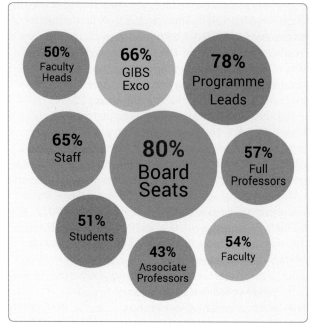

Source Author

Aradhna Krishna and Yesim Orhun, writing in Harvard Business Review in 2020, strongly championed for the utilisation of female instructors, faculty and role-models as "a possible silver-bullet to closing the academic performance gap", since female faculty increase "female students' interest and performance expectations in quantitative courses and are viewed as role models" (Krishna & Orhun, 2020). Therefore, logic would dictate that walking the talk when it comes to representation in business schools will automatically attract more female students, who in turn will go on to advance in corporate positions around the world and break through the glass ceiling. This has certainly been true of the GIBS experience.

At GIBS we believe that female students are drawn to a way of learning and mutual support that is nurtured under a more inclusive and yet rigorous culture – balancing accountability with empathy. For instance, in 2020, female students made up 45.3% of GIBS's MBA students, rising to 46.8% in 2023. Postgraduate diploma senior management female students, equivalent to a Master of Science in other jurisdictions, leapt from 40% in 2020 to 49.4% in 2023, with postgraduate diploma for mid-level management female students rising from 48.8% in 2020 to 58.8% in 2023, a slight retreat from a high of 63% in 2022. While overall female students currently make up 51% of the GIBS student body, there is still progress to be made when it comes to doctoral enrolments (which stand at 41.6% in 2023) and the research-based Master of Philosophy numbers, which dropped off from 51% in 2022 to 41.1% in 2023.

Annual Research Volume 2 – Complex Societal Impact Projects Requiring Tri-Sector Collaboration and Cooperation

The Female Leader: Experiences from the Gordon Institute of Business Science, South Africa
Morris Mthombeni
....

OUR PLACE IN SOCIETY

These numbers tell a positive story but they are not the goal. They are an outcome of several interventions and investments undertaken over time by successive leadership teams at GIBS. Therefore, they do not reflect leadership success but cultural success instead. As we listen to this data, we are less concerned with what it is screaming at us but more concerned with the whispers that are leading us to fine-tune and accelerate our efforts to support and encourage female leadership in business schools to streamline their career progression. In part, this requires us to have a clear, systemic view of our role in society.

Recognising that the goal of advancing female leaders in business and society is part of a system-wide realignment, over the years GIBS has established a number of programmes, mechanisms, think-tanks and social collaborations through which we partner with other stakeholders to address and shift the reality for women at a grassroots level. With South Africa often crudely dubbed the 'rape capital of the world', there is no denying that the vulnerability and abuse suffered by females in South Africa is among the highest in the world, according to Statistics South Africa (Statistics SA, 2021). Furthermore, as KPMG probed in a 2014 report (KPMG, 2014), the economic costs of gender-based violence impact the South African economy by around 0.9% and 1.3% of GDP annually.

The report also showed that as females increasingly improved their formal education and relative wealth, the prevalence of violence reduced; although it was still clearly in evidence. Accepting the link between deeply rooted social, cultural and systemic marginalisation of women, the GIBS Centre for Business Ethics (CfBE) works with international and local partners to address problems plaguing women in our context. Internationally, the GIBS CfBE works with Nottingham Trent University and non-governmental bodies to undertake ongoing research into the problem of gender-based violence and make strategic inputs which can be implemented by businesses. In South African, the GIBS CfBE works with large retailer Woolworths to empower more than 200 of its leaders about gender-based violence using the GIBS Women's Equality & Digital Access: Right to Expression (WE-DARE) framework.

Also, the GIBS CfBE actively ensures that senior females in business and society have a strong voice in socially relevant reports and research such as the anti-corruption focused '2022 Zondo for Business' report compiled for Business Leadership South Africa. In the report, four eminent female leaders – Tsakani Maluleke (Auditor-General SA), Nicky Newton-King (former CEO of the Johannesburg Stock Exchange), Claudelle von Eck (former CEO of the Institute of Internal Auditors) and Ansie Ramalho (King IV project lead) – provided significant inputs, alongside Rob Rose (editor of the Financial Mail) and analyst Stuart Theobald. In so doing, these leaders are shaping business and public discourse, as well as policy.

Other examples of initiatives on women in leadership include efforts by our Entrepreneurship Development Academy (EDA) which, in 2022, continued its work to empower women entrepreneurs, by the rolling-out of an app-based programme for approximately 3,500 female business owners in South Africa on behalf of the Cherie Blair Foundation for Women (Gordon Institute of Business Science, 2022). This move also highlights the openness of GIBS faculty to embrace new technologies and platforms which allow us to create training and education offerings that reach broad sections of the typical GIBS population.

Since 2020, the EDA's Social Entrepreneurship Programme (SEP) has proved a particularly positive example of the reach and impact that can be achieved by focusing our attention on addressing female-specific issues – and, in the African context, helping black females. Since 2020, 76 out of the 104 individuals who participated in the SEP (or 73%) were females. Of that 76, 64 – representing 61% - were black females. The reason women are increasingly attracted to a programme of this nature, is that it doesn't sugar-coat the issues and challenges female entrepreneurs face; including the difficulties balancing multiple roles across family, work and personal development.

Annual Research Volume 2 – Complex Societal Impact Projects Requiring Tri-Sector Collaboration and Cooperation

The Female Leader: Experiences from the Gordon Institute of Business Science, South Africa
Morris Mthombeni
....

OUR CONTRIBUTION TO PEDAGOGY AND SCHOLARSHIP

Following feedback from each of the peer-review teams from AACSB, AMBA, and EQUIS, which visited us during the COVID-19 era, we at GIBS made a decision as an Africa-based business school to ensure that our research strategy and agenda were firmly aligned with the needs of our continent. As such, we honed our output to focus on four pillars: African markets and management; entrepreneurship in Africa; leadership and performance in Africa and ethical business in complex contexts.

While Africa is our focus and our guide, much of our published research has relevance for other emerging markets. This is evident when considering a peer-reviewed business case published by Emerald in 2022 by two GIBS academics, Amy Moore and Dr Tracey Toefy. Mitti Café: Enabling Disability Inclusion in India through Scalable Business Model (Moore & Toefy, 2022) offers sustainability and social inclusion insights for social entrepreneurs and businesses in India and abroad, and fittingly went on to win in The Case for Women category at the 2021 Emerald case-writing competition. Moore joined the editorial board for Emerald Publishing Emerging Markets Case Studies as an associate editor in January 2023.

Many of GIBS's research outputs in recent years are thanks to the likes of international renowned scholars like Professor Helena Banard and Professor Anastacia Mamabolo. Barnard and Mamabolo won 2022 Best Paper Award and Best Phenomenon-Based Paper Award from the Journal of World Business for their article titled "On Religion as an Institution in International Business: Executive' Lived Experiences in Four African Countries". The most prolific however is Professor Scheepers who won the Outstanding Contribution to the Case Method title at the European Case Centre's 30th Awards in 2020. Scheepers became the fourth female winner in the 10 years this global award has been bestowed. It was also only the second win for an African institution in the history of the awards (University of Pretoria, 2020a).

Scheepers, who frequently co-authors with other female faculty members and students, also makes a point of featuring female protagonists and actors in her case studies and, due to her field of study in organisational behaviour and development and female entrepreneurship, she publishes academic articles that focus on gender issues. Recently this has included a 2021 case published by Ivey Publishing by Scheepers and GIBS junior faculty, Motshedisi Mathibe, which profiles a female entrepreneur in the male-dominated retail fuel sector (Scheepers and Mathibe, 2021). In 2019 and 2020 respectively, Scheepers teamed up with Tracey Toefy to create another award-winning case on female-led domestic award-winning start-up, SweepSouth South Africa (University of Pretoria, 2020b). Also, with GIBS doctoral candidate Philandra Govender, she co-authored a case to probe the buyout offer dilemma facing the female founder of Candi&Co, South Africa's first ethnic hair salon franchise (Scheepers and Govender, 2022).

Mindful of the small permanent faculty size at GIBS, of the 57 journal articles published in 2022 by GIBS, five were authored solely by females and 20 were co-authored with male colleagues. This compares to 53 journal articles published in 2018, of which only two were authored by females and 24 that were co-authored. When it comes to case studies, of the 11 published in 2022, five were by females alone and a further five by teams of females and males. Of the book chapters contributed in 2022 – a total of 14 – three were written by females alone, and 10 were co-authored by females. The collective use of these artifacts in our classrooms, as well as countless other classrooms the world over, has a direct impact on our students and broader stakeholders.

IN CONCLUSION: CLOSING THE LOOP

These efforts allow us to take great pride in celebrating our female alumni who are making a positive contribution to society. These include, but are not limited to, Stacey Brewer (MBA class of 2011), Tashmia Ismail-Saville (MBA class of 2010), Raisibe Morathi (MPhil Corporate Strategy class of 2020), and Anastacia Mamabolo (PhD class of 2013). Brewer is founder and CEO of SPARK Schools, which was inspired by her MBA studies, with a network of 24 schools serving 15,000 students. Ismail-Saville is founder and former CEO of the Youth Employment Service (YES), which has created over 100,000 jobs since its founding and is now influencing youth-led innovation in Canada, first through the MaRS urban innovation hub and, more recently, as a board member of innovation catalyst Mitacs. Morathi is Chief Financial Officer of Vodacom Group, which connects tens of millions of people through mobile technology, the most impactful of which is its mPesa business in East Africa. Mamabolo is an associate professor and National Research Foundation-rated researcher, and she recently won the South African Women in Science Awards (SAWiSA) Distinguished Young Women Researchers in humanities and social sciences, an award of the South African National Governments Department of Science and Technology. These women are but a drop in the ocean of countless inspiring stories of the 3,081 (42%) of female alumni since GIBS' founding in 2000, when numbers of female students were appreciably lower. They are a timely reminder of why we make the choices we do.

Annual Research Volume 2 – Complex Societal Impact Projects Requiring Tri-Sector Collaboration and Cooperation

The Female Leader: Experiences from the Gordon Institute of Business Science, South Africa
Morris Mthombeni
....

Responding to the ever-changing dynamics of doing business in a changing world is a daunting task for business schools. There are no easy choices. The fact is that organisations around the world are losing female leaders at unprecedented rates since the 2020 COVID-19 pandemic, as female leaders who previously broke through the glass ceiling are now facing the glass cliff (Groeneveld *et al.*, 2020). This situation clearly highlights a disconnect between what most business schools teach and what the evolving market requires. Without widespread organisational and societal change – which truly embraces EDIR in all its forms – then the few females who do make it to the top are faced with the daunting task of fighting against a rising tsunami of societal challenges. Our role as business schools must be to create a groundswell of female leaders who can fundamentally drive EDIR across society. This, in turn, will lead to greater female ownership and management underscoring collective commitments to SDG 5, gender equality. The microcosm we create within our business schools today will ultimately be reflected in the quality and diversity of our societies in the future. Best we tread purposefully, with clear intent, and urgency.

References

AAUW (2016) Barriers and Bias: The Status of Women in Leadership. https://www.aauw.org/app/uploads/2020/03/Barriers-and-Bias-nsa.pdf

Aiston, S.J. (2019) Behind the silence and silencing of academic women. *University World News*, 15th March. https://www.universityworldnews.com/post.php?story=20190314071633193

Bisoux, T. (2021) Elevating the equity curve. *AACSB*, 8th March. https://www.aacsb.edu/insights/articles/2021/03/elevating-the-equity-curve#:~:text=But%20even%20so%2C%20just%2025.7,23%20percent%20of%20dean%20positions.

Doyle, C. and P. Hind (1998) Occupational stress, burnout and job status in female academics. *Gender, Work & Organization, 5*(2), 67-82. https://doi.org/10.1111/1468-0432.00047.

EFMD (2017) Creating impact with purpose. *Global Focus: The EFMD Business Magazine, 2*(11). https://issuu.com/efmd/docs/efmd_global_focus_1102_online.

Ennser-Kananen, J. (2019) Are we who we cite? On epistemological injustices, citing practices, and# metoo in academia. *Apples-Journal of Applied Language Studies, 13*(2) pp.65-69

Gordon Institute of Business Science (2022) HerVenture App is set to boost 3,500 women's businesses in South Africa. https://www.gibs.co.za/news-events/news/pages/herventure-app-is-set-to-boost-3,500-women%E2%80%99s-businesses-in-south-africa!-.aspx. 5th May

Grant Thornton (2022) Women in business 2022: Opening the door to diverse talent. https://www.grantthornton.global/en/insights/women-in-business-2022/

Groeneveld, S., V. Bakker and E. Schmidt (2020). Breaking the glass ceiling, but facing a glass cliff? The role of organizational decline in women's representation in leadership positions in Dutch civil service organizations. *Public Administration, 98*(2) pp.441-464

Gwaelane, N. (2020) Covid-19 and women leadership struggles in South Africa. *Polity*, 3rd June. https://www.polity.org.za/article/covid-19-and-women-leadership-struggles-in-south-africa-2020-06-03#:~:text=South%20Africa%20also%20scores%20poorly,only%2032%25%20of%20executive%20positions.

Hinson, R. E. (2020) Female business school dean brands are on the rise. *University World News*, 23rd July. https://www.universityworldnews.com/post-mobile.php?story=20200720144348102

Hunt, M. (2022) Women Leaders Index: why gender parity in South Africa's public service isn't just a numbers game. *Global Government Forum* 6th December. https://www.globalgovernmentforum.com/women-leaders-index-why-gender-parity-in-south-africas-public-service-isnt-just-a-numbers-game/

Annual Research Volume 2 – Complex Societal Impact Projects Requiring Tri-Sector Collaboration and Cooperation

The Female Leader: Experiences from the Gordon Institute of Business Science, South Africa
Morris Mthombeni
....

KPMG (2014) Too costly to ignore – the economic impact of gender-based violence in South Africa. https://assets.kpmg.com/content/dam/kpmg/za/pdf/2017/01/za-Too-costly-to-ignore.pdf

Krishna, A. and Y. Orhun (2020) How business schools can help close the gender gap. *Harvard Business Review*, 23rd December. How Business Schools Can Help Close the Gender Gap (hbr.org)

Leander, L. and R.M. Watson (2021) Academic leadership already lacked women representation pre-pandemic. Now what? *Harvard Business School Publishing*. https://hbsp.harvard.edu/inspiring-minds/academic-leadership-already-lacked-women-representation-pre-pandemic-now

Moore, A.F. and T. Toefy (2022) *Mitti Café: Enabling Disability Inclusion in India through Scalable Business Model*. Emerald Publishing Limited. https://doi.org/10.1108/CFW.2022.000003

Parlak, S., O. Celebi Cakiroglu and F. Oksuz Gul (2021) Gender roles during COVID-19 pandemic: The experiences of Turkish female academics. *Gender, Work & Organization, 28*, pp.461-483. doi: 10.1111/gwao.12655

Rowe, M.P. (1990) Barriers to equality: The power of subtle discrimination to maintain unequal opportunity. *Employee Responsibilities and Rights Journal, 3*, pp.153-163. https://doi.org/10.1007/BF01388340

Scheepers, C. B. and M. Mathibe (2021) *SASOL fuel retail franchise: Contextualising entrepreneurship's role in women empowerment (Case No. 9B21M070)*. Ivey Publishing

Scheepers, C. B. and P. Govender (2020) *Candi&Co South Africa: Entrepreneurial woman's leadership in revolutionalizing the ethnic hair industry (Case No. 9B20C027)*. Ivey Publishing

Statistics SA. (2021) Crimes against women in South Africa, an analysis of the phenomenon of GBV and femicide. https://www.parliament.gov.za/storage/app/media/1_Stock/Events_Institutional/2020/womens_charter_2020/docs/30-07-2020/A_Statistical_Overview_R_Maluleke.pdf

University of Pretoria. (2020a, February 26) Lecturer from UP's GIBS wins Outstanding Contribution to the Case Method at the European Case Centre's 30th Awards. https://www.up.ac.za/news/post_2875957-lecturer-from-ups-gibs-wins-outstanding-contribution-to-the-case-method-at-the-european-case-centres-30th-awards-

University of Pretoria. (2020b, June 12) GIBS lecturers scoop award for the Best African Business Case at the 2019 EFMD Case Writing Competition. https://www.up.ac.za/news/post_2902267-gibs-lecturers-scoop-award-for-the-best-african-business-case-at-the-2019-efmd-case-writing-competition-

About the Author

Professor Morris Mthombeni is Dean of the Gordon Institute of Business Science in Johannesburg, South Africa; the top-ranked African business school for executive education. He has a wealth of experience in the corporate world, as an active researcher at the intersection of corporate governance and strategy, and is active in influencing the evolution of the business education sector towards responsible business and management education.